# JESUS

Everything You Need
to Know to Figure Him Out

# JESUS

## Everything You Need
## to Know to Figure Him Out

### Mark Littleton

Westminster John Knox Press
Louisville, Kentucky

Scripture quotations from the Holy Bible, New International Version. Copyright © 1973, 1978, 1984 International Bible Society. Used by permission of Zondervan Bible Publishers.

Scripture quotations marked NASB are taken from the *New American Standard Bible*, © 1960, 1962, 1963, 1968, 1971, 1972, 1973, 1975, 1977 by The Lockman Foundation. Used by permission.

*Book design by Sharon Adams*
*Cover design by Paz Design Group*
*Cover illustration: Andy Warhol*

*First edition*
Published by Westminster John Knox Press
Louisville, Kentucky

This book is printed on acid-free paper that meets the American National Standards Institute Z39.48 standard. ∞

PRINTED IN THE UNITED STATES OF AMERICA
01 02 03 04 05 06 07 08 09 10 — 10 9 8 7 6 5 4 3 2 1

Cataloging-in-Publication Data is on file at the Library of Congress, Washington, D.C.

ISBN 0-664-22245-5

# Introduction

Who was Jesus? What did he do during his lifetime? What effect has he had on history? What legends and stories arose in later years about him that are appealing but probably not true? What do modern writers say about Jesus?

Answers to these questions are found in this book. Here, for instance, you will find the answer to the question: Did Jesus ever weep? Look up "Weeping," read the entry, and you will find every instance we know of where Jesus actually wept and for what reasons.

Perhaps you wonder: Have modern rock groups ever written about Jesus? Consider the entries under "Music" for interesting lyrical references to Jesus in modern rock, from Simon and Garfunkel's "Mrs. Robinson" (He Loved Her More . . .) to U2's "I Still Haven't Found What I'm Looking For" (Rock Idols Who Idolize Jesus).

What were the circumstances of the composing of Handel's *Messiah*? Look up "Music: Compelled to Stand." Fascinating information is provided about the composer's faith in Christ.

This book is not meant to be a scholarly treatment of the history of Jesus, an exhaustive dictionary about everything connected to Jesus, or even a theological treatment. I have attempted to be factually accurate. However, the purpose of this book is to delight and interest you as the reader and to encourage you to begin at the beginning and read through to the end, much as you would any other nonfiction book. The alphabetical arrangement makes it easy for those who desire information on a specific topic. But this book is meant more as a devotional/coffee table/gift book than a reference book. I have chosen what I consider the most "fascinating" facts and stories about Jesus, rather than everything he ever did, which in many cases includes many redundancies. For instance, I don't go through every healing episode, though there were many. Thus, I've done some selecting to include only the information that you as the reader will likely find most interesting. If you want a more exhaustive or complete dictionary, any of the scholarly works out there will probably do. This book is meant more to entertain and stir your thinking, rather than defend the faith or critique the text of the Bible.

Another matter is the use of the Bible in this book. I personally believe that the Bible is God's Word, inspired and full of spiritual power. I don't believe that you can pick and choose which texts you'll believe and/or discard simply because you like them or don't like them, or you have "scholarly" reasons for doing so: "This sounds like something the later church manufactured and put in the mouth of Jesus."

My suggestion is simply to read what the Bible says and take it at face value. That is primarily why I have given so many quotations directly from the Bible—so that you can see precisely what it says and not just take my word for it.

What is my view of the authority of the Bible? I see it as the only nearly complete resource we have of the life of Jesus. There are references to him in secular literature from close to his time, but they are sketchy and few. If we, for so-called scholarly or other reasons, end up throwing out most of what the Bible says Jesus said or did, we will be throwing out the only resource we have about him. In such a case, trying to understand and "figure him out," as my title suggests, will be futile indeed.

On the other hand, if you have serious problems with the Bible's accuracy and authenticity, I don't think this book will be a problem for you. I don't try to embellish what it says or prove its accuracy in most cases. I've just tried to use it as a source book, much as you would use a good magazine or newspaper or biography to do research on a personality. If you come to the Bible with the same interest and open-mindedness that you bring to reading a magazine you trust, you will have stepped most of the distance expected of you by the scriptures. I don't think God expects you to "believe" without at least looking at what the Bible says from a purely "interested bystander" perspective. God doesn't expect you to take a "leap of faith" without history, cultural resources, or other information on which to base your faith. But God can take what you read in God's word and put it into your heart in a way that no one completely understands. If that happens to you as it has happened to me, I think you will find this book interesting and transforming.

It is my hope that both religious and nonreligious people will find this book full of fascinating information about Jesus Christ and his legacy. Although I have written from a theologically conservative point of view, I've included a wealth of insights from an array of sources, whether liberal, agnostic, atheistic, or conservative. It's up to you to determine whether you believe everything or anything.

Have fun, and keep your hands on the wheel.

**Abba**—"Abba" was Jesus' personal name for his Father in heaven, according to Mark 14:36. Jesus used the name in the Garden of Gethsemane as he asked to be released from having to go to the cross. He said: "Abba, Father, . . . everything is possible for you. Take this cup from me. Yet not what I will, but what you will." God did not release Jesus, however, and he went to the cross willingly and in obedience to his Father's will.

Later in the New Testament, Paul speaks of the same term as an address of intimacy and familiarity to God from God's children. "Abba" is the Near Eastern term for "Papa" or "Daddy." Paul refers to it twice in the following passages:

*Romans 8:15–16:* "For you did not receive a spirit that makes you a slave again to fear, but you received the Spirit of sonship. And by him we cry, 'Abba, Father.' The Spirit himself testifies with our spirit that we are God's children."

*Galatians 4:6:* "Because you are sons, God sent the Spirit of his Son into our hearts, the Spirit who calls out, 'Abba, Father.'"

**Accession of Kings**—It was believed, after the reign of Constantine, that kings derived their power and authority from Christ. See, for example, Romans 13:1: "Everyone must submit himself to the governing authorities, for there is no authority except that which God has established. The authorities that exist have been established by God." Thus, on Christmas Day, A.D. 800, Charlemagne was crowned emperor by Pope Leo III. Political sovereignty passed from God to Christ, from Christ to the apostle Peter (on whom Christ said he would build his church—Matt. 16:18), from Peter to his successors (the popes), and from them to emperors and kings.

**Actors: Jesus, a Good Example?**—Marcello Mastroianni, the famed Italian actor, once said: "Jesus Christ is an admirable example, but he's too remote from men of today to be a model. Or he's too much of one to be understood and followed. A man who dies for others is moving and admirable, but how many followers can he have in a world filled with people who will hardly help you across the street, let alone die for you?"

Mastroianni's opinion is countered somewhat by an article in *Time Magazine* at the turn of the second millennium by Reynolds Price.

Price says: "It would require much exotic calculation, however, to deny that the single most powerful figure—not merely in these two millenniums but in all human history—has been Jesus of Nazareth. Not only is the prevalent system of denoting the years based on an erroneous sixth century calculation of the date of his birth, but a serious argument can be made that no one else's life has proved remotely as powerful and enduring as that of Jesus. It's an astonishing conclusion in light of the fact that Jesus was a man who lived a short life in a rural backwater of the Roman Empire, who died in agony as a convicted criminal, and who may never have intended so much as a small portion of the effects worked in his name" (*Time Magazine*, 6 December 1999, 86).

**A.D.**—From the Latin "Anno Domini," which means "In the Year of the Lord," in contrast to B.C. ("Before Christ"). The dating is based on a calculation on when the birth of Christ occurred (believed to be A.D. 0) by Dionysius Exiguus in A.D. 527. A.D. and B.C. are the anchors of the Gregorian Calendar, which was put forth by Pope Gregory XIII in 1582.

**Adopted?**—In the first few centuries after the time of Christ, a school of theological thought known as Adoptianism believed that Jesus was not born the Son of God but became the Son of God by adoption at his baptism when the Spirit of God descended upon him and God the Father spoke from heaven: "This is my Son, whom I love; with him I am well pleased" (Matt. 3:17). This contradicts somewhat the thought of Gabriel the Archangel when he announced to the Virgin Mary: "'You will be with child and give birth to a son, and you are to give him the name Jesus. He will be great and will be called the Son of the Most High. The Lord God will give him the throne of his father David, and he will reign over the house of Jacob forever; his kingdom will never end'" (Luke 1:30–33). This school of thought also believed that Jesus was not declared God incarnate until his resurrection. See Romans 1:4, which says, "who through the Spirit of holiness was declared with power to be the Son of God by his resurrection from the dead." Both views are considered incorrect by most interpreters, but undoubtedly there are some who subscribe to those views today.

**Ancestors**—Jesus' genealogy in Matthew 1:1–17 contains an impressive list of some of Israel's finest personages, including the patriarchs: Abraham, Isaac, and Jacob; Israel's greatest king, David; and the whole line of Israel's kings thereafter. What is amazing is the character of some of these people. Consider this listing:

*Abraham*—lied twice to protect himself in a way that almost caused his wife to commit adultery.

*Isaac*—lied once to protect himself in the same way his father Abraham did.

*Jacob*—cheated his brother and many others on his way "up the corporate ladder." His name, "Jacob," means "cheater."

*Judah and Tamar*—he mated with her, his daughter-in-law, because he thought she was a prostitute. They produced twins, one of whom was Jesus' ancestor.

*Salmon and Rahab*—she was a harlot from Jericho and was one of Jericho's only survivors after the walls fell under Joshua.

*Boaz and Ruth*—she was a Moabite, a people founded by Moab, the son of Lot's union with his own daughter when she got him drunk. (His other daughter did the same thing and produced Ammon, the patriarch of another line.)

*David*—adulterer with Bathsheba and murderer of Bathsheba's husband. God did not let him build the Temple because he was a man who had "shed much blood."

*Solomon*—idolater and the world's greatest polygamist with three hundred concubines and seven hundred wives.

*Uzziah*—became a leper because of disobedience to God.

*Manasseh*—mass murderer.

*Jeconiah*—so wicked that God cursed the line from him on.

Clearly, Jesus was no blueblood!


**Angels Ministering to Jesus**—On several occasions, angels appeared to minister to Jesus and his family through difficult times. The occasions are these:

*Luke 1:26*, in which the angel Gabriel appeared to Mary, telling her she would bear the Messiah: "In the sixth month, God sent the angel Gabriel to Nazareth, a town in Galilee."

*Matthew 1:20–21*, where an angel appears to Joseph to assure him of Mary's virgin pregnancy with Jesus: "But after he had considered this, an angel of the Lord appeared to him in a dream and said, 'Joseph son of David, do not be afraid to take Mary home as your wife, because what is conceived in her is from the Holy Spirit. She will give birth to a son, and you are to give him the name Jesus, because he will save his people from their sins.'"

*Matthew 2:13*, when an angel warned Joseph in a dream to flee from Israel: "When they had gone, an angel of the Lord appeared to Joseph in a dream. 'Get up,' he said, 'take the child and his mother and escape to Egypt. Stay there until I tell you, for Herod is going to search for the child to kill him.'"

*Matthew 2:19–20*, in which an angel advised Joseph in a dream that it was all right to return to Israel because Herod was dead: "After Herod died, an angel of the Lord appeared in a dream to Joseph in Egypt and said, 'Get up, take the child and his mother and go to the land of Israel, for those who were trying to take the child's life are dead.'"

*Matthew 4:11*, where angels came and ministered to Jesus after his trial in the wilderness. There Jesus was tempted by Satan: "Then the devil left him, and angels came and attended him."

*Luke 22:43*, where an angel appeared to strengthen Jesus while he was praying in the Garden of Gethsemane about his impending death: "An angel from heaven appeared to him and strengthened him."

*Matthew 28:2*, in which an angel rolls away the rock at Jesus' tomb: "There was a violent earthquake, for an angel of the Lord came down from heaven and, going to the tomb, rolled back the stone and sat on it."

*Matthew 28:5*, where either one or two angels appeared to tell the women that Jesus had risen from the dead: "The angel said to the women, 'Do not be afraid, for I know that you are looking for Jesus, who was crucified.'"

**Angels Singing Hallelujah Chorus at Jesus Birth?**—Contrary to tradition, when the angels appeared to shepherds in the fields above Bethlehem at Jesus' birth, they did not sing; they spoke. This is what the passage says: "Suddenly a great company of the heavenly host appeared with the angel, praising God and saying, 'Glory to God in the highest, and on earth peace to men on whom his favor rests'" (Luke 2:13–14). But go ahead, you can sing anyway, if you like!

**Anger: Jesus Got Mad!**—There are only a few places in scripture where Jesus expresses anger. The first is found in John 2:13–16: "When it was almost time for the Jewish Passover, Jesus went up to Jerusalem. In the Temple courts he found men selling cattle, sheep and doves, and others sitting at tables exchanging money. So he made a whip out of cords, and drove all from the Temple area, both sheep and cattle; he scattered the coins of the money changers and overturned their tables. To those who sold doves he said, 'Get these out of here! How dare you turn my Father's house into a market!'" Clearly, Jesus was angry on this occasion, though John the writer does not use that word.

The only text that says directly that Jesus was angry is found in Mark 3:1–6, where Jesus finds opposition from the leading Jews because he healed on the Sabbath. They believed doing any "work" was forbidden, according to the Fifth Commandment of Moses (Exod. 20:8–11). Jesus challenged their interpretation and deliberately healed frequently on the Sabbath. These actions became a source of hot contention. In this episode, though, Mark says that Jesus was indeed angry: "He looked round at them in anger and, deeply distressed at their stubborn hearts, said to the man, 'Stretch out your hand.' He stretched it out, and his hand was completely restored" (Mark 3:5).

The third occasion, even though there are undoubtedly others, occurred at the second cleansing of the Temple, shortly before Jesus' death. There we find a situation similar to the first one above where Jesus cleared the Temple of the money changers and others (see Matt. 21:12–13; Mark 11:15–17; and Luke 19:45–46).

There were other times when Jesus may have been angry in spirit, such as when he denounced the Pharisees in Matthew 23:1–39. What is evident is that Jesus became angry about several things: disrespect for God the Father (the Temple episodes); putting traditions and personal interpretations of God's Word ahead of compassion and human decency (the healing episodes); and leading others astray on the basis of one's own beliefs (the denunciations of the Pharisees).

**Annas: Priestly Enemy**—Annas was the high priest from A.D. 6–15 until Valerius Gratus removed him from office: a primary leader in the mock trial of Jesus by the ruling Jews of the Sanhedrin. Annas maintained much power and gained wealth through the extorting practices in the Temple worship. Five of his sons and his son-in-law, Caiaphas, also served as high priests at one time or another. He was the first to examine Jesus at his trial (see John 18:12–14, 19–23), after which Annas sent Jesus on to stand before the present high priest, Caiaphas, and the whole Sanhedrin (see Matt. 26:57–68).

**Antichrist**—This term usually refers to a figure pictured in the Book of Revelation as the final political leader seeking to end Christ's influence and power in the world. He will display himself as being God incarnate, and the whole world will follow him except for those who believe in Christ (see 2 Thess. 2:1–4). He will persecute and kill Christians. One of his acts will be to use the number 666 as some special symbol of his person and position. It will be done in a way that will be obvious to people of his time, but a way that scholars have to date never understood. On the basis of the scripture referring to it, 666 will be a "calculation," perhaps by assigning numerical values to the letters of the Antichrist's name. However, such people as Adolph Hitler, Joseph

Stalin, Richard Nixon, John F. Kennedy, and Ronald Reagan have all been mentioned (in their times) as Antichrists. The real one will give a "mark" to all who follow him. This mark will appear either on the forehead or on the hand, and without it a person will not be able to buy or sell anything the world over. He is the ultimate incarnation of evil, sets himself up as "being God," and leads all astray who do not believe the truth (see Revelation 12–14). Following him is a sure ticket to hell, according to John's statement in Revelation 14:11: "And the smoke of their torment rises for ever and ever. There is no rest day or night for those who worship the beast and his image, or for anyone who receives the mark of his name."

**Apostles**—"Apostle" means "sent one" in Greek. There were the original twelve disciples who became the eleven apostles (after the defection, betrayal, and suicide of Judas Iscariot). Jesus also had other disciples he sent to proclaim the gospel of the kingdom. At one point there were seventy of these, according to Luke 10:1. Later, after the conversion of Paul, there were other apostles, including Paul, Barnabas, Silas, and undoubtedly others. An apostle had a special spiritual gift from heaven in which he was able to (1) do miracles, healings, and other acts of power; (2) speak the Word of God and write it down without error; and (3) go all over the world of that time and preach so that many became Christians and established churches. Many leaders today believe that the office of apostle no longer existed once the New Testament was completed. Others, especially Pentecostals and charismatic Christians, believe that people can still be especially anointed apostles today.

**Apostolic Succession**—How did Christ pass on his authority so that the leaders of the church are authentically his appointed rulers? About the third century, when all the original apostles were long dead, church leaders like Tertullian and Cyprian came up with the idea of apostolic succession. Jesus appointed the apostles (Peter, Andrew, James, John, etc.); these apostles appointed elders and bishops, and they in turn appointed others to rule after them. Today, the Roman Catholic Church continues to assert apostolic succession in the appointment of the pope. Some Protestant and Orthodox churches also follow this practice, though there is no indication from the New Testament that Jesus instituted such a practice.

**Appearance: What Did Jesus Look Like?**—Scripture contains not one description of Jesus' appearance, looks, demeanor, or body. However, a description that scholars believe appeared in the thirteenth century contains a startling physical portrait of Jesus. This is the description given by Lentulus, supposedly an official of the Roman Empire stationed in Judea during the reign of Tiberius. He writes that he saw Jesus in person and witnessed many of his miracles.

> There has appeared in these times, and still is, a man of great power named Jesus Christ, who is called by the Gentiles the prophet of truth, whom His disciples call the Son of God; raising the dead and healing diseases, a man in stature middling tall, and comely, having a reverend countenance, which they that look upon may love and fear; having hair of the hue of an unripe hazel-nut and smooth almost down to his ears, but from the ears in curling locks somewhat darker and more shining, waving over his shoulders, having a parting at the middle of the head according to the fashion of the Nazarenes; a brow smooth and very calm, with a face without wrinkle or any blemish, which a moderate color makes beautiful; with the nose and mouth no fault at all can be found; having a full beard of the color of his hair, not long, but a little forked at the chin, having an expression simple and mature, the eyes grey, glancing, and clear; in rebuke terrible, in admonition kind and lovable, cheerful yet keeping gravity; sometimes he has wept but never laughed; in stature of body tall and straight, with hands and arms fair to look upon; in talk grave, reserved and modest (so that he was rightly called by the prophet), fairer than the children of men. (*The Jesus Book*, edited by Calvin Miller)

This description is certainly a fabrication; moreover, we are left without one piece of physical description of Jesus in the New Testament. The only place we come close to a few details is from the prophet Isaiah. In chapter 53, verse 2, Isaiah wrote: "He had no beauty or majesty to attract us to him, nothing in his appearance that we should desire him."

Although this does not indicate that Jesus was ugly or repulsive, it certainly suggests that he did not resemble in any way the many handsome "artist conceptions" of him that we find today in religious bookstores, Sunday School literature, and Bible leaves. Over and over from the Bible records, it is Jesus' personality and character that shine through from his life in the Bible. It's as if the writers were saying, "Forget what he looks like; this is what he was."

**Ascension: How Did Jesus Get to Heaven?**—Acts 1:6–11 records the ascension of Jesus into heaven. It occurred on the Mount of Olives outside Jerusalem:

> So when they met together, they asked him, "Lord, are you at this time going to restore the kingdom to Israel?"
>
> He said to them: "It is not for you to know the times or dates the Father has set by his own authority. But you will receive power when the Holy Spirit comes on you; and you will be my witnesses in Jerusalem, and in all Judea and Samaria, and to the ends of the earth."
>
> After he said this, he was taken up before their very eyes, and a cloud hid him from their sight.
>
> They were looking intently up into the sky as he was going, when suddenly two men dressed in white stood beside them. "Men of Galilee," they said, "why do you stand here looking into the sky? This same Jesus, who has been taken from you into heaven, will come back in the same way you have seen him go into heaven."

**Ascension Day: When Did Jesus Go to Heaven?**—According to Acts 1:3, Jesus appeared to his disciples for forty days following his resurrection and then ascended into heaven. Thus, Ascension Day is always celebrated on the fifth Thursday after Easter Sunday, when Jesus arose from the dead and began the resurrection appearances.

**Ash Wednesday**—You've seen them, people coming out of church with a blotch of ash on their foreheads on the first day of Lent. The practice started in the seventh or eighth centuries, and today it is followed in the Roman Catholic, Anglican, and other liturgical churches. The ashes are obtained by burning the palm leaves from the previous Palm Sunday. The ashes are applied to the forehead with the words, "Remember, man, that thou art dust and to dust thou shalt return."

**Aslan: A Potent Portrait of Jesus in Fiction**—C.S. Lewis's series of children's books, The Chronicles of Narnia, have charmed many. In them, Lewis, who was a devout Christian, uses his characters and story to portray Christian truths and principles. His lead character in all the books, Aslan, is a huge lion who comes and goes as he pleases. He is the "son of the king from across the sea" and often rescues the children out of terrible circumstances. Many have found great comfort in the portrayal, for Aslan is not only bold, courageous, and strong, but gentle, kind, and sacrificial. They see in Aslan a side of Jesus that doesn't always come out in the spare writing of the New Testament stories.

**Asperges: Sprinkle It with Holy Water**—This is the Roman Catholic tradition of sprinkling new churches or houses for consecration. The congregation is also sprinkled during the mass. The purpose is inward purification by the merciful Lord. A strange offshoot of this custom is that when exorcists come to a house or person to exorcise demonic presences, witches, or other instruments of the devil, they will sprinkle holy water in various spots to cleanse the area. There is no precedent in the New Testament for such a practice.

**Baptism of Jesus: Why?**—Jesus never committed any sins, so why was he baptized? When Jesus appeared to John the Baptist for baptism, John knew instantly who Jesus was. John said, "I need to be baptized by you, and do you come to me?" Jesus replied, "Let it be so now; it is proper for us to do this to fulfill all righteousness" (Matt. 3:13–15). The reason for the act of baptism, normally done for the repentance of sin, was not so that Jesus could repent of his sins, but in order for Jesus to identify completely with the sinners he came to die for. In this situation, most interpreters agree that the baptism John practiced was by immersion (submersion in a river) and represented one's repentance for sin. Later, baptism would come to represent union with Christ and was the outward indication of the inward cleansing. Scholars would argue for centuries, and still do, whether baptism is supposed to be *in* water (immersion) or *by* water (sprinkling). They would also debate, with no agreement in sight, about whether baptism is only for conscious believers (people who are old enough to make a conscious and clearheaded decision about following Christ) or for anyone born into a believer's family, including babies. When babies are baptized by sprinkling, it usually means they are included in God's protection and covenant until they reach an age when they can make a conscious decision to follow Christ.

**Battle Hymn of the Republic**—Julia Ward Howe (1819–1910) was born in New York City into an Episcopalian family. In 1843, she married Samuel G. Howe, who was a teacher of the blind and editor of the abolitionist paper, *The Commonwealth*. She was an advocate of children's welfare, world peace, women's suffrage, and prison reform in her latter days, but before and during the Civil War, she was ardently anti-slavery. Her poem "Battle Hymn of the Republic" was published in 1862 in *The Atlantic Monthly*. It was written to the tune of the well-known song (at that time), "John Brown's Body."

The "Battle Hymn," which became a marching song for the North during the Civil War, sounded forth the trumpet call of the return of Christ to right all the wrongs done in the name of slavery. The following is the first stanza:

> Mine eyes have seen the glory of the coming of the Lord;
> He is trampling out the vintage where the grapes of wrath
>     are stored;
> He has loosed the fateful lightning of his terrible swift
>     sword:
> His truth is marching on.

**B.C.**—"Before Christ." Dating of the Gregorian Calendar. See **A.D.**

**Ben Hur: Civil War General Spins a Tale of Cosmic Dimensions**—*Ben Hur*, at one time a best-selling novel and later an Oscar-winning movie starring Charlton Heston, was written by Lew Wallace, a general during the Civil War who was challenged in a conversation with the atheist Robert Ingersoll to prove that Christ was relevant to people living today. Wallace, a nominal, occasional Christian, wrote the novel on that premise, to show how Christianity works out in real life and that Jesus really was God incarnate. While he did research for the novel, he converted to true Christianity, attempted to use the story to dispel Ingersoll's theories about the "myth" of Jesus' divinity, and became an ardent Christian thereafter.

**Betrayal: Betrayed by a Kiss**—Jesus really was betrayed by a kiss. According to Mark 14:44, Judas Iscariot, one of Jesus' disciples who had become disaffected with Jesus for reasons we do not know, arranged a signal with the leaders of the Jews that he would use to show which person was Jesus when the soldiers and crowd came to arrest him. Judas said, "The one I kiss is the man; arrest him and lead him away under guard." Judas led the soldiers and leaders to Jesus after he had been praying in the Garden of Gethsemane. A fuller text is found in Luke 22:47–48. Here we find these words: "While he was still speaking a crowd came up, and the man who was called Judas, one of the Twelve, was leading them. He approached Jesus to kiss him, but Jesus asked him, 'Judas, are you betraying the Son of Man with a kiss?'" Apparently, the people who came to arrest Jesus didn't know him by sight, or at least were uncertain because of the darkness and needed someone to point Jesus out. Why did Judas choose a kiss? It seems strange to us today, even preposterous, but this was the most intimate, loving greeting a person could give in the Middle East in those days. Perhaps his own guilt about what he was about to do compelled Judas to do this as a sign of his deep hatred of Jesus, for he could not have chosen a more despicable way to betray Jesus. Perhaps it was a fulfillment of a prophecy in Psalm 41:9 in which David said, "Even my close friend, whom I trusted, he who shared my bread, has lifted up his heel against me." In the story of Jesus' final days, Jesus shared bread with Judas as his honored guest at the Last Supper. And it was Judas whom Jesus greeted as friend (see Matt. 26:50).

**Birth Date: Isn't December 25 Christ's Birth Date?**—It could be, but there's no proof that it is. The date was chosen by Dionysius Exiguus, who created the "Easter Tables" and placed Jesus' birth date as December 25. This date was also the day of celebration of the great day of the sun, a pagan holiday that the Romans provided as a day of feasting and fun for their people. After Constantine's conversion to Christianity in A.D. 312, he tried to make various Christian events coincide with pagan holidays so that he could effectively "Christianize" paganism. Until Dionysius's dating, January 6 was the chosen date of Christ's birth. However, neither date is provable as the birth of Christ, for there is no indication in scripture that his birth occurred in winter, in December or January, and certainly not on a feast dedicated to the sun. Nonetheless, the irony is not missed, for Jesus called himself "the light of the world" (John 8:12) and might appropriately be considered the new "sun" of God!

**Birth Date: Jesus Was Not Born in A.D. 0!**—Though the original dating for Christ's birth was A.D. 0, the dividing line between B.C. and A.D., this date was later discovered to be erroneous and based on mistakes of the original mathematician, Dionysius Exiguus (A.D. 527). Later, scholars examined records and compared data such as what Luke gives in his Gospel—that Jesus was born during the reign of Herod the Great (Matt. 2:1) after a decree for taking a census went out from Caesar Augustus (the best date we have for that is from some Egyptian records from 8 B.C.). Luke also says that Christ was born when a man named Quirinius was governor of Syria. For many years scholars thought Luke was mistaken, because the only record we had of Quirinius being governor was from A.D. 6–9. However, a stone fragment found in 1764 near Tivoli (a town close to Rome) indicates that someone fitting Quirinius's description was military governor of Syria twice during the reign of Augustus Caesar, first during the civil governorship of a man named Varus. Because Herod the Great died in 4 B.C., it appears that Christ was born sometime after Augustus's decree for a census in 8 B.C., but before Herod's death. Thus, many scholars estimate Christ was born sometime around 6–4 B.C.

**Birth of Jesus: Prophets Present**—Two prophets were present at the time of Jesus' birth—a man, Simeon, and a woman, Anna. In Luke 2:25–35, it is written that Joseph and Mary brought the eight-day-old Jesus to the Temple to be circumcised. There, a prophet named Simeon had arrived in anticipation of the event. He had been told by the Spirit of God that he would not die until he had seen the Messiah. Simeon saw Jesus and knew by revelation that this was the "anointed one," and he picked the baby up and said, "Sovereign Lord, as you have promised, you now dismiss your servant in peace. For my eyes have seen your salvation, which you have prepared in the sight of all people, a light for revelation to the Gentiles and for glory to your people Israel"(Luke 2:29–32). After that, Simeon spoke to the parents, saying, "This child is destined to cause the falling and rising of many in Israel, and to be a sign that will be spoken against, so that the thoughts of many hearts will be revealed. And a sword will pierce your own soul too"(Luke 2:34–35).

After this, Anna, a prophetess who had been married for seven years and then widowed for eighty-four, also blessed the child and his parents, giving thanks to God and speaking to the people regarding who and what Jesus was. Luke is the only Gospel writer who makes reference to these events.

**Birthplace**—All reverent Jews knew where the Messiah was to be born—in Bethlehem, the home city of David, the greatest king of the Jews. They based this on a prophecy spoken by Micah in the Old Testament. He said, "But you, Bethlehem Ephrathah, though you are small among the clans of Judah, out of you will come for me one who will be ruler over Israel, whose origins are from of old, from ancient times"(Mic. 5:2). When the wise men came to Jerusalem in search of this Messiah, King Herod asked the Jews where this person was to be born, and they quoted to him this prophecy of Micah (see Matt. 2:5–6).

One might think, because God supernaturally appeared to both Mary and Joseph to tell them they would be the parents of the Messiah, that they'd speed down to Bethlehem to make sure the prophecy was fulfilled. They were both from Nazareth, a small city of Galilee that had no prophetic significance at that time. But it's apparent from Luke's and Matthew's data on the birth of Jesus that neither Mary nor Joseph considered it their duty to fulfill prophecy, if they even knew the details of Micah's statement.

So what got them to Bethlehem? A decree of Caesar Augustus! From both biblical and also outside records, we know that Augustus decreed that a census of all the Roman Empire was to be started in 8 B.C. The purpose of this was for discovery of young men to be drafted into the Roman army and also to locate the homes of Roman citizens. The census was to be repeated every fourteen years. A previous census had done just that, but Palestine was excluded because Jews were exempt from military service. However, in 8 B.C., Augustus wanted more. He wanted a universal census to number each nation by family and tribe. This required that everyone return to his family home, which, in Joseph's case, being descended from King David, meant Bethlehem. Apparently, this was a serious matter, for Joseph had to make this hazardous journey from Nazareth over rough terrain with a wife who was in her ninth month of pregnancy. One might quibble, but it appears that the sovereign God got Joseph and Mary to Bethlehem just in time to fulfill an important prophecy that, left unfulfilled, would have rendered Jesus' whole ministry and work invalid. One might even go so far as to think that God the Father accomplished this through Augustus Caesar, the ruler of most of the world at that time, who probably, on something of a whim, decided to include the Jews in his latest census!

**Birthplace Stable: Silver Star Marking**—A silver star marked the supposed stable in which Christ was born in Bethlehem, even though there is no indication in Luke's or Matthew's stories that Jesus was born in a stable. People thought that Jesus was placed in a "manger," or feed trough, which was for feeding animals in a stable. Tradition, however, says that Jesus was born in a cave possibly used for housing animals. Today, the Church of the Nativity erected by Helena in the reign of Constantine has traditionally been the site of Jesus' birth: but the Emperor Hadrian destroyed the original site of Bethlehem in second century A.D., and little was built there for two centuries. Whether Helena's church is the actual site of Christ's birth is open to debate.

Regardless of the traditions, though, the silver star became a matter of dispute between the Eastern Orthodox and Roman Catholic Churches in the 1800s. The Orthodox Church wanted to replace it with its own star. Soon both sides were appealing to governments, and from 1853 to 1856 Russia warred against Turkey, France, England, and Italy in the Crimean War over the issue. In 1858 the silver star was permanently removed.

**Births: Miraculous**—Jesus' was not the only miraculous birth in his lineage. In fact, God had to engineer a number of miraculous births to bring Jesus to planet earth. The first happened with the Father of the Jews, Abraham, and his wife, Sarah. God appeared to Abraham (which means "father of nations"), who was then called "Abram" (which means "father"), when he was seventy-five years old and Sarah ("princess"), then called Sarai, was sixty-five. Sarah had been barren and unable to bear children all her life. God intervened, however, and Sarah conceived in her old age at ninety and Abraham at one hundred. Isaac was born—his name means "laughter"—the first Hebrew miracle baby.

But that wasn't the end. Isaac himself married Rebekah, who was also barren for many years until Isaac prayed for her and she gave birth to twins, Jacob and Esau (see Gen. 25:20–21).

Next, Jacob (whose name means "cheat" or "supplanter" and would later be changed by God to "Israel," which means "God strives") would also have a barren wife, Rachel, his first and greatest love, although he ended up with two wives and two concubines. Rachel was barren for many years until she pled with God to help her conceive (see Gen. 30:1–2, 22–24). She then gave birth to Joseph and later to Benjamin. However, these latter two were not in Jesus' line, for the son of Jacob through whom Jesus' line came was Judah, the fourth son of Leah, Jacob's first wife.

One other miraculous birth was that of John the Baptist, who was Jesus' cousin. He was the son of Zechariah and Elizabeth, both elderly folks who had never had children (see Luke 1:13–25).

Jesus' birth, however, was the only birth that did not have a human father.

**Bones of John the Baptist**—Churches all over the European continent contain relics of John the Baptist, including three shoulder blades, four legs, five arms, and fifty index fingers. In such a scenario, either John was a most grotesque person, or some Middle Easterners made great deals selling artifacts to Christian tourists!

**Born Again**—The words "born again" have become part of the American tongue, and Americans use the term in many ways. Michael Jordan's basketball career was "born again" after his hiatus into professional baseball. Madonna has been "born again" several times as she has "reinvented" her persona for her public. But Jesus was the first to use the term. It's found in John 3:3 as Jesus talks clandestinely by night to a Pharisee teacher named Nicodemus, who, apparently, wanted to know the truth but didn't want to go public with it if he could avoid it. Jesus said to him, "I tell you the truth, unless a man is born again, he cannot see the kingdom of God." Jesus repeats the idea in John 3:7, and it is also found in a letter from Peter (see 1 Pet. 2:23). The phrase "new birth" is also found in 1 Peter 1:3.

What did Jesus mean by the phrase? He clarifies it in John 3:5 by saying that a person must be born of "water and the Spirit." In Jesus' understanding of salvation, a person had to undergo a complete transformation effected by "starting over" as a new person. Paul calls this being a "new creation"(2 Cor. 5:17). When one is born again, one's eyes are opened in a spiritual way, and one is enabled to see the "kingdom of God" in a new way. It is an utterly spiritual experience, and those who go through it—all people who come to believe in Jesus—enter into a special relationship with God so that they become (are "born into") part of God's family.

**Bosses: Deal Fairly**—Jesus, through the apostle Paul, had several strong words for bosses. Among them are these:

*Ephesians 6:9:* "And masters, treat your slaves in the same way. Do not threaten them, since you know that he who is both their Master and yours is in heaven, and there is no favoritism with him."

*Colossians 4:1:* "Masters, provide your slaves with what is right and fair, because you know that you also have a Master in heaven."

**Bumper Sticker: Honk Twice**—A bumper sticker of some years ago sounded out to all who would notice, "Honk twice if you love Jesus." Some said they honked, and the driver with the sticker only got angry, thinking that the honker meant to move him out of the way! Another bumper-slogan said, "Jesus is coming again, and man is He ever going to be ripped." The bumper sticker is the classic "sound bite." But Jesus was also a bumper-sticker kind of speaker. Some of his sayings that might have become bumper stickers are these:

"Blessed are the peacemakers" (Matt. 5:9).
"Seek first God's kingdom and all these things will be given to you" (Matt. 6:33).

"Do not worry about tomorrow. Each day has enough trouble of
its own" (Matt. 6:34).

"Do to others what you would have them do to you" (Matt. 7:12).

"Enter through the narrow gate" (Matt. 7:13).

"You must be born again" (John 3:7).

**Burial of Jesus: Buried in a Rich Man's Tomb**—It was prophesied
in Isaiah 53:9 that the Messiah would die a horrible death in order to
bear the sins of the world. The verse says, "He was assigned a grave
with the wicked, and with the rich in his death, though he had done no
violence, nor was any deceit in his mouth." This is an interesting
prophecy, for it pertains to the actual events of Jesus' death. According
to John 19:31, the Jews intended that Jesus be buried in disgrace with
the two thieves who were crucified on either side of him. "Now it
was the day of Preparation, and the next day was to be a special Sabbath. Because the Jews did not want the bodies left on the crosses during the Sabbath, they asked Pilate to have the legs broken and the
bodies taken down." Normally, Romans left a crucified man to die by
natural means (loss of blood and asphyxiation). This could take several
days. Then they left the bodies on the crosses to rot and be devoured
by vultures.

In this case, however, because Jesus was crucified on a Friday, the
leading Jews were concerned about honoring the Sabbath (see Deut.
21:22–23). They wanted to speed death by asphyxiation and take the
bodies down. However, the soldiers found Jesus already dead and
speared his side to make sure. The leading Jews then would have had
the three bodies thrown into a common grave or possibly even into
Gehenna (the garbage pit on the edge of Jerusalem) to rot and be con-
sumed by rats and vultures.

This didn't happen, for a man named Joseph of Arimathea, one of
the leading Jews himself but also a believer in Jesus, offered his own
tomb for Jesus' body (see Matt. 27:57–61). Thus the prophecy was
fulfilled in two unique ways—the Jews made his "grave with the
wicked," but they were ultimately foiled. Moreover, Jesus was buried
"with the rich," for Joseph of Arimathea was a rich man and owned the
best kind of tomb, a cave hewn into rock near Calvary, a place only the
wealthiest could afford.

**Burial Sheet**—Jesus' burial sheet, according to scripture, was lying in
his tomb when Peter and John visited the tomb after several of the
women reported to them that Jesus' body was gone. In John 20:6–7, we
find these words: "Then Simon Peter, who was behind him, arrived and

went into the tomb. He saw the strips of linen lying there, as well as the burial cloth that had been around Jesus' head. The cloth was folded up by itself, separate from the linen." Normally, at burial, preparers wrapped the dead body in cloths and secreted spices and myrrh into the folds to cover the stench that rose with decay. In this case, the cloths were found lying there in the hewn niche of Jesus' tomb. The reading does not say they looked like they were unwrapped. It seemed that Jesus' body "passed through" the linen wrappings, leaving them in place like a cocoon.

The head wrappings were found neatly folded up, "separate from the linen." Apparently, Jesus, after rising from the dead, had folded up this part of the wrappings. Today, many believe we have the exact burial shroud. It is called the Shroud of Turin and is in Turin's Cathedral of St. John the Baptist in Italy (see **Shroud of Turin**).

# C

**Caiaphas: High Priest**—This man became high priest in the Jewish religion in A.D. 18. He was appointed by the Roman prefect Valerius Gratus and remained in office until A.D. 36 when he was deposed by the Romans at the same time that they removed Pontius Pilate. Caiaphas was the leader present during Jesus' trial that led to his crucifixion. A Sadducee, Caiaphas had tremendous wealth and influence, having made his fortune by extorting money and by investing heavily in the Temple practices of money changing and providing sacrificial animals at high prices. Part of the reason he opposed Jesus so fiercely was that Jesus posed a threat to his money flow when Jesus cleaned out the Temple on two occasions and tried to bring the people back to sincere worship of God. Annas, another priestly leader, was Caiaphas's father-in-law who had been high priest from A.D. 7–14. The two were heavily invested in the "extorting" going on in the Temple and were implacable enemies of Jesus.

**Calendar: Jewish**—Jesus was born in 3761, according to the Jewish calendar, which starts with creation.

**Carpenter**—According to Mark 6:3, when Jesus was teaching, several of those listening said, "Isn't this the carpenter? Isn't this Mary's son and the brother of James, Joses, Judas and Simon? Aren't his sisters here with us?" From this passage, we deduce that Jesus was a carpenter, and his father had been a carpenter also (see Matt. 13:55). One might wonder what Jesus made as a carpenter—fine chairs and tables and desks? Perhaps an ornate hutch or something like that?

Unfortunately, according to a writing of Trypho, an early Christian, Justin Martyr (A.D. 100–165) said Jesus made mainly ploughs and yokes!

Whatever he made, we can be sure Jesus understands the plights of the blue collar worker, the apprentice, the craftsman, and the average businessman. Perhaps Jesus even used modern sales techniques in order to sell his wares!

**Cars: Jesus on Your Dashboard**—Affixed to the dashboards of the cars of many people are small plastic figures of Jesus. He's supposed to bring blessing, good luck, and protection for the journey.

**Catacombs: Musty but Decorated Places**—The catacombs were originally constructed as burial grounds for dead Christians, but as the Roman persecutions intensified under Nero, Domitian, and other emperors, Christians fled to the catacombs as secret places where they could hide and have their worship meetings in peace. They often decorated the tombs—dug into walls and covered with slabs of marble, slate, or earthenware—with Christian symbols such as the fish, anchor, and cross. (See **Fish Symbol** and **Cross**.)

**Christ of the Andes**—This huge statue in the Andes in Uspallata Pass was dedicated on March 13, 1904, and commemorates a series of treaties between Chile and Argentina. It is a huge stone carving of Jesus.

**Christ of the Christus Gardens**—In Gatlinburg, Tennessee, this sculptured head of Christ has eyes that appear to "see" you no matter what angle you look at them.

**Christ of the Ozarks**—A giant statue of Christ is found in Eureka Springs, Arkansas, which many tourists visit yearly.

**Christian: How to tell if You're One**—How do you tell if a person is really a "Christian"? The apostle John, in his First Letter, notes several tests that should be applied:

*1 John 2:4–6:* "The man who says, 'I know him,' but does not do what he commands is a liar, and the truth is not in him. But if anyone obeys his word, God's love is truly made complete in him. This is how we know we are in him: Whoever claims to live in him must walk as Jesus did."

*1 John 2:9:* "Anyone who claims to be in the light but hates his brother is still in the darkness."

*1 John 3:6:* "No one who lives in him keeps on sinning. No one who continues to sin has either seen him or known him."

*1 John 3:10:* "This is how we know who the children of God are and who the children of the devil are: Anyone who does not do what is right is not a child of God; nor is anyone who does not love his brother."

*1 John 4:8:* "Whoever does not love does not know God, because God is love."

*1 John 4:15:* "If anyone acknowledges that Jesus is the Son of God, God lives in him and he in God."

**Christian: The Insult**—The word "Christian" is first found in the Book of Acts where it says, "The disciples were first called Christians at Antioch"(Acts 11:26). The term was originally an insult and means "Little Christ." King Agrippa later used the term in Acts 26:28 to indicate he understood what the apostle Paul was trying to persuade him to do, but perhaps the king meant it there as an insult too. He said, "Do you think that in such a short time you can persuade me to be a Christian?"

**Christian Fiction**—The book market today is burgeoning with fictional depictions of Jesus and his world, from *Two from Galilee*, by Marjorie Holmes (about Joseph and Mary), to *The Book of God*, by Walter Wangerin, which tells the stories of the Bible in a fresh way, using fiction techniques to bring home the power of the story. Now many authors have entered the field, with the most popular being books such as *In His Steps*, by Charles Sheldon, and the *Left Behind Series*, by Tim LaHaye and Jerry Jenkins.

**Christmas: First Celebrated**—The first Christmas celebration resembling those we have today occurred on the shores of Haiti, when Christopher Columbus's ship, the Santa Maria, was wrecked off the coast. Columbus had been searching for gold along the coast of America. The sailors built a fort, La Natividad ("The Nativity") so they could be sheltered while Columbus rebuilt the ship. They had a celebration, gifts, and feast on December 25.

**Christmas Candles**—Why do we light candles at Christmas? Christ claimed be the "light of the world" (John 8:12). Durandus of St. Pourcain

(1270–1332)—a Christian writer, Dominican theologian, and bishop of several cities in France—wrote of the custom of lighting candles at Christmas. He said that the wax of the candle represented Christ's body, the wick his soul, and the flame his "imperishable, divine nature." A candle placed in the window at Christmas welcomed both the Christ child to shelter as well as any other pilgrim. Some also say the candle represents the star that led the Magi to Bethlehem to worship Jesus.

**Christmas Card**—A museum director named Henry Cole initiated the first Christmas card in 1843 when he didn't have time to write a nice message to each friend on a list. He printed the cards and sent them out. Soon the custom spread all over the United States until Hallmark Cards came along and turned it into a necessity!

**Christmas Pageants: The Greatest Pageant Ever**—In her wonderful children's story *The Greatest Christmas Pageant Ever,* Barbara Robinson tells the story of how the Herdman children, the local white trash, take over the debonair children's pageant one year at the local church. The very worst of the Herdmans, Imogene, wins the role of Mary. Her brother Ralph is Joseph, and other members of the family are Wise Men. The Herdmans are the family the church sends all their leftovers and giveaways to. They never attend church, but when they do they draw mustaches on all the disciples in the children's illustrated Bible and do many other "horrible" things. When the angels announce to the shepherds that Jesus is born, they don't say "Glory!"; they protest that it doesn't sound cool and want to say, "Shazam!" In the end, they shout, "Hey! Unto you a child is born!" The Herdman Wise Men think gold, frankincense, and myrrh are pretty stupid gifts for a baby, so they bring a large ham from the gift box the church sent the family at Christmas. Imogene, in her Mary costume, smokes cigars in the girls' bathroom. In the end, though, after everything looks ruined by the Herdmans, Imogene sits holding the baby Jesus and weeps as the church sings "Silent Night." It's a holy moment, and the onlookers appear stunned and awed. All agree it was the best Christmas pageant ever.

**Church: Don't Miss a Single Service, Buster!**—The Sandemanians, a fundamentalist sect founded in 1725 by John Glas, had some strict rules, among them church attendance every Lord's Day. They strongly believed in Christ's salvation as a gift of grace. Michael Faraday, who invented the first electric motor, the first dynamo, and the first transformer, and is sometimes known as the father of electricity, was a member of this sect. On one occasion, Queen Victoria invited him to dinner on a Sunday in 1844, which meant he would miss services. He agonized about this decision, but in the end felt he owed some allegiance to the queen. He went, and his church excommunicated him, allowing him back only after a rather excessive penance. What would they have done if Jesus broke one of their rules, as he did with the ultra-strict Pharisees? The Sabbath was a huge issue for the leaders of the Jews, and Jesus broke their rules by healing on the Sabbath, allowing his disciples to pick grain and eat it, and numerous other no-no's. How far we've come!

**Church: Get These Guys to Build Your House**—Many churches the world over commemorate the presence and worship of God in majestic beauty and architectural magnificence. However, the French took it a bit more seriously than most. From 1170 to 1270, French artisans, because of their stout belief in Christ and commitment to his kingdom, built over eighty huge cathedrals and over five hundred smaller ones throughout their small nation. Notre Dame, the greatest of Gothic cathedrals, was begun in 1163 and finished in 1300.

**Church: A Million Strong**—The largest church in the world is in Seoul, Korea, pastored by Dr. Paul Yongghi Cho. It presently has over a million members, and services are held in stadiums and other huge auditoriums.

**Church: Rich**—In the early days after Christ's life and death, Christians rarely owned buildings. Often they gave what holdings they did have to feed the poor and help needy people. As time wore on, though, the church prospered, especially after it became the state religion under Constantine, and many great churches were built. Often, much of a nation was owned by the church. Such an example is Portugal, a poor country by many standards. In the eighteenth century, two thirds of all the land was owned by the Roman Catholic Church as a sign of the nation's commitment to Christ.

**Church Denominations Using Christ's Name**—Denominations have arisen under all sorts of guises. Baptists go back to the baptistic practices of John the Baptist. Presbyterians base their name on the Greek word for "presbyter" or "elder." Episcopalians also have such a heritage, with their name derived from the Greek *episcopos*, which means "bishop." However, some churches, perhaps wanting a more spiritual edge, have put Christ's name in their denominational title. Thus, we find such names as: Church of Christ, United Church of Christ, Disciples of Christ, Christadelphian, Christian and Missionary Alliance, Christian Catholic Church, Christian Methodist Episcopal, Christian Reformed Church, Christian Science, and many others.

**Churches: Jesus' Followers Have Flowered**—There are approximately 375,000 churches in the United States. Of them, over 100,000 have fewer than fifty people in attendance. Only three hundred have more than two thousand in total attendance on a Sunday morning. (From "Attendance: Winning the Values War in a Changing Culture," by Leith Anderson [Bethany House, 1994]; *Leadership*, Vol. 16, #2.) The percentage of Americans who claim membership in a church or synagogue is 69 percent. The number who believe it is important to be a church member is 84 percent. (From "Church Membership," Princeton Religion Research Center's *Emerging Trends*, 2/90; "The Church Today: Insightful Statistics and Commentary," Barna Research Group, 1990; *Leadership*, Vol. 12, #2.) About 44 percent of U.S. adults are unchurched, neither belonging to a church nor visiting one in the last six months, except for holidays, weddings, or funerals. This finding came from a Gallup study, "The Unchurched American," in 1988, which also reported that 72 percent of these unchurched believe Jesus is the Son of God; 63 percent believe the Bible is God's Word; and 77 percent pray to God (41 percent daily).

Surprisingly, 58 percent of unchurched adults say they're open to joining a church if they find the right one. Yet in the year of the poll, only 38 percent were actually invited to one by any church member. (*Leadership*, Vol. 10, #1)

**Cities Named after Christ**—Some of the world's great cities named after Christ are Corpus Christi, Texas; Christmas, Florida; Christmas Atoll; Christmas Island; Christiansted; Christiania (Norway); Christchurch (New Zealand); and Chrissiesmeer (Transvaal).

**Claims to Be Christ**—Jesus prophesied in Matthew 24:5 that "many will come in my name, claiming, 'I am the Christ,' and will deceive many." In recent times, more people have made this declaration than perhaps at any other time in history. Some of the most famous people who have claimed to be God or Jesus or both are Charles Manson, David Koresh, Jim Jones, Sun Myung Moon, Rasputin, Mahara Ji, Bhagwan, Herbert Armstrong, Adolph Hitler, Father Divine, and many others.

**Comics: Christ in the Comics**—Jesus has made it into the comics of a number of Christian illustrators, including Charles Schulz ("Peanuts"), Johnny Hart ("B.C."), Jeff MacNelly ("Shoe"), and Gary Trudeau ("Doonesbury").

**Commandments: What Were the Most Important Commandments to Jesus?**—One might think Jesus would have concentrated on repeating, teaching, and parsing the Ten Commandments of Moses. But Jesus rarely mentioned them. Instead, he concentrated on what he called the Great Commandments, of which there were two. In Matthew 22:35–40, we find this exchange between Jesus and a scribe: "One of them, an expert in the law, tested him with this question: 'Teacher, which is the greatest commandment in the Law?' Jesus replied: 'Love the Lord your God with all your heart and with all your soul and with all your mind.'" This is the first and greatest commandment. And the second is like it: "'Love your neighbor as yourself.'" Jesus concluded that "'all the Law and the Prophets hang on these two commandments.'" That included the Ten Commandments as well as the other 613 commandments found in the laws of Moses.

**Constantine: Jesus Conquered an Empire, and Finally an Emperor**—As Christianity turned the Roman world upside down in the first three centuries, many said that no emperor would ever give in to Christ's influence. At least ten emperors mercilessly persecuted Christians and tried to wipe them out, from Nero (A.D. 54–68) through Domitian (81–96) and all the way through to Diocletian (284–305). One day, however, as Constantine (who began his reign in 306) faced his greatest battle for empire against Maxentius in A.D. 312, he prayed to his god, Apollo, the Unconquered Sun. In a dream he saw a "cross of light" above the sun bearing the inscription "CONQUER BY THIS." Constantine claimed that the whole army saw it. When he won the battle the next day, he was soundly converted to the Christian faith. He immediately began a campaign to declare Christianity legal and, later, by the Edict of Milan, the state religion. Some said this became the greatest advance for the Christian faith. Others say that because people became "believers" simply by being Romans and part of the State, conversion became meaningless.

**Conversion: Romans Converted**—The first Romans to become followers of Christ were those officiating at the execution of Jesus. Luke says in Luke 23:47 that "the centurion, seeing what had happened, praised God and said, 'Surely this was a righteous man.'" Matthew writes: "When the centurion and those with him who were guarding Jesus saw the earthquake and all that had happened, they were terrified, and exclaimed, 'Surely he was the Son of God!'" (Matt. 27:54). These were the same soldiers who, as they nailed Jesus to the cross, heard him say directly to them, "Father, forgive them, for they do not know what they are doing" (Luke 23:34).

**Conversion: St. Augustine's Conversion to Christ Out of a Life of Debauchery**—St. Augustine of Hippo (354–430) is considered by many to be the first great theologian of the church. His early life, however, according to his *Confessions* was one far away from religion, Christian faith, and commitment to holiness. In this passage from his *Confessions* he tells of his conversion from that way of life to that of Christ:

> The very toys of toys and vanities of vanities still held me; they plucked at the garment of my flesh and whispered softly, "Will you cast us off forever? And from that moment shall we no longer be with you—forever?" And I hesitated, for a strong habit said to me, "Do you think you can live without them?"
>
> But continence said to me, "Why do you rely on yourself and so waver? Cast yourself upon him, fear not, he will not withdraw himself and let you fall, he will receive you and heal you."
>
> So I rose and, throwing myself down under a certain fig tree, wept bitterly in contrition of heart. Suddenly I heard from a neighboring house the voice of a child, singing over and over again, "Take up and read, take up and read."
>
> Checking my weeping I got up and went back to where I had been sitting, and had laid down the volume of the apostle, and read the first passage which met my eyes: "Not in rioting and drunkenness, not in impurity and wantonness, not in strife and envy, but put on the Lord Jesus Christ, and make no room for the flesh, to fulfill its lusts."
>
> I needed to read no further, for suddenly, as it were by a life infused into my heart, all darkness vanished away.

**Cousins of Jesus: John the Baptist Was Jesus' Cousin**—According to Luke 1:36, Elizabeth, the barren wife of Zechariah, was a "relative" of the Virgin Mary. Elizabeth, miraculously pregnant by normal means with John the Baptist, was visited by Mary during Elizabeth's sixth month. She gave Mary an amazing confirmation of God's Word and the angel Gabriel's visit where Mary was told she would bear the Son of God. This means that John the Baptist and Jesus were cousins. Does prophecy run in families? Rarely, as Jewish history shows, were prophets descended or related to one another. Even Elijah and Elisha were strangers. But this is one case where the Sovereign God brought two of the most famous men of history together by passion, belief, and blood.

**Cross: Jesus Felt Forsaken**—On the cross, Jesus revealed the depth of his pain in his cry: "*'Eloi, Eloi, lama sabachthani?'*—which means, 'My God, my God, why have you forsaken me?'"(Matt. 27:46). The purpose of Jesus' death is stated many times in scripture as "for the sins of the world." His physical pain on the cross was part of that payment, but only a small part. The greatest shame and horror for him was this moment when he was "separated" from his Father. For the first time in his life, Jesus felt as if his Father had forsaken him. In that moment, Jesus knew what it was to be condemned to eternal hell, bereft forever of the presence, love, and peace of God.

**Cross: A King in Three Languages**—Attached to the top of Jesus' cross was a bit of paper declaring that Jesus was the King of the Jews. According to John 19:19–20, Pontius Pilate "had a notice prepared and fastened to the cross. It read: JESUS OF NAZARETH, THE KING OF THE JEWS. Many of the Jews read this sign, for the place where Jesus was crucified was near the city, and the sign was written in Aramaic, Latin and Greek." The leading Jews who had engineered the execution of Jesus were outraged that Pilate had placed this declaration about Jesus as though it was correct. They went to Pilate and demanded that he retract what he had written and replace it with a different sign. In John 19:21–22, we find: "The chief priests of the Jews protested to Pilate, 'Do not write "The King of the Jews," but that this man claimed to be King of the Jews.' Pilate answered, 'What I have written, I have written.'" Was Pilate somehow being "led" by God to participate in the ultimate plan of Jesus' death where he would become the eternal King of the Jews? The Spirit of God has done that in other cases. For instance, Caiaphas, the high priest, said in John 11:49–52: "Then one of them, named Caiaphas, who was high priest that year, spoke up, 'You know nothing at all! You do not realize that it is better for you that one man die for the people than that the whole nation perish.' He did not say this on his own, but as high priest that year he prophesied that Jesus would die for the Jewish nation, and not only for that nation but also for the scattered children of God, to bring them together and make them one." There are other occasions where unbelievers or lost men have prophesied or acted in God's providence without intending it (see Balaam in Numbers 22–24, Acts 4:27–28).

**Cross: Six Hours on the Cross, or More?**—How long was Jesus on the cross? The crucifixion began about 9 A.M. (see Mark 15:25), called "the third hour" because morning started with the "first hour" at 6 A.M., according to the Jewish method of counting hours in the day. (The Roman method began with midnight, so that the third hour in their system was 3 A.M.) Jesus died at the "ninth hour," which was about 3 P.M. Thus, he was on the cross about six hours, typically a short time for an execution to take place. Many crucifixions lasted several days. The victim usually died from loss of blood, exhaustion, asphyxiation, fever, or thirst. Often, the victim was left on the cross to be eaten alive by birds and beasts of prey.

**Cross: The Wood of the Cross**—What was the cross made of? Nothing in scripture reveals a definite answer, but legend has it that the cross was the aspen, a tree that trembles and shakes in the wind in a noisy and unique way. The legend says that to this day the aspen quakes and trembles its leaves because of whom it once held. Another legend says the wood was from the mistletoe, which at one time was a large tree but shrank for shame ever after.

**Crossing Your Fingers**—Originally, some sociologists believe, the act of crossing your fingers, which was an act of wishing for luck ("I've got my fingers crossed") or wiping out the guilt of a lie ("Hey, I had my fingers crossed"), was actually an early Christian custom. It depicted Jesus' cross and was a sign Christians used to identify one another in public.

**Crossing Your Heart**—This custom, preserved in Roman Catholicism, was an early Christian gesture signifying one's sincerity ("Cross my heart and hope to die"). It invoked Jesus as witness to the gravity of a statement or act.

**Crown of Thorns, Christ's Thorn**—This thorn was believed to be used in the circlet placed on Christ's head at his humiliation at the hands of the Romans.

**Crusades: Take Back the Holy Land for Christ**—The Crusades, from the eleventh to the thirteenth centuries, were begun in order to take back the holy land from the Muslims. The First Crusade (1095–1099) ended in triumph, with the armies under several monarchs taking Jerusalem. However, in succeeding crusades, the holy land was continually lost back to the Turks, and the Second through the Fifth Crusades all ended in various forms of disaster. At one point, in 1212, the Children's Crusade, in which thousands of children set out for the holy land, led to slavery, disease, and death for most of the young people in it.

**Dancing: Did Jesus Ever Dance?**—In the Gospels, shortly before Jesus' arrest in the Garden of Gethsemane, he and his disciples depart the Upper Room and sing a hymn. No one knows for sure what hymn they sang or what else they did. However, in one of the books passed down through the ages known as *The Acts of John*, we have a story of what that hymn was and what Jesus did. This book is part of the *New Testament Apocrypha* and is not considered authoritative or even necessarily true, so we cannot be sure anything like this happened. However, it is interesting to see what the author tried to convey. As Jesus and his disciples proceed out of the site of the Last Supper, Jesus says, "Let us dance!" Then he bids them all join hands in a circle, and Jesus cries, "Glory be to the Father!" The company responds, "Amen."

This dance and singing results:

> "Glory be to Thee, Word." "Amen."
> "I would be born and I would bear!" "Amen."
> "I would eat and I would be eaten!" "Amen."
> "Thou that dancest, see what I do, for thine is this passion
>     of the manhood, which I am about to suffer!" "Amen."
> "I would flee and I would stay!" "Amen."
> "I would be united and I would unite!" "Amen."
> "A door am I to thee that knocketh on me . . . a way am I
>     to thee, a wayfarer."

When Jesus ended the dance, he walked into the garden where he would soon be arrested.

**Darkness the Day Jesus Died**—When Jesus died on the cross, the Bible says a strange darkness covered the land (see Matt. 27:45) from the sixth hour (12 P.M.) to the ninth hour (3 P.M.). Thallus, a Samaritan historian writing around A.D. 52, referred to this darkness, which apparently was seen all over Israel and possibly the Roman Empire, and said it was an eclipse of the moon, though scientists have since found this was impossible. No one knows the cause of the darkness except as a judgment of God upon the murderers of Jesus, warning them that he was no ordinary man. God has used darkness before as a judgment, notably on the Egyptians when God sent the ninth plague of darkness, a "darkness that can be felt" (Exod. 10:21). God appeared to Israel and spoke the commandments to them from a deep darkness (see Deut. 4:11), and darkness was considered a judgment of God for disobedience (see Deut. 28:29; Isa. 8:22). When God stopped the Egyptian army at the edge of the Red Sea so they couldn't kill the Israelites trying to cross, God threw them into turmoil by surrounding them with a darkness (see Josh. 24:7). Darkness was considered the time when evil reigned, as Jesus said in Luke 22:53. One of God's final judgments on humankind because of wickedness is to be "plunged into darkness" where men will "gnaw their tongues in agony"(Rev. 16:10). Clearly, for whatever reason the darkness appeared, it was a sign of God's displeasure and judgment upon those who had crucified Jesus.

**Da Vinci Erred**—Leonardo da Vinci (1452–1519) made his fame as the quintessential "Renaissance man." Architect, scientist, inventor, writer, and painter, he mastered many arenas of intellect. He is most famous for two paintings, the "Mona Lisa" and the "Last Supper." In the latter, da Vinci made a major mistake. He pictures Jesus in the middle, seated at a table with his twelve disciples who are also seated. The problem is that Jews of Jesus' day did not sit at tables, but reclined on their elbows with pillows supporting them around a mat or very low table. Many paintings of that era make the same mistake, including the most recent one by Salvador Dali.

**Death: Jesus Couldn't Even Carry the Cross**—One of the ways Roman executioners humiliated their victims was to make them carry their means of execution—the top crossbar of the cross (the posts were left in the ground so that all that was needed for a particular execution was the top T). This piece of wood could weigh as much as two hundred pounds. After Jesus' scourging and beating at the hands of several different groups of people (the Sanhedrin, Herod's guard, the Roman soldiers), Jesus had undoubtedly lost much blood and might have been in a state of mild shock by the time he was forced to walk the Via Dolorosa ("Way of Sorrows") to the place of execution on Calvary, which means "skull" in Latin, or Golgotha, which means "place of the skull." On the way, Jesus fell and could not continue on under the weight of the cross, so the guard of four Roman soldiers conscripted a man named Simon from Cyrene, a city of North Africa, to take the crossbar the rest of the way (see Matt. 27:32). This Simon may have been the Simon called Niger, referred to in Acts 13:1, because "Niger" means "black" and indicates he might have been an African. No direct evidence supports this theory, though. Jesus' weakness in this situation indicates his human need and difficulty, a point that makes him able to identify with and help people in weakness, pain, and all sorts of other situations (see Heb. 4:14–16).

**Death: Jesus Didn't Want to Die**—Although Jesus' stated purpose was to come into the world to "seek and to save the lost" by his death on the cross for the sins of the world, just hours before he was to be tried, he attempted to persuade his Father to let him off the hook! In the Garden of Gethsemane, Matthew 26:39 says: "Going a little farther, he fell with his face to the ground and prayed, 'My Father, if it is possible, may this cup be taken from me. Yet not as I will, but as you will.'" He clearly did not want to face the agonizing death on the cross that he knew he would ultimately face. In fact, he asked his Father three times to allow him not to go to the cross. But on each occasion, he added, "Yet not as I will, but as you will."

This truth should be great encouragement to anyone who has flinched from taking on some godly task that seems daunting or even painful. Jesus himself did not relish God's will for his life, but he chose to do it anyway because he knew what would be accomplished as a result (see Heb. 12:1–4).

**Death: Prediction of**—Jesus predicted his death in detail, and the disciples protested. Matthew writes: "From that time on Jesus began to explain to his disciples that he must go to Jerusalem and suffer many things at the hands of the elders, chief priests and teachers of the law, and that he must be killed and on the third day be raised to life" (Matt. 16:21). Jesus informed his disciples on many occasions (see Matt. 20:17–19; Mark 9:31–32; Luke 24:46) that his death was imminent. He also described how he would die. The disciples did not understand what Jesus meant. On at least one occasion, Simon Peter rebuked him for thinking such things, saying, "Never, Lord! . . . This shall never happen to you!" Jesus regarded this as an attempt of Satan to derail him from his destined course. He said to Peter, "Out of my sight, Satan! You are a stumbling block to me; you do not have in mind the things of God, but the things of men" (Matt. 16:22–23). It is impossible to know how and when we will die in most cases, but this is a clear case where Jesus knew exactly what would happen and did not try to stop it.

**Death of Christ: To Satisfy God's Justice or to Pay Off the Devil?**—For centuries, theologians believed that Jesus' death was largely a ransom paid to the devil. This ransom freed his believers from having to pay the devil with their own death and confinement in hell. Anselm of Canterbury (1033–1109), at one time Archbishop of Canterbury, proposed a different interpretation that finds many adherents today. Anselm believed that Jesus died to satisfy God's justice, holiness, and righteousness, all of which demanded that sinners pay a penalty for their sins.

**Death of Christ: You Wouldn't Think So Much Could Happen in One Day**—Jim Bishop's classic, *The Day Christ Died*, a best-seller, details everything that happened on Jesus' last day. It movingly depicts Christ's passion as well as the people of his times and influence. It was a day filled with terror, pain, passion, and death.

**Death Warrant: What Was Written on Jesus' Death Warrant?**— In 1810, excavators at the city of Amitorum (now Aguila) in the Kingdom of Naples discovered a marble vase in which was concealed a copper plate, written on one side in Hebrew letters and on the other, also in Hebrew, "A similar plate is sent to each tribe." It was discovered to be the "death warrant" of Jesus Christ. The relic was then placed into an ebony box and held in the sacristy of the Carthusians. The warrant reads as follows:

> Sentence rendered by Pontius Pilate, acting governor of lower Galilee, stating that Jesus of Nazareth shall suffer death on the cross. In the seventeenth year of the reign of the Emperor Tiberius and on the twenty-seventh day of March, in the most holy city of Jerusalem, during the pontificate of Annas and Caiaphas, Pontius Pilate, governor of lower Galilee, sitting in the presidential chair of the praetorium, condemns Jesus of Nazareth to die on the cross between thieves, the great and notorious evidence of the people saying:
>
> 1. Jesus is a seducer.
> 2. He is seditious.
> 3. He is the enemy of the Law.

4. He calls himself falsely the Son of God.
5. He calls himself falsely the King of Israel.
6. He entered into the Temple followed by a multitude bearing palm branches on their heads.

Orders the first centurion, Quintus Cornelius, to lead him to the place of execution. Forbids any person whomsoever, either rich or poor, to oppose the death of Jesus Christ.

The witnesses who signed the condemnation of Jesus are:

1. Daniel Robani, a Pharisee
2. Joannus Robani
3. Raphael Robani
4. Capet, a citizen

Jesus shall go out of the city of Jerusalem by the Gate of Struenus. (*The Jesus Book*, edited by Calvin Miller)

There are several flaws in this document: (1) No plate like this is known in archaeology. (2) Such a plate, if authentic, would have been included in the New Testament. (3) No competent scholar has ever reported seeing such a plate, nor has any museum or institution claimed to own such a plate. (4) The twelve tribes and their history broke down over 750 years earlier (B.C.), after the destruction of Israel by Nineveh. (5) That a Roman would feel compelled to justify himself to Jews is inconceivable.

**Deity of Christ: Was Christ God?**—(See also entries under "Human," "Incarnation," and "Messiah.") The deity of Christ has been argued, scorned, rejected, and believed in for centuries. It is unlikely that this small entry will sway people one way or another. However, it does seem worthwhile to provide the biblical evidence of why Christians believe Jesus was God.

One way to come at it is to offer the primary scriptural evidence:

1. Jesus was called "God"(Heb. 1:8), the "Son of the living God" (Matt. 16:16), "Lord"(Matt. 22:43–45), and "King of kings and Lord of lords"(Rev. 19:16).
2. He possessed several of the primary characteristics of Godhood:
   Omnipotence ("all-powerful"): Matt. 28:18.
   Omniscience ("all-knowing"): John 1:48.
   Omnipresence ("everywhere present"): Matt. 18:20.

Life: John 1:4.
Truth: John 14:6.
Immutability: Heb. 13:8.
Light: compare John 8:12 and 1 John 1:5.
Power over death: John 11:25.
Eternality: John 1:2.

3. He performed deeds and works only God could do:
      The power to create (John 1:3).
      The power to sustain creation (Col. 1:17).
      The authority to forgive sin (Luke 7:48).
      The power to raise the dead (John 5:25; 11:43–44).
      The power to heal diseases and perform miracles (all through the Gospels).
      Power over Satan and demons (Matt. 8:28–34).
      Power to perform miracles like walk on water (Matt. 14:24–33), stop a storm (Matt. 8:23–27), and multiply food to feed thousands of people (John 6:5–13).
      The authority to judge others (John 5:27).
      The authority to send the Holy Spirit (John 15:26).
      The right to receive worship: by angels (Heb. 1:6); by people (Matt. 14:33); by everyone from all time (Phil. 2:10).

4. He was equal to God the Father and the Holy Spirit; he was a member of the Trinity (John 14:23; Matt. 28:19; 2 Cor. 13:14).

This is not an exhaustive list, but it might be wise to ask one more question: If God were to come among people into human history, what might we expect to happen? Several thoughts:

1. His coming among us would be announced beforehand.
2. He would come in a unique way.
3. He would be perfect and sinless.
4. He would speak the greatest words ever spoken.
5. He would be different from all others and would recognize that difference.
6. He would admit he was God incarnate.
7. He would provide a way for anyone, from the smallest child to the most sinful adult, to find salvation and gain eternal life.
8. He would perform miracles.
9. He would solve the problem of human sin and ultimate evil.
10. He would have a lasting impact on our world.
11. He would conquer death.
12. He would make his presence known personally to all who seek him.
13. His story would be the greatest story ever told.

For any ordinary person, these characteristics are fantastic, impossible. But in Jesus they all come together. The Old Testament prophesied his coming. Many events in his life were fulfillments of prophecy, including his birth (Isa. 7:14), where he would be born (Mic. 5:2), when he would be born (Dan. 9:27), how he would die (Psalm 22), and that he would rise from the dead (Psalm 16).

He was born of a virgin in a lowly stable. His birth was announced by a strange star, heralded by angels, and visited by kingmakers (the Magi) (see Matthew 1–2 and Luke 1–2). He never committed a sin. His words are timeless, his deeds astonishing. He healed lepers, banished demons to the pit, stilled the winds and sea, and fed thousands, all at a mere word from his lips. No other person has impacted the world as he has. His name and teachings have influenced billions. His story has been published and told by every generation of humankind. Billions of people will eagerly tell of his personal impact on their lives.

He solved the problem of evil and sin on the cross, and three days later, he conquered death once and for all. He has made his salvation available to all who will listen and believe. He turns away no one, invites everyone, and promises wealth, honor, and blessing in heaven to those who will follow him.

There is no one like Him, and it is unlikely there will ever be anyone to rival him.

If Jesus was not God come among us, then what else could he have been?

**Demon-possession: 2000 of Them**—On one occasion, two demon-possessed men met Jesus on a lonely road. They had come out of the tombs and had fallen at Jesus' feet, begging him to cast out their demons. This was in the country of Gadarenes, which was a small town opposite Tiberius on the other side of Galilee. When Jesus started to speak the words to cast out the demons, the demons suddenly spoke up, begging him not to send them into the pit where other demons were confined (see 2 Pet. 2:4 and Jude 6). They asked Jesus to cast them out into the herd of pigs standing on the hill above them. Jesus complied and sent them into the pigs. The two thousand hogs went wild, ran off the cliff, and drowned in the sea (see Mark 5:13).

Was it possible that these men actually had two thousand demons inside them? It seems impossible, but when Jesus asked the demons for their name, they replied, "Legion, for we are many." A Roman Legion was composed of six thousand foot soldiers. This response indicated there had to be a huge number of these demons present and that they were probably rather militant, as was indicated by the brute strength these men possessed (see Mark 5:3–5). Jesus gives this warning in Matthew 12:43–45: "When an evil spirit comes out of a man, it goes through arid places seeking rest and does not find it. Then it says, 'I will return to the house I left.' When it arrives, it finds the house unoccupied, swept clean and put in order. Then it goes and takes with it seven other spirits more wicked than itself, and they go in and live there. And the final condition of that man is worse than the first." Apparently, it was quite possible for one person to be possessed by many demons, at least in the time of Jesus.

**Demons: One More Way to Hassle Jesus**—Jesus frequently cast out demons from people who were oppressed or possessed by evil beings. Although we don't know precisely what this involved, Jesus obviously believed these were spirit beings who had taken up residence in a human's body. The demons did not leave willingly, though apparently at Jesus' command they had no choice. As a "parting shot," these demons would often cry out, "You are the Son of God!" (see Mark 3:11 and Luke 4:41). This was a tactic perhaps to discredit Jesus, because people knew these were demons and would believe they were lying, or mocking, or pulling some other trick. That is probably the reason Jesus "rebuked them and would not allow them to speak," according to Luke 4:41.

**Devil's Sneaky Plan**—Jesus understood well how his archenemy, Satan, intended to subvert his plan to establish God's kingdom on earth. In his parable of the tares, Jesus illustrated how Satan makes fake "believers" look like the real thing (see Matt. 13:24–30). In this parable, Jesus speaks of a man who sows normal wheat in a field. That night, an enemy walked through his field and sowed "tares," probably a kind of darnel, which was a weed that resembles wheat very closely until the final head appears at harvest time. Jesus tells how the servants of the wheat-field owner wanted to weed out the tares, but Jesus counseled to leave them until the harvest time when the tares would be more obvious. He expressed fear that the "servants" would uproot the true wheat shoots.

The meaning of the parable is fairly obvious. It's about how Satan sows "false" or "pretend" believers in the church and uses them to cause problems for church leaders. They're hard to tell apart, because often these people look very much like the real thing, even as the tares closely resembled the wheat, until the end, when God's angels gather the true believers out of the world and take them to heaven. Jesus explains all these details when he shows the meaning of the parable to his disciples later in the chapter (see Matt. 13:36–43).

**Disciples Deserted Him**—Jesus warned his disciples that they would all betray him on some level by deserting him in his final hours. He said in Matthew 26:31 to the eleven remaining disciples, after Judas Iscariot's defection, "This very night you will all fall away on account of me, for it is written: 'I will strike the shepherd, and the sheep of the flock will be scattered.'" This was a quotation of a prophecy found in the Book of Zechariah, which said, "'Awake, O sword, against my shepherd, against the man who is close to me!' declares the LORD Almighty. Strike the shepherd, and the sheep will be scattered, and I will turn my hand against the little ones" (Zech. 13:7). Three times Peter denied he even knew Jesus personally (see Luke 22:31–34). This took place as Peter stood by at Caiaphas's house while Jesus was tried before the Sanhedrin. All the other disciples would vanish into the night, except John, who appeared with Jesus' mother Mary while Jesus hung on the cross (see John 19:25–27).

**Disciples Died Horribly**—Jesus told his disciples many times that they would be persecuted. He even prophesied how Peter would die. According to John 21, Peter would die by crucifixion. How then did the disciples meet their ends? Here is a listing:

*Andrew:* He was crucified by order of a Roman governor named Aegeates, at Patrae in Achaia. Apparently, he was bound, not nailed, to a cross, so his sufferings would last longer. He died during the reign of Nero, on November 30, A.D. 60.

*Bartholomew:* He died supposedly at Albanopolis in Armenia. Some traditions say he was beheaded; others say he was flayed alive and crucified, head downward, because he converted Polymius, King of Armenia.

*James (brother of John):* James was the first to be martyred, in A.D. 44, by order of Herod Agrippa I. In order to please the leading Jews, he persecuted the church during Passover of that year. According to Acts 12:1–2, he chose to have James killed with the sword. According to one tradition from Eusebius, which he received from Clement of Alexandria, the accuser who led James to judgment was touched by James's confession. He accepted Christ on the spot, and the two were beheaded together.

*James the Less:* It is unknown how he died, but it is believed he was martyred.

*John (brother of James):* John was banished to Patmos during the reign of the Emperor Domitian (81–96). According to Tertullian, though, John was thrown into a vat of boiling oil in Rome. He suffered no injury. After Domitian's death, he returned to Ephesus where he'd been an elder. He died there about A.D. 100, the only disciple not martyred violently.

*Judas Iscariot:* His guilt over betraying Jesus led Judas to commit suicide shortly after Jesus' death.

*Matthew:* It is unknown where Matthew was martyred or what kind of torture he received. It is believed he was either burned, stoned, or beheaded.

*Peter:* A tradition offered by Tertullian at the end of the second century and also by Origen says that Peter suffered crucifixion. Origen wrote: "Peter was crucified at Rome with his head downwards, as he himself had desired to suffer." Peter did this because he did not believe himself worthy to be crucified in the same manner as was Christ.

*Philip:* The apocryphal "Acts of Philip," regarded as legend, say Philip died at Hieropolis by martyrdom.

*Simon the Zealot:* According to Moses of Chorene, Simon faced martyrdom in Weriosphora in Iberia.

*Thaddeus:* No clear tradition states the manner of his death. Jerome states that he was sent on a mission to Abgar, king of Edessa. But nothing more is known of his work after his years with Jesus.

*Thomas:* A strong tradition that says that Thomas preached in "India" is found in such authors as Ephraem Syrus, Ambrose, Paulinus, Jerome, and Gregory of Tours. Some believe that Thomas preached in Mylapore, not far from Madras, and there was martyred.

What stands out from these traditions (none found in the Bible, except James and Judas) is that all the disciples paid the price of death—and in many cases, torture—for their belief in Christ, his life, salvation, resurrection, and reign in heaven. Although many people throughout the world have died to support their beliefs (as, for instance, an American soldier in World War II), few in history have died because of their beliefs. Any one of these disciples could easily have recanted his belief in the message and history of Christ. That none of them did is a powerful testimony to the truth of that message and history.

**Disciples Doing Miracles**—Jesus commissioned his twelve disciples early in their ministry to cast out demons, heal the sick, cleanse lepers, and raise the dead. At one point, Jesus sent out seventy disciples to do the same thing (see Luke 10:1). They were so amazed when they were able to do these things that they came back to Jesus to give a report and said, "Lord, even the demons submit to us in your name." Jesus replied, "I saw Satan fall like lightning from heaven. I have given you authority to trample on snakes and scorpions, and to overcome all the power of the enemy; nothing will harm you. However, do not rejoice that the spirits submit to you, but rejoice that your names are written in heaven" (Luke 10:17–20).

On one occasion, however, the disciples ran into real trouble. When they tried to exorcise a demon in a certain time and place, they couldn't. Jesus had to step in and finish the job. After Jesus cast out the demon, the disciples approached him in private and said, "Why couldn't we drive it out?" He replied, "Because you have so little faith. I tell you the truth, if you have faith as small as a mustard seed, you can say to this mountain, 'Move from here to there' and it will move. Nothing will be impossible for you" (Matt. 17:19–20).

**Disciples Were Egomaniacs**—The disciples of Jesus frequently argued about who was the greatest in his kingdom. This became such a hot issue among them that James and John finally sent their own mother to ask Jesus for seats at his left hand and right hand in his kingdom (Matt. 20:20–28). This kind of egomania did not sit well with Jesus. He told them, "You know that the rulers of the Gentiles lord it over them, and their high officials exercise authority over them. Not so with you. Instead, whoever wants to become great among you must be your servant, and whoever wants to be first must be your slave—just as the Son of Man did not come to be served, but to serve, and to give his life as a ransom for many" (Matt. 20:25–28).

Apparently, Jesus' answer didn't sink in very deeply, because the disciples were still arguing the point at the Lord's Supper shortly before Jesus was arrested and crucified (see Luke 22:24).

**Disciples Were Generally Stupid and Stupefied**—The disciples Jesus chose were common men, uneducated, and, in some cases, complete outcasts. James, John, Simon, and Andrew were all fishermen. Nathaniel was something of a dreamer, Philip a vagabond, Simon the Zealot a member of the rebelling sect of the Zealots, Matthew a tax gatherer. It's not even known whether most of them could read and write, or whether they knew the scriptures that well. But Jesus clearly saw something in each of them that he felt was necessary to fulfill his ministry and plant the church, which would grow to over a billion strong today. Jesus knew many people he could have chosen as disciples who were educated and important: Nicodemus, a leader and teacher of the Jews; Joseph of Arimathea, a rich man; the rich young ruler who came to Jesus and asked how he could be saved (see Matt. 19:16–26); and Mark, the writer of the second Gospel and possibly a Roman nobleman. Nonetheless, Jesus chose the twelve he did. Through them, plus the apostle Paul and others, Jesus' name and fame were spread so powerfully and so far that at one point people said, "These men who have caused trouble all over the world have now come here" (Act 17:6).

These men, however, were often foolish and bumbling, making serious and stupid mistakes. For instance, when Jesus walked on water and Peter asked to walk out to him, the disciple stepped out of the boat and promptly sank after he saw the winds and the waves. Jesus had to rescue him (see Matt. 14:22–33). When Peter, James, and John saw Jesus transfigured on the mountain with Moses and Elijah, the only thing Peter could think to say was that he could build tents for each of them so they could stick around (see Matt. 17:1–8). When Jesus told his disciples to feed the five thousand, they had no idea how they could do it until a little child offered his lunch (John 6:5–13). They didn't seem to "get most of it" until after Jesus rose and ascended into heaven and the Holy Spirit came to dwell in them, illuminating their minds about all that had happened.

**Discrimination Against Catholics**—Religious discrimination has always been part of the world scene. It happened to Jesus and his immediate followers and for many years thereafter. The Puritans came to America originally to gain religious freedom from the oppression in England. However, after they got here, they and their successors began setting up new laws of discrimination. In fact, laws against citizenship for Roman Catholics were found everywhere in the United States until 1835 when the last anti-Catholic law was repealed. Since then, discrimination was supposed to have ceased, but in the modern day there still remain many forms of discrimination and intolerance despite the fact that Jesus was the first to take the Jewish faith to the Gentiles when he welcomed some Greeks brought by Philip in John 12:20–22: "Now there were some Greeks among those who went up to worship at the Feast. They came to Philip, who was from Bethsaida in Galilee, with a request. 'Sir,' they said, 'we would like to see Jesus.' Philip went to tell Andrew; Andrew and Philip in turn told Jesus." Jesus welcomed these men, and later Christianity became one of the first religions to embrace people from every culture and place. Jesus told his disciples in Acts 1:8 that they would go to "the ends of the earth" with his message of love, peace, and salvation.

**Divinity: Did Jesus Ever Claim to Be God?**—Although the Book of John is replete with Jesus' references to his divinity, the three other Gospels are almost completely silent on the matter. However, in at least one instance, Jesus made his position very clear. In Matthew 26:62–66, this conversation takes place as Jesus stands before Caiaphas, the high priest, and the Sanhedrin, the high court of Israel:

> Then the high priest stood up and said to Jesus, "Are you not going to answer? What is this testimony that these men are bringing against you?" But Jesus remained silent.
> The high priest said to him, "I charge you under oath by the living God: Tell us if you are the Christ, the Son of God."
> "Yes, it is as you say," Jesus replied. "But I say to all of you: In the future you will see the Son of Man sitting at the right hand of the Mighty One and coming on the clouds of heaven."
> Then the high priest tore his clothes and said, "He has spoken blasphemy! Why do we need any more witnesses? Look, now you have heard the blasphemy. What do you think?"
> "He is worthy of death," they answered.

This passage, perhaps one of the oldest on record, indicates that Jesus believed he was the Son of God, God incarnate, the Messiah. When the high priest asked him point blank, he had to answer, knowing that this was the issue on which they would send him to the cross. If Jesus had been playing games about the issue or had any misgivings about who he was, or even if everything he'd said about it previously had been misunderstood, this passage appears unequivocal. If there was any question about what he meant, the leading Jews didn't see it. They immediately called what he said blasphemy, a specific Jewish term used against someone who disrespected the name of God in any way. Claiming to be God was the ultimate blasphemy in the mind of a Jew.

The Book of John contains several of the most important passages in which Jesus claims divinity:

*John 5:17–18:* "Jesus said to them, 'My Father is always at his work to this very day, and I, too, am working.' For this reason the Jews tried all the harder to kill him; not only was he breaking the Sabbath, but he was even calling God his own Father, making himself equal with God."

*John 8:54–59:* "Jesus replied, 'If I glorify myself, my glory means nothing. My Father, whom you claim as your God, is the one who glorifies me. Though you do not know him, I know him. If I said I did not, I would be a liar like you, but I do know him and keep his word. Your father Abraham rejoiced at the thought of seeing my day; he saw it and was glad.' 'You are not yet fifty years old,' the Jews said to him, 'and you have seen Abraham!' 'I tell you the truth,' Jesus answered, 'before Abraham was born, I am!' At this, they picked up stones to stone him, but Jesus hid himself, slipping away from the temple grounds."

In this passage, Jesus uses the name of God, "I am," as his own, which was considered the utmost blasphemy. The Jews did not mistake his meaning, either, for they picked up stones to stone him on the spot.

*John 10:30–33:* Jesus answered, . . . "'I and the Father are one.' Again the Jews picked up stones to stone him, but Jesus said to them, 'I have shown you many great miracles from the Father. For which of these do you stone me?' 'We are not stoning you for any of these,' replied the Jews, 'but for blasphemy, because you, a mere man, claim to be God.'"

*John 14:8–11:* "Philip said, 'Lord, show us the Father and that will be enough for us.' Jesus answered: 'Don't you know me, Philip, even after I have been among you such a long time? Anyone who has seen me has seen the Father. How can you say, "Show us the Father"? Don't you believe that I am in the Father, and that the Father is in me? The words I say to you are not just my own. Rather, it is the Father, living in me, who is doing his work. Believe me when I say that I am in the Father and the Father is in me; or at least believe on the evidence of the miracles themselves.'"

These are some of the best passages in which Jesus asserts his deity without embellishment.

**Divorce: Jesus' Parents Almost Divorced**—When Joseph learned his betrothed Mary was pregnant (by the Holy Spirit), he planned to divorce her—indicating he didn't believe her story from Gabriel about the Holy Spirit impregnating her. There were two ways he could have accomplished this: by having Mary publicly humiliated and possibly stoned for her sin of adultery; or by quietly giving her a "certificate of dismissal," as Moses allowed in Deuteronomy 24:1–4. Joseph, according to the passage in Matthew 1:18–25, chose the latter route. However, God intervened and sent an angel in a dream who informed Joseph of what had really happened. Joseph then took Mary as his wife and made no more argument.

This is a proof that Joseph was no gullible fool and not one simply to believe Mary's story, if she even told him, against reason and the normal way such things happen. God did not expect Joseph to believe this either; God obviously decided to intervene to make sure the marriage resulted.

**Divorce: When Was It Permissible?**—What did Jesus have to say about divorce? He allowed for divorce only under one condition, when one's spouse commits adultery or sexual sin (see Matt. 5:31–32 and Matt. 19:1–12).

**Dostoyevsky: What Did the Great Russian Author Think of Jesus?**—In Fyodor Dostoyevsky's novel *The Brothers Karamasov*, the author tells the fable of the Grand Inquisitor in order to explain the real meaning of what happened between Jesus and Satan in the wilderness. In the Dostoyevsky story, Jesus returns to earth to visit Spain and is arrested and condemned because he has rejected three things that can control men: the ability to make bread; authority; and mystery. With bread you can feed men, and they will follow you for it. With authority, men obey you because you reward them. With mystery, men want to believe in someone who is different, august, and powerful. Satan tempted Jesus to use one or all of these methods to win the souls of men, but Jesus rejected them all. He informed the Grand Inquisitor that he would accept men following him only out of genuine love and devotion or not at all. This was the very attitude the perpetrators of the Inquisition had to destroy. Why? Because they believed no one would have accepted Christ otherwise.

Thus, Dostoyevsky tells how Jesus' coming had spoiled the work of the Inquisition. He made the same mistake he made with Satan in the wilderness. First, he refused to turn stones into bread; second, he wouldn't leap off the pinnacle of the Temple and so become truly mysterious; and third, he would not worship Satan in order to gain authority over the world. For this, the Grand Inquisitor informed Jesus that he would be burned at the stake.

When the Inquisitor finished judging Jesus, laying out the sentence as they stood facing one another in a prison cell, Jesus merely walked across the floor and kissed the Inquisitor. The Grand Inquisitor was so astonished and then humbled that he opened the cell door and asked Jesus to go. In the Dostoyevsky parable, Jesus was never seen again.

Dostoyevsky was saying that Christ, even on pain of death, will not use the world's (or Satan's) methods to claim a following.

**Doubt: Even Jesus' Disciples Didn't Believe Him!**—In our day we think of Peter and James and John as the greats of the faith. But they also had a difficult time believing the things Jesus said. In particular, they never seemed to understand that Jesus' primary mission in life was to die on the cross.

On one occasion, Jesus told Peter and the others that he would indeed die soon and then rise from the dead three days later. Peter took Jesus aside and rebuked him, saying he shouldn't talk like that. Jesus was so incensed by Peter's words that he rebuked his number one disciple, "Out of my sight, Satan! You do not have in mind the things of God, but the things of men" (Mark 8:33).

When Jesus was dying on the cross, only John stood by grieving with Jesus' mother and other friends; the other disciples had fled. And when Mary Magdalene reported that the tomb was empty and that an angel had told her Jesus had arisen, the disciples still didn't believe until they saw Jesus in person and he presented to them several proofs of his resurrection, including letting them touch him, eating a piece of fish, and appearing to them numerous times over a period of forty days.

Being a believer, plainly, doesn't mean never doubting.

**Doubt: Even John the Baptist Doubted Jesus**—Jesus called John the Baptist the greatest man who had ever lived. However, John's faith, great as it was, wavered on at least one occasion. After Herod Antipas had thrown John into prison for preaching against Herod's marriage to his brother's wife, John suffered pangs of fear and doubt. He sent his disciples to Jesus to ask if he really was the Messiah or whether they should expect someone else. Jesus replied, "Go back and report to John what you hear and see: The blind receive sight, the lame walk, those who have leprosy are cured, the deaf hear, the dead are raised, and the good news is preached to the poor. Blessed is the man who does not fall away on account of me"(Matt. 11:4–6).

When John asked this question, he was probably looking for some confirmation from scripture, and in this passage Jesus gave it to him. Jesus was paraphrasing a well-known passage about the Messiah that said, "The Spirit of the Sovereign LORD is on me, because the LORD has anointed me to preach good news to the poor. He has sent me to bind up the brokenhearted, to proclaim freedom for the captives and release for the prisoners, to proclaim the year of the LORD's favor" (Isa. 61:1–2). Although John might not have been convinced simply by the things Jesus did, he would be convinced by the corroboration of scripture to the miracles Jesus was doing.

**Doubt: When Thomas Doubted, Jesus Didn't Rebuke Him, but Gave Him Proofs!**—Is doubt wrong? Preachers and poets have claimed that to doubt is sin, but Jesus himself did not so much as chide the greatest doubter of all, his disciple Thomas. This disciple was not with the other ten when Jesus first appeared to them. They told Thomas about Jesus' appearance and resurrection, but Thomas replied, "Unless I see the nail marks in his hands and put my finger where the nails were, and put my hand into his side, I will not believe it" (John 20:25). When Jesus appeared the next time with Thomas present, Jesus immediately said to the lone doubting disciple, "Put your finger here; see my hands. Reach out your hand and put it into my side. Stop doubting and believe." Thomas was so amazed, he fell at Jesus' feet and worshiped, crying, "My Lord and my God!" Jesus concluded with the words, "Because you have seen me, you have believed; blessed are those who have not seen and yet have believed" (John 20:27–29).

When we doubt, Jesus apparently does not rebuke us, but he is willing to answer our questions with stout proofs and encouraging words.

**Dreams: Everyone Dreamed Except Jesus**—There are many dreams in scripture in which God appeared to people to inform them of God's plan or will for a certain situation. You will find them in the stories of Jacob, Joseph, Daniel, the Wise Men who visited Jesus at his birth, and Paul the apostle. The prophet Joel prophesied that in the last days God would "pour my Spirit on all people. Your sons and daughters will prophesy, your old men will dream dreams, your young men will see visions" (Joel 2:28). Jesus' own father (really, stepfather), Joseph, was led by God on several occasions through dreams (see Matt. 1:20–21; 2:13; 2:19–22), thus preserving his and his family's lives. However, although all these people dreamed tremendous dreams, there is no record of a dream that Jesus had.

Did he dream? If Jesus was fully human, he undoubtedly did. But whether those dreams were the kind that his Father used to lead him into the plan for his life, we don't know.

**Dunce**—John Duns Scotus (1265–1308) was the first theologian to defend the idea of Mary's immaculate conception. This later was turned into Roman Catholic doctrine by Pius IX in 1854. He wrote a papal bull that said, "From the first moment of her conception, the Blessed Virgin Mary was, by the singular grace and privilege of Almighty God, and in view of the merits of Jesus Christ, Savior of Mankind, kept free from all stain of Original Sin." This meant that Mary was born without a "sin nature," unlike all other people except Jesus. It did not mean she also was born of a virgin. Duns Scotus's hairsplitting ideas, however, were originally discredited by the humanists of the Renaissance, especially Thomas Aquinas, who called Duns Scotus's followers Duns or Dunces. In time, a dunce came to mean a person who is so stupid he shouldn't even be conversed with.

**Easter: The Dateless Holiday**—Most holidays are fixed to certain dates, but Easter is always celebrated, after directives at the Council of Nicaea in A.D. 325, according to the Gregorian Calendar, on the Sunday after the first full moon of spring, which can be anywhere from March 22 to April 25.

**Easter Egg**—Easter, the celebration of Christ's resurrection, was derived from an Anglo-Saxon term for the earth goddess, Easter, according to the Venerable Bede (673–735). The sharing of eggs symbolized the process of rebirth as well as the idea that Jesus would emerge from his tomb, resurrected and alive.

**Easter Lily**—A symbol of Christ's purity and perfection, the lily is also a picture of resurrection. This was based on the fact that when you plant the bulb, out of the bulb springs the lily. This process is much like Christ's planting of his dead body in a tomb and then emerging alive. The lily also resembles a trumpet, which is reminiscent of the angel Gabriel's great "awakening trumpet," the "last trumpet" of 1 Corinthians 15:52 that announces the "Catching Up" in the air or Rapture of the church to meet Christ in the air.

**Eating After Resurrection**—When Jesus first appeared to his eleven remaining disciples, they thought he was a ghost or spirit. To prove he was really alive, full-bodied and real, Jesus ate a piece of fish in front of them. The passage in Luke 24:41–44 records the event: "And while they still did not believe it because of joy and amazement, he asked them, 'Do you have anything here to eat?' They gave him a piece of broiled fish, and he took it and ate it in their presence. He said to them, 'This is what I told you while I was still with you: Everything must be fulfilled that is written about me in the Law of Moses, the Prophets and the Psalms.'"

**Eclipse During a Full Moon**—Impossible! That's what Phlegon, a first-century historian, says happened the day Christ was crucified.

However, an eclipse during a full moon is impossible, because the moon has to be on the far side of the earth in order to be illuminated fully to observers below.

**Emerson, Ralph Waldo (1803–1882), a Deist, Saw Jesus' Significance**—As a Transcendentalist, Emerson believed that Christ was a mere human being whose faith we should emulate; however, Jesus never meant us to put our faith in him personally. Emerson was very strong on man's goodness, ideas that go against the teachings of Jesus. Nonetheless, as a scholar he couldn't fail but notice the impact of Jesus on the world, and he is quoted as saying, "The name of Jesus is not so much written as plowed into the history of the world."

**Encyclopedia Entry**—The *Encyclopedia Britannica* entry on Jesus devotes over twenty thousand words to him, more than to any other person, including George Washington, Martin Luther, Julius Caesar, Buddha, Muhammad, and others.

**End of the World**—Many have predicted the end of the world, who, as we can see (if you are reading this), were wrong. One of the most successful was William Miller in New England, who began preaching in 1831 that the world would end on April 3, 1843. He claimed he had thoroughly studied the Bible and had ascertained this date. Thousands believed him, and when the date arrived, his followers gathered all over the country on housetops, in cemeteries (to see the rising of the dead), and on hilltops. Many had disposed of their possessions and were destitute. When April 3 came and went with no arrival of Christ, Miller named a second date: October 22, 1844. After that date passed without Christ's coming, the Millerite movement died out.

**End of the World: Jesus Speaks**—When his disciples asked Jesus how the world would end, he gave them a sermon on the subject that is found in Matthew 24–25. He predicted such things as famines, earthquakes, diseases, bitter wars, family members turning against each other, and many other actions that would come at the end of time. He predicted that many would come pretending to be him. Lawlessness would increase, people's hearts would be cold, and things would look pretty grim. But it would be in that time that Jesus would return again to set up his kingdom and reign forever and ever. For that reason, Jesus repeatedly warned his followers not to be afraid, but to be "watchful." Many today believe that the Book of Revelation is Jesus' final answer about what precisely will happen in the last days of planet earth.

**End Times: The Great Faith Turnaway**—Referred to by the apostle Paul in 2 Thessalonians 2:3, the end times is a time at the end of human history when people will turn away from faith in Christ and embrace the Antichrist as the one true God and ruler of the universe. Scholars interpret the passage in various ways, but Paul makes it clear that Jesus Christ will not return "until the rebellion occurs and the man of lawlessness (Antichrist) is revealed, the man doomed to destruction."

**Enemies of Jesus Criticize**—The relogous leaders were always enraged when Jesus did things on the Sabbath, but healing was one that particularly incensed them. For instance, on one occasion (Luke 13:10–17), Jesus healed a crippled woman on the Sabbath. His bitter exchange with the leaders goes like this:

> On a Sabbath Jesus was teaching in one of the synagogues, and a woman was there who had been crippled by a spirit for eighteen years. She was bent over and could not straighten up at all. When Jesus saw her, he called her forward and said to her, "Woman, you are set free from your infirmity." Then he put his hands on her, and immediately she straightened up and praised God.
> Indignant because Jesus had healed on the Sabbath, the synagogue ruler said to the people, "There are six days for work. So come and be healed on those days, not on the Sabbath."
> The Lord answered him, "You hypocrites! Doesn't each of you on the Sabbath untie his ox or donkey from the stall and lead it out to give it water? Then should not this woman, a daughter of Abraham, whom Satan has kept bound for eighteen long years, be set free on the Sabbath day from what bound her?"
> When he said this, all his opponents were humiliated, but the people were delighted with all the wonderful things he was doing.

Often, Jesus countered the criticism he received with profound wisdom that embarrassed his opponents, showing them to be fools, unkind and nasty people. This made their hatred even more implacable—and unreasonable.

**Essene: Was Jesus One?**—The Essenes were an ascetic sect who lived in the desert. Under pressure in the early first century when Rome destroyed Jerusalem and the Israelite nation, the Essenes in desperation hid many of their sacred writings at Qumran. These were later discovered in 1947 and are called the "Dead Sea Scrolls." Some scholars have proposed that Jesus was one of the Essenes. Their faith was character-ized by asceticism, communal living and having everything "in com-mon," and refusing to perform animal sacrifices, an important tenet of Judaism. Little is known about them, even with the discovery at Qum-ran, because they kept their rites and beliefs secret. If Jesus was one of them, he violated one of their primary practices, which was to keep everything they did secret from the public. There is no strong evidence that Jesus was an Essene, nor was John the Baptist, despite the exten-sive "proofs" by some scholars today.

**Eternal Existence of Christ: Has Jesus Always Been?**—Scripture claims that Jesus existed before his first coming into the world and that he has always existed. This is a mark of his divinity, for if he is not eter-nal, he cannot be divine. Several scriptures support this idea (support-ing element in italics):

*Micah 5:2:* "But you, Bethlehem Ephrathah, though you are small among the clans of Judah, out of you will come for me one who will be ruler over Israel, *whose origins are from of old, from ancient times.*"

*Isaiah 9:6:* "For to us a child is born, to us a son is given, and the gov-ernment will be on his shoulders. And he will be called Wonderful Counselor, Mighty God, *Everlasting Father,* Prince of Peace."

*Matthew 28:20:* "'Surely *I will be with you always, to the very end of the age.*'"

*John 1:1–3, 14:* "In the beginning was the Word, and the Word was with God, and the Word was God. He was with God in the beginning. Through him all things were made; without him nothing was made that has been made. . . . The Word became flesh and lived for awhile among us. We have seen his glory, the glory of the one and only Son, who came from the Father, full of grace and truth."

*Colossians 1:16–17:* "For by him all things were created: things in heaven and on earth, visible and invisible, whether thrones or powers or rulers or authorities; all things were created by him and for him. *He is before all things,* and in him all things hold together."

*Hebrews 13:8:* "*Jesus Christ is the same yesterday and today and forever.*"

**Excuses: They All Made Excuses**—One of God's primary points of contention with the human race is that when God decides to do some-thing—send a message by a prophet, send God's Son, even throw a party—people pay little attention and make excuses when confronted. Jesus' parable of the wedding feast shows that many are too busy to pay attention to God's invitation. In Matthew 22:1–14, Jesus tells the parable of the wedding feast, where many people were invited to the marriage of the king's son. Jesus says in Matthew 22:3–7:

> "[A king] sent his servants to those who had been invited
> to the banquet to tell them to come, but they refused to
> come.
> "Then he sent some more servants and said, 'Tell those
> who have been invited that I have prepared my dinner:
> My oxen and fattened cattle have been butchered, and
> everything is ready. Come to the wedding banquet.'
> "But they paid no attention and went off—one to his field,
> another to his business. The rest seized his servants,
> mistreated them and killed them. The king was
> enraged. He sent his army and destroyed those murder-
> ers and burned their city."

Jesus illustrates how God reacts to those who reject him and make excuses about things like faith, church, commitment, and worship.

**Extraordinary Statement**—Perhaps Jesus' most extraordinary statement in the Sermon on the Mount was to "love your enemies"(Matt. 5:43–45). Many people in Jesus' community had some strong ideas about loving their enemies, even though Moses said in Leviticus 19:18, "Do not seek revenge or bear a grudge against one of your people, but love your neighbor as yourself. I am the LORD." By their teaching, the Pharisees and other leaders of the Jews developed an interpretation of this passage that Jesus quotes in his sermon. Jesus says, "You have heard that it was said, 'Love your neighbor and hate your enemy'" (v. 43). This expression was never found in scripture and could not be built on anything God said in scripture. In fact, in Proverbs 25:21 God said that people should do good to their enemies. Conservatives in Jesus' community avoided such ideas and pushed forth their own, which became the occasion for Jesus' opposition to them.

**Failure: Jesus Knew Peter Would Fail, Warned Him, and Let Him**—Failure, either in business, marriage, social, and moral affairs or other situations, can devastate a life. It can become the point at which one life completely reverses itself in the eyes of history and God. One such example of a gross failure is that of King David and Bathsheba, where he commits adultery and has Bathsheba's husband murdered. Until that point in King David's life, the story in 1 and 2 Samuel just seems to go from victory to victory and success to success. But that event marks a line of demarcation in David's life. From that point on, all is turned downhill, and things go wrong at every turn.

David's life in that respect is a powerful caution to anyone who would commit rank sin. On the other hand, another scriptural failure is Peter. In Luke 22:31–34, Luke tells the details of how Jesus warned Peter he was about to commit a huge mistake. Jesus says: "Simon, Simon, Satan has asked to sift you as wheat. But I have prayed for you, Simon, that your faith may not fail. And when you have turned back, strengthen your brothers." But he replied, "Lord, I am ready to go with you to prison and to death." Jesus answered, "I tell you, Peter, before the rooster crows today, you will deny three times that you know me."

This passage offers powerful warning and also marvelous hope to anyone who has ever failed in some stupendous way. One, Jesus reveals that Satan is after Peter, but Satan has to ask permission from God to get a chance at him. In other words, Satan can't touch anyone without God's permission. Two, Jesus prays for those who will be so tested, not that they wouldn't fail, but that their "faith may not fail." Big difference. The actual failure is not the mistake, but losing faith in the face of it is. Three, Jesus tells Peter that after he has come to his senses, he should get back to the business at hand, helping his brothers.

Though heavy with warning and caution, for those who follow Christ, this passage shows that failure is only a minor detour to learn from and then get past.

**Faith, Childlike**—Jesus often told his disciples that they had to believe like a child in order to inherit the kingdom of God. What did he mean? Matthew 18 reports Jesus as saying to the Twelve: "I tell you the truth, unless you change and become like little children, you will never enter the kingdom of heaven. Therefore, whoever humbles himself like this child is the greatest in the kingdom of heaven. And whoever welcomes a little child like this in my name welcomes me" (Matt. 18:3–5). Becoming like a "little child" is what faith is all about. That calls for a willingness to believe a parent or leader without too much question, a determination to obey, and a desire to listen to the parent as the one who can possibly save that child's life.

**Faithful: Who Are the Faithful in Jesus' Eyes?**—In Matthew 25:14–30, Jesus offers some powerful words about those he considers the truly believing and faithful. In this parable, Jesus pictures three people being given different amounts of money that they can use and invest in order to please their master. The money is clearly on loan, and the master who gave it expects a return on his gifts.

The first man was given five "talents" (a talent was 75–150 pounds of gold or silver, depending on what kind of talent it was, common or royal). If these were gold, they had a modern value of over six million dollars! This man went out, invested the money, and doubled it while his master was on a journey. Likewise, a second man was given two talents. He invested them and doubled his money. The third man, though, receiving only one talent, went out and "dug a hole in the ground and hid his master's money." When the master returned, he praised the first two men for their wise investments and said, "Well done, good and faithful servant! You have been faithful with a few things; I will put you in charge of many things. Come and share your master's happiness!" But to the third man, who protested he was afraid of the master, the master said, "You wicked, lazy servant! So you knew that I harvest where I have not sown and gather where I have not scattered seed? Well then, you should have put my money on deposit with the bankers, so that when I returned I would have received it back with interest. Take the talent from him and give it to the one who has the ten talents. For everyone who has will be given more, and he will have an abundance. Whoever does not have, even what he has will be taken from him. And throw that worthless servant outside, into the darkness, where there will be weeping and gnashing of teeth."

What then is faithfulness? Investing and using the gifts God gives you for the profit and advancement of God's kingdom. Such people God promises to reward heavily!

**Faith That Pleases Jesus**—What kind of faith pleases Christ? In one story of a woman suffering from vaginal bleeding, Jesus reveals the secret. This woman knew about Jesus and believed that all she had to do was touch his coat to be healed (see Matt. 9:20–22). Jesus at the time was passing through a crowd, but at one point he stopped and asked who had touched him. His disciples were astounded, for many people were touching him. But Jesus knew that power had gone out of him. He soon found the culprit, this woman with the bleeding problem. The story spills out and Jesus responds, "Take heart, daughter, your faith has healed you." The woman was healed that instant.

What then is this faith that pleased Jesus? It was from a woman who believed Jesus was so great and powerful that all she had to do was touch his cloak to be healed.

**Family: Did Jesus' Family Believe He Was the Messiah?**—Jesus often said that no one honors a prophet from one's hometown. He knew what he was talking about, for his own brothers didn't believe he was the Messiah, a prophet, or anything else. In fact, they thought he was crazy! John wrote in John 7:5 "For even his own brothers did not believe in him." And in Mark 3:21, Mark says, after Jesus told the people of Nazareth that he was a fulfillment of one of Isaiah's prophecies about the Messiah: "When his family heard about this, they went to take charge of him, for they said, 'He is out of his mind.'"

**Family of Jesus**—Did Jesus have family? Though some might believe that the Virgin Mary remained a virgin all her life, scripture does not support that assumption. In Mark 6:3, while Jesus is teaching in his hometown of Nazareth, some of the listeners take offense at his words, saying, "Isn't this the carpenter? Isn't this Mary's son and the brother of James, Joses, Judas and Simon? Aren't his sisters here with us?" Clearly, these people understood that Jesus was Mary's son. They also knew he had brothers and sisters, some of whom they name. In fact, the Books of James and Jude at the end of the New Testament were written by two of Jesus' brothers. Where were these siblings from? To call them brothers and sisters, they had at least to have been the progeny of Joseph and/or Mary. If Joseph, then they really couldn't have been siblings, because Joseph wasn't Jesus' real father. If not Mary, then they would not have been real brothers. It's possible these siblings were adopted, but that is remote, considering the number of them. It's also possible that these listeners were using the words "brothers" and "sisters" loosely, not really knowing the details, but that also is remote. Other passages reveal similar ideas; thus it appears that Jesus had quite a large family that he grew up with, most of whom if not all became believers in him after his resurrection.

**Famous Conversion**—John Wesley (1703–1791), another great evangelist and English divine, was actually a seeker of Christ for many years before finding him. He attended Oxford University and founded, with his brother Charles, a group of students eager to learn more about and build a closeness to Jesus Christ. It was called "The Holy Club." In 1735, Wesley left for the thirteen colonies by ship in order to evangelize the Native Americans there. He met with abject failure as a speaker and evangelist and felt great guilt over his own inability to secure a genuine relationship with Christ. He wrote, "I went to America to convert the Indians, but, oh, who shall convert me?"

On the ship over to America, Wesley met a group of Moravians whose vibrant faith amazed him. Even in the midst of a terrible storm, when all aboard the ship feared for their lives, these believers exhibited a surpassing and supernatural peace that Wesley couldn't get out of his mind. When he returned to London in 1738, he met another Moravian, Peter Boehler, and began meeting with him to learn of the one true faith. This is what Wesley wrote, on May 24, 1738, the day that his long seeking would be answered by the Lord:

> I think it was about five this morning that I opened my Testament on three verses, "There are given unto us exceeding great and precious promises, even that ye should be partaken of the divine nature." Just as I went out, I opened it again on those words, "Thou art not far from the kingdom of God." In the afternoon I was asked to go to St. Paul's. The anthem was, "Out of the deep have I called unto thee, O Lord. O let thine ears consider well the voice of my complaint. If thou, Lord, wilt be extreme to mark what is done amiss, O Lord, who may abide it? For there is mercy with thee; therefore shalt thou be feared. O Israel, trust to the Lord: for with the Lord there is mercy, and with him is plenteous redemption. And he shall redeem Israel from all his sins."
>
> In the evening I went very unwillingly to a society in Aldersgate Street, where one was reading Luther's preface to the Epistle to the Romans. About a quarter before nine, while he was describing the change which God works in the heart through faith in Christ, I felt my heart strangely warmed. I felt I did trust in Christ, Christ alone, for my salvation; and an assurance was given me that He had taken away my sins, even mine, and saved me from the law of sin and death. (*The Jesus Book*, edited by Calvin Miller)

Wesley went on to found Methodism, preach through the country of England in open-air meetings, and lead a tremendous revival in England and America. He traveled over 240,000 miles by horseback and preached over 40,000 sermons, often several different messages a day, most of them published.

**Fasting: No Food for Forty Days and Forty Nights**—Early in Jesus' ministry, right after his baptism by John the Baptist, Jesus "was led by the Spirit into the desert to be tempted by the devil" (Matt. 4:1). To prepare for this time of testing, Jesus fasted for forty days and nights. This seems an incredible amount of time to go without food, but it wasn't unprecedented. When Moses went up on Mt. Sinai to receive the Ten Commandments, he also fasted for forty days, according to Exodus 34:28; in fact, Moses didn't even drink water during that time. Elijah also experienced such a fast after he ran for his life from Queen Jezebel. He was fed by God with "angel food." Elijah then went to Mt. Horeb to see God's power displayed (see 1 Kings 19:8).

**Feasting on Christ's Body**—One of the most sacred feasts of the Roman Catholic Church is called the "Feast of Corpus Christi," or the "Feast of the Body of Christ." It was established in 1264 by Pope Urban IV, not long after the doctrine of transubstantiation came into being by the Fourth Lateran Council in 1215. In the feast, the bread and wine representing Christ's body and blood are carried in a procession while those present sing hymns. Indulgences were given to those who watched.

Because Martin Luther and the other Reformers rejected both transubstantiation and the sale of indulgences, Protestants do not celebrate this feast, though Roman Catholics continue to this day.

**Fighting Back: Jesus Didn't Hesitate to Fight Back**—Jesus told his followers to "turn the other cheek" (see Matt. 5:39) and "love your enemies" (Matt. 5:44). Many got the idea that Christians should never "fight back" when persecutors attack them. However, Jesus' statements did not preclude making a defense when you are attacked. "Turning the other cheek" applied to insults, not mortal threats. Jesus fought back when people attacked him on a number of occasions, including at his trial before the hostile leaders of the Jews (see John 18:23).

**First Disciple**—Jesus' first disciple was Andrew, the brother of Peter (then called "Simon"). In John 1:37–42, Andrew and another unnamed follower of John the Baptist followed Jesus after he was pointed out by John the Baptist as the "Lamb of God." When Jesus turned to ask what the two wanted, one asked where he was staying. Jesus then invited them to his home, and they stayed there all night, presumably discussing all the questions the two had about him, his mission, and perhaps many other things. Andrew then went to Simon, told him he'd found the Messiah, and brought Simon to Jesus. Immediately, Jesus gave Simon a new name, Peter, which means "stone" or "rock."

**First Miracle**—Jesus' first miracle occurred at Cana during a wedding reception and feast (see John 2:1–11). Normally, such proceedings could last up to a whole week. The bride and groom provided the food and wine for the feast. At this particular party, the wine ran out. Jesus was there with some of his disciples. Mary his mother solicited him to "do something" about the wine, because it was humiliating to run out, for it showed that the newlyweds were either cheap or poor. Jesus replied, "My time has not yet come." Perhaps he was saving his first miracle for something truly stupendous. However, Mary simply turned to the servants and told them to do whatever Jesus said. Jesus apparently decided he had to help out, so he instructed them to fill some waterjars with water, up to fifty gallons each. When the servants returned, Jesus told them to take a cup to the master of ceremonies. The master was so amazed at the taste of this water become wine that he said, "Everyone brings out the choice wine first and then the cheaper wine after the guests have had too much to drink; but you have saved the best till now." It appears in this case that Jesus put his own interests aside and rose to the occasion to help a friend in need.

**Fishing: Was Jesus Good at It?**—Jesus seemed to have a strong interest in fishing, though why we do not know. He told his fisherman disciples—Peter, Andrew, James, and John—that if they'd follow him he'd make them fishers of men. On at least three occasions, he performed miracles that involved fishing.

The first happened as Jesus taught in Simon Peter's boat on the Lake of Galilee. After his lecture, Jesus told Simon to put his boat out and use the nets to fish. Simon answered that they'd fished all night and caught nothing. But, he added, he would do so because Jesus said to. A few minutes later, Simon and his partners caught so many fish that the boats nearly sank. Simon came ashore, fell down at Jesus' feet, and said, "Go away from me, Lord; I am a sinful man!" But Jesus simply informed him that from then on he'd be "fishing for men" (see Luke 5:1–11).

On a second occasion, Jesus and Simon Peter were discussing taxes. Jesus instructed Peter that they should still pay them. He told Peter to go down to the sea and throw in a hook. The first fish he would catch would have a four-drachma coin in its mouth with which to pay the poll tax, both for Peter and Jesus (see Matt. 17:24–27).

The third time happened after Jesus' resurrection. Several of the disciples, including Peter, went back to fishing. Jesus appeared (his third appearance, according to John 21:14) on the beach and told them to try on the right side of the boat. The men had fished all night without success. When they complied, however, they caught so many fish the nets could barely hold them—all 153! (see John 21:1–14).

**Fish Symbol: What Was That All About?**—Most people have probably seen the symbol of the fish drawn with a few simple strokes. Christians put the symbol on their cars, doorways, and other places. It was at one time a secret symbol used by Christians to indicate to traveling ministers and strangers that Christians resided in such a place, and that they would find hospitality and welcome.

The fish was used as a symbol much like the cross, but it actually had a deeper meaning. The letters forming the Greek word for fish were ICHTHUS, or I for Iota, CH for Chi, which looked like our X, TH for Theta, which was a zero with a horizontal line through it, U for Upsilon, and S for Sigma, which looks like an M sideways. Iota-Chi-Theta-Upsilon-Sigma spelled out the first letters of five words important to Christians:

> Iota—I—Iesus or Jesus
> Chi—X—for Christos—Christ
> Theta-Upsilon for Th—Theos—God, U—Uios—Son for Son of
>   God
> Sigma—S—Soter for Savior

Thus, the Greek word for fish spelled out the statement: Jesus Christ, Son of God, Savior.

**Florence Nightingale's Dedication**—When she was thirty years old, Florence Nightingale wrote, "I am thirty years of age, the age at which Christ began His mission. Now no more childish things, no more vain things. Now, Lord, let me think only of Thy will."

**Food Miracles**—Jesus performed at least two major food miracles in which he took small amounts of fish and bread and multiplied them miraculously so that they ended up feeding thousands. The first, the feeding of the five thousand, is revealed in Matthew 14:14–21 and also much more extensively in John 6:1–59. The text says five thousand men were present, but this did not include women and children (Jews never counted women and children when they made "head counts"), which would have meant there might have been as many as fifteen thousand people present. In that passage, Jesus takes "five small barley loaves and two small fish" (John 6:8) and feeds everyone with them. In the same passage, he calls himself "the bread of life" (John 6:35). The second feeding involved four thousand men and occurred under similar conditions. It's found in Matthew 15:32–39.

**Footprints**—Margaret Fishback Powers has gained fame and fortune through her simple story of the footprints, based on Hebrews 13:5: "Never will I leave you; never will I forsake you."

> One night I dreamed a dream. I was walking along the beach with my Lord. Across the dark sky flashed scenes from my life. For each scene, I noticed two sets of footprints in the sand, one belonging to me and one to my Lord. When the last scene of my life shot before me I looked back at the footprints in the sand. There was only one set of footprints. I realized that this was at the lowest and saddest times of my life. This always bothered me, and I questioned the Lord about my dilemma. "Lord, you told me when I decided to follow You, You would walk and talk with me all the way. But I'm aware that during the most troublesome times of my life there is only one set of footprints. I just don't understand why, when I need You most, You leave me." He whispered, "My precious child, I love you and will never leave you, never, ever, during your trials and testings. When you saw only one set of footprints, it was then that I carried you."

**Footprints of Christ**—There is a marble stone with Christ's supposed footprints on it in the Church of St. Sebastian in Rome.

**Forbidden to Speak**—When Jesus healed a couple of blind men, he told them not to tell others he was the Son of God, which they had been shouting out to get his attention. It's unclear exactly why Jesus asked them to stop saying this, though perhaps it was because calling him "the Son of God" incited so much anger and criticism that for him it wasn't worth the trouble. The two men, though, went out and told everyone about it! (see Matt. 9:27–31).

**Forgiving Others Who Repeatedly Sin Against You**—In a discussion on forgiveness, Peter questioned Jesus regarding how many times you should forgive someone who has sinned against you and then repented. The rabbis said four times, which they considered rather forthcoming. Peter decided to be a little liberal and suggested, "Up to seven times." Jesus replied, "I tell you, not seven times, but seventy-seven times." The numbers can also be translated "up to seventy times seven times" or 490 times! (see Matt. 18:21–22). Jesus' point was not that one should count how many times he's forgiven a sinner, but that one should forgive him as many times as it takes. To the people of Jesus' day, this was unprecedented and even "kooky."

**Forgiving Sins by Fiat!**—A big bone of contention between Jesus and the Pharisees was their treatment of crippled and broken people. They often subscribed to the belief that people who were sick, crippled, or blind, or had other defects had them because of previous sins, either the victim's or his parents or ancestors (see John 9:1–5). Jesus always explained that people with such afflictions did not have them because of sin but in order that "the work of God might be displayed in his life" (John 9:3). Jesus was also very liberal in forgiving sins, sometimes without the person even asking for forgiveness. A good example occurs in Matthew 9:1–8, where some friends bring a paralytic to Jesus for healing. The first thing Jesus said to the paralytic was that his sins were forgiven. Immediately, several of the scribes and Pharisees present began to complain inwardly, saying, "Who can forgive sins but God alone?" Jesus knew what they were thinking and replied, "Why do you entertain evil thoughts in your hearts? Which is easier: to say, 'Your sins are forgiven,' or to say, 'Get up and walk'? But so that you may know that the Son of Man has authority on earth to forgive sins. . . ." Then he said to the paralytic, "Get up, take your mat and go home." The man immediately got up and walked home.

Jesus' point was made!

**Forgiving Those Who Nailed Him to the Cross**—Perhaps Jesus' greatest act of forgiveness was to the Roman soldiers as they nailed him to the cross. Jesus cried out, "Father, forgive them, for they do not know what they are doing" (Luke 23:34). The Romans paid no attention and immediately began dividing up Jesus' possessions—trophy hunting really—and cast lots to see who would win what. Later, after six hours on the cross, the soldiers, amazed at watching Jesus die, came to believe he was the Son of God (see Matt. 27:54).

**Friendship: "Are You Jesus?"**—A boy on crutches waited in the subway for the next train at Christmas. He carried several packages and was obviously weighed down, but also poor and alone. When the train came, the crowd rushed in so quickly that the boy was knocked over, his crutches flying, his packages kicked here and there. As the deck cleared, a businessman noticed the boy and stooped down to help him, getting him his crutches and packages and helping him onto the train.

When they both stood aboard, the boy looked up into the man's face and asked, "Please, sir, are you Jesus?"

**Funerals**—Jesus didn't much like funerals, as evidenced from his few encounters with dead people. He raised Jairus's daughter despite the ridicule of the mourners (Matt. 9:18–26), the widow of Nain's son (Luke 7:11–15) to the amazement of all concerned, and Lazarus (John 11:34–44). In the third case, particularly, Lazarus had been dead four days. Jesus purposely did not make an attempt to heal Lazarus when he learned his friend was sick, even though he was not far away. We know that Jesus could have healed Lazarus without actually traveling to him, because Jesus did this once before with a Roman centurion's paralyzed servant (see Matt. 8:5–13). So why did Jesus tarry and let Lazarus die?

Although the scripture does not specifically say, there are two things to consider. One, Jesus told his disciples when he first learned of the problem: "This sickness will not end in death. It is for God's glory so that God's Son may be glorified through it" (John 11:4). From that and considering the conclusion of the event, it must have been Jesus' intent all along to raise Lazarus from the dead.

But why four days? A Jewish belief existed at the time that the spirit of a dead person hovered around the body for four days. After that, it left for the afterlife and there was no chance of resuscitation. All the other resuscitations in the Bible occurred shortly after death, but Lazarus's resuscitation was perhaps an attempt by Jesus to show that he truly had power over any kind of death.

**Gambling for His Garments: Those Gambling Romans Fulfilled Prophecy**—As the Roman soldiers divided up their "trophies" at the foot of Jesus' cross, they found his cloak, which was fairly valuable because it was "seamless." They decided not to tear it up, but instead to cast lots to see who would get the whole thing. This they did and one soldier won. (The famous book by Lloyd Douglas, *The Robe*, is a fictional rendition of this man's life after his winning of the cloak.)

These men, of course, had no idea that they were fulfilling a curious prophecy King David wrote that eerily describes crucifixion before it was even invented. David refers to the unique pain of crucifixion and the circumstances Jesus faced. Then David says: "I am poured out like water, and all my bones are out of joint. My heart has turned to wax; it has melted away within me. My strength is dried up like a potsherd, and my tongue sticks to the roof of my mouth; you lay me in the dust of death. Dogs have surrounded me; a band of evil men has encircled me, they have pierced my hands and my feet. I can count all my bones; people stare and gloat over me. They divide my garments among them and cast lots for my clothing" (Psalm 22:14–18).

There is nothing in history that corroborates such an experience in King David's life. So what was he writing about? The above passage is a fairly accurate description of a crucifixion, which was not to be invented until centuries later by the Romans. In the passage, David clearly states that the person's executioners would divide up his garments and cast lots for his clothing. This is exactly what the Roman soldiers did, according to John 19:23–24: "When the soldiers crucified Jesus, they took his clothes, dividing them into four shares, one for each of them, with the undergarment remaining. This garment was seamless, woven in one piece from top to bottom. 'Let's not tear it,' they said to one another. 'Let's decide by lot who will get it.' This happened that the Scripture might be fulfilled."

**Gandhi Revered Him**—Mohandas Gandhi, though deeply distrustful of Christians and their hypocrisy, still had great respect for Jesus. He wrote: "Jesus, a man who was completely innocent, offered himself as a sacrifice for the good of others, including his enemies, and became the ransom of the world. It was a perfect act."

**Garden of Gethsemane**—The Garden of Gethsemane (which means "garden of the oil press") can still be found on the Mount of Olives outside Jerusalem. This is the place where Jesus prayed that God not make him go to the cross. He often prayed there, according to Luke 22:39. When he prayed, Jesus knelt and talked to the Father. The Christian tradition of kneeling as we pray is from Jesus' example in Gethsemane.

**Gardening: Did Jesus Know a Lot About It?**—Jesus possessed a remarkable ability to draw on the common experiences of his listeners. One of his favorite subjects was taking images from gardening and farming. Consider some of these examples:

Story of the Sower (Matt. 13:5–8)
Story of the Wheat and Tares (Matt. 13:24–30)
Story of the Mustard Seed (Matt. 13:31–32)

Story of the Laborers in the Vineyard (Matt. 20:1–16)
Story of the Wicked Husbandman (Matt. 21:33–46)
Story of the Seed Growing Secretly (Mark 4:26–29)
Story of the Barren Fig Tree (Luke 13:6–9)

From these it is obvious that Jesus was an acute observer of his times and the work and people he lived among.

**Genealogies of Jesus**—There are two genealogies of Jesus' lineage in the New Testament. The one in Matthew is his royal lineage, descended through Joseph (see Matt. 1:1–17). Scholars believe that the second genealogy in Luke is the actual line through Mary (see Luke 3:23–38), for she was descended from Nathan, one of the sons of King David and a half-brother of Solomon. Interestingly enough, God had a problem with Jesus' line. God had promised Abraham, Isaac, Jacob, and finally David that God would give them a "Son" whose kingdom would never end. However, because of idolatry in the line of David after Solomon, God actually cursed that line and said they would have no son reigning on the throne because of the sins of the last king of Israel, Jeconiah (see Jer. 22:24, 28; 37:1). Thus, although Jesus was the legal heir of Joseph, who was in David's and Solomon's line, he could never have successfully reigned because of this curse. But because he was also a natural heir of Mary, who was also in the Davidic line, Jesus could reign and still fulfill all prophecies relating to David and others!

**Gibran, Kahlil, and Jesus**—The famed author of *The Prophet* and other writings, Kahlil Gibran (1883–1931), Lebanese poet and novelist, wrote this about Jesus:

> I often wonder whether Jesus was a man of flesh and blood like ourselves, or a thought without a body, in the mind, or an idea that visits the vision of man.
>
> Often it seems to me that he was but a dream dreamed by countless men and women at the same time in a sleep deeper than sleep and dawn more serene than all dawns. . . .
>
> But in truth he was not a dream. We knew him for three years and beheld him with our open eyes in the high tide of noon. . . .
>
> He was a mountain burning in the night, yet he was a soft glow beyond our hills. He was a tempest in the sky, yet he was a murmur in the mist of daybreak.

*Godspell:* **In Reaction to *Superstar*—**Another play depicting Jesus' life in song, *Godspell* was written partly as a reaction to *Jesus Christ Superstar. Godspell* was conceived and adapted by a university student, John-Michael Tebelak, and its songs are by a then-young Stephen Schwartz. Telebak, then a 21-year-old student at Carnegie-Mellon University, first came up with the idea of a rock musical dealing with love, charity, and Christian virtues at a sunrise service when he was stopped and frisked for drugs by a Pittsburgh policeman in the nave of St. Paul's Cathedral. Schwartz went on to write the music and lyrics for such shows as *Pippin,* the Disney movies *Pocahontas* and *The Hunchback of Notre Dame,* and he contributed several songs to the recent film, *The Prince of Egypt.*

The rock musical adaptation of the Gospel According to St. Matthew was an immediate success when it opened in the spring of 1971 at an off-Broadway theater. Ticket sales were brisk for three years. Between 1971 and 1973, productions of the musical opened in Los Angeles, London, Paris, Boston, Washington, D.C., Toronto, San Francisco, Melbourne, Sydney, Hamburg, and Berlin.

The *Godspell* cast album won a Grammy Award for Best Score and became, in 1972, the only cast album on the charts.

The play is a whimsical view of Jesus, who is dressed like a clown with a red nose, a red heart painted on his forehead, and a Superman shirt. His followers and disciples reenact parables and scenes from Jesus' life with enormous energy. Several songs from the show, including "Day by Day," became hits.

**Government: Defender of the Faith**—Ten years before King Henry VIII broke from the Roman Catholic Church and established the Church of England, he wrote a tome called "Defence of the Seven Sacraments," defending faith in Christ as the true faith and disputing Martin Luther's Theses and Tracts. He claimed complete allegiance to the pope. The pope was so impressed, he granted Henry a title, "Defender of the Faith." Henry kept it when ten years later he ended Roman Catholicism in England.

**Government: Establish Jesus' Way Politically?**—What might happen if a national government decided to incorporate Jesus' principles into its tenets and laws? Throughout history, most governments set up on religious principles ended up limiting freedom and becoming tyrannical, a sham. Christianity has had such supporters. One of them was John Calvin (1509–1564), the Reformer, who convinced the Council of Two Hundred (the leading political governing body in

Geneva, Switzerland, at the time) to live according to the laws of the Reformation and the person and teachings of Christ. They enacted this into law on February 2, 1554. The experiment, though, was a failure, with harsh punishments and an "iron rule" destroying human freedom and imagination.

**Government: A Little Murmur**—Thomas à Becket (1118–1170) was chancellor to Henry II of England. They were best friends until Henry, in an attempt to gain more control over the church in his country, appointed Becket Archbishop of Canterbury. Becket went from being a stalwart supporter of the king and his policies to becoming a champion of the church, his faith in Christ inflamed and vigorous. In order to gain greater power over the church, Henry issued the Constitutions of Clarendon. Becket supported them at first, then recanted and fled to Europe where he met with the pope and gained the power to excommunicate churchmen in England who supported Henry's Constitutions. Becket returned to England where, in a fit of anger, Henry murmured that he wished someone would rid him of the archbishop. Four knights, overhearing the indiscretion, took matters into their own hands and murdered Becket in the cathedral. T.S. Eliot's play *Murder in the Cathedral*, the movie *Becket*, and other media have glorified Becket's role, though many historians argue over whether Becket was truly a saint (he was canonized in 1173), traitor, fanatic, or politician.

**Grave: Three Days and Nights in the Grave?**—How long was Jesus dead? Jesus repeatedly told his disciples he would spend "three days and three nights" in the grave. However, from the records, he hung on the cross from 9 A.M. to 3 P.M. and was taken down dead shortly thereafter. He was buried in the tomb of Joseph of Arimathea, a rich man and member of the Sanhedrin that had condemned Jesus to death. (He dissented that decision.) Thus, Jesus was placed in the tomb in the early evening on Friday. When his female followers arrived at the tomb early on Sunday morning, they found it open and his body gone, resurrected from the dead. It appears that although Jesus did spend three actual days—Friday, Saturday, and Sunday—in the tomb, the period certainly didn't involve three days from morning till night. In effect, if Jesus was entombed on Friday shortly after 3 P.M. and rose on Sunday in the early morning, just after the sun came up, about 5 A.M., then he was really in the tomb a total of thirty-eight hours, not even two full days. The problem is resolved when we understand that Jews used the expression "day and night" to refer to any part of a single day. Jesus, using the Jewish expression, was not offering the idea of seventy-two hours in the tomb, but was just using the normal Jewish expression for three days.

**Greatest Short Story Ever Told**—Some have called the parable of the prodigal son (Luke 15:11–32) the greatest short story of all time. It involves an interesting plot, but uses only 22 verses, approximately 535 words in a modern English translation. It also incorporates the classic "twist" ending, depicting the anger of the elder son who didn't like what the father did with the prodigal when he returned.

*Greatest Story Ever Told*: **The Movie**—This movie, starring Max von Sydow, was the definitive movie on the life of Jesus until the 1970s, when other movies about Christ's life came out. It was called *The Greatest Story Ever Told*, based on the book by Fulton Oursler, a Roman Catholic writer and radio preacher. Von Sydow said he was particularly moved and transformed through playing the role of Jesus.

**Greatness: A Lesson for Those Who Crave Greatness**—When Jesus' disciples disputed which among them was the greatest, Jesus gave them a lesson. In Matthew 18:3–6 (NASB), when his disciples asked him who was the greatest in the kingdom of heaven, he had a child stand in front of them, and he said: "Truly I say to you, unless you are converted and become like children, you shall not enter the kingdom of heaven. Whoever then humbles himself as this child, he is the greatest in the kingdom of heaven. And whoever receives one such child in My name receives Me; but whoever causes one of these little ones who believe in Me to stumble, it is better for him that a heavy millstone be hung around his neck, and that he be drowned in the depth of the sea." What does it mean to "become like children"? Presumably Jesus was talking about the issue of trust. In a normal family, where the father and mother treat their children with kindness and love, children will trust their parents almost without question, implicitly. They can't imagine their parents doing anything to hurt them.

In the same way, to believe as a little child is to exhibit such complete trust in God that you go to God for every need, every secret, every concern, and every joy, because you know God will listen and smile and help.

**Handel: 23 Days to Glory**—George Fredrich Handel composed *Messiah* in twenty-three days straight, often going without food. When he reached the composition of the "Hallelujah Chorus," he said, "I did think I did see all Heaven before me, and the great God Himself." Many scholars today believe that Handel was in a vivid state of musical "inspiration," perhaps from God, that enabled him to write so well, so quickly, and so beautifully.

**Harvard: Jesus' Influence on Early Harvard Grads**—Many universities today have forgotten their roots, but some of the most famous were actually formed and based on dedication to the "principles of Christ." In 1646, Harvard University professed these "Rules and Precepts": "(1) Every one shall consider the main end of his life and studies to know God and Jesus Christ which is eternal life. (2) Seeing the Lord giveth wisdom every one shall seriously by prayer in secret seek wisdom of him. (3) Every one shall so exercise himself in reading the Scriptures twice a day that they be ready to give an account of their proficiency therein, both in theoretical observations of languages and logic in practical and spiritual truths."

Fifty-two percent of seventeenth-century graduates of Harvard became Christian ministers!

**Headaches and Healing**—One might think some illnesses would be too trivial for Christ to be concerned with: headaches, back pain, arthritis. In one episode recorded in Matthew 8:14–15, we read, "When Jesus came into Peter's house, he saw Peter's mother-in-law lying in bed with a fever. He touched her hand and the fever left her, and she got up and began to wait on him." We don't know the depth or extent of the fever, or if it was life threatening, though in Jesus' time any fever could be serious. It's plain, however, that whatever its nature, it wasn't too inconsequential for Jesus to fix.

**Healer Statue**—A majestic statue of Jesus as the healer stands in the foyer of Johns Hopkins Hospital. It features him standing with arms outstretched, beckoning all to come to him for healing. About twelve feet tall on a pedestal and carved out of white-gray marble, it was unveiled on October 14, 1896. It was sculpted by Theobald Stein after an original by Danish sculptor Thorwaldsen (1768–1844). It was a gift from William Wallace Spence to the hospital at the request of Johns Hopkins University president Daniel Coit Gilman.

**Healing: Did You Have to Ask?**—Many people believe that in order to be healed, one must go somewhere or to the right person or source and state one's request plainly and directly. Jesus debunked this issue many times when he healed people without their even asking or indicating an interest in such a thing. In some cases, they might not have known who Jesus was and that he was capable of healing. A good example is found in John 9:1–7. Jesus, along with his disciples, was passing by a blind man as he sat and begged. They noticed the man there and asked, "Who sinned, this man or his parents, that he should be born blind?" This indicated an old Jewish belief not unlike the Hindu Law of Karma in which it was believed that people were punished by God in this life for past sins. Jesus immediately rejected the idea and answered, "*It was* neither *that* this man sinned, nor his parents; but *it was* in order that the works of God might be displayed in him" (John 9:3, NASB). Clearly, the whole reason for this man's blindness was that God might work in him and show that work to the world. Then Jesus healed the blind man by spitting on the ground and mixing dirt with the spittle. Placing it on the blind man's eyes, he said, "Go, wash in the pool of Siloam." The blind man obeyed and was able to see. In this case, Jesus took the initiative in healing, perhaps because he cared about the man enough not to wait for the man to ask.

**Healing a Blind, Mute, and Demon-Possessed Man**—The world is full of strange and terrible sicknesses. But what is a worst-case scenario? How bad can it get? An answer might be built around Jesus' healing of the blind, mute, and demon-possessed man in Matthew 12:22. It's not clear what the cause of the man's condition was, but his situation was obviously very bad. Jesus healed all three elements of his medical situation in one gesture. Even today, one might write off some of the horrid conditions people face—AIDS, Lou Gehrig's Disease, terminal cancer—as unhealable. Clearly, God does not heal in most cases. But there's no reason to rule out any disease. If Christ can heal a man like the above, surely he can help or even heal in many other terrible circumstances.

**Healing at a Distance**—Did Jesus have to be right there to heal a person? Usually, in psychosomatic cases where a person receives healing through a mental transaction, one must be assured and helped by the doctor to see that this is possible. In a case found in Matthew 8:5–13

(NASB), a centurion came to Jesus and asked him to heal a servant who was paralyzed and suffering great pain. When Jesus offered to accompany the centurion home and heal the servant, the centurion responded, "Lord, I am not worthy for You to come under my roof, but just say the word, and my servant will be healed. For I, too, am a man under authority, with soldiers under me; and I say to this one, 'Go!' and he goes, and to another, 'Come!' and he comes, and to my slave, 'Do this!' and he does *it*." Jesus was so amazed at the centurion's obvious faith, he said, "Truly I say to you, I have not found such great faith with anyone in Israel. And I say to you that many shall come from east and west, and recline *at the table* with Abraham, Isaac, and Jacob, in the kingdom of heaven; but the sons of the kingdom shall be cast out into the outer darkness; in that place there shall be weeping and gnashing of teeth." Then Jesus said to him, "Go your way; let it be done to you as you have believed." The passage concludes, "And the servant was healed that *very* hour." Perhaps this story was meant to indicate that Jesus' powers of healing were not restricted to being present at the actual place where he would heal. This also indicates that his healings were not simply psychological responses to his powerful presence.

**Heaven: Jesus Went to Heaven to Prepare Homes for His Followers**—Why did Jesus go to heaven? Scripture reveals many reasons. We find one in John 14:1–3 (NASB): "Let not your heart be troubled; believe in God, believe also in Me. In My Father's house are many dwelling places; if it were not so, I would have told you; for I go to prepare a place for you. And if I go and prepare a place for you, I will come again and receive you to Myself; that where I am, *there* you may be also." Clearly, Jesus is there now to prepare the places where his people will live in the afterlife. The interesting thing is that in Genesis one pictures God creating the heavens and earth in six days. What then could God accomplish in the two thousand years that Jesus has been in heaven?

**Hell: Was It the Town Dump?**—When Jesus spoke of "hell" in the scriptures, he usually used the word "gehenna," which was the town dump outside of Jerusalem. Fires always burned in it, and strange ugly worms lived in the refuse. Thus Jesus spoke of hell as being like Gehenna, "Where their worm does not die, and the fire is not quenched"(Mark 9:44–48, NASB).

**Hell and Heaven by Jesus**—When you compare the amount of words Jesus spent on talking about hell and heaven, the former wins. Among them are these (NASB):

*Matthew 5:22:* "But I say to you that everyone who is angry with his brother shall be guilty before the court; and whoever shall say to his brother, 'Raca' [You good-for-nothing], shall be guilty before the supreme court; and whoever shall say, 'You fool,' shall be guilty *enough to go* into the fiery hell."

*Matthew 5:29:* "And if your right eye makes you stumble, tear it out, and throw it from you; for it is better for you that one of the parts of your body perish, than for your whole body to be thrown into hell."

*Matthew 10:28:* "And do not fear those who kill the body, but are unable to kill the soul; but rather fear Him who is able to destroy both soul and body in hell."

*Matthew 23:33:* "You serpents, you brood of vipers, how shall you escape the sentence of hell?"

In addition, several whole parables speak directly about the consequences of not obeying the Word of God:

The Wise and Foolish Builders (Matt. 7:24–27)
The Tares (Matt. 12:24–30)
The Sower (Matt. 13:3–23)
Net Cast into the Sea (Matt. 13:47–50)
The Unmerciful Servant (Matt. 18:23–35)
The Wicked Husbandmen (Matt. 21:33–45)
The Marriage Feast (Matt. 22:2–14)
The Faithful and Evil Servants (Matt. 24:45–51)
The Ten Virgins (Matt. 25:1–13)
The Talents (Matt. 25:14–30)
The Rich Fool (Luke 12:16–21)
The Rich Man and Lazarus (Luke 16:19–31)
The Pounds (Luke 19:12–27)
The Good Shepherd (John 10:16)
The Vine and the Branches (John 15:1–5)

**Hellfire and Brimstone!**—Jesus was meek and mild, but on occasion he cut loose with some real hellfire and brimstone on his listeners. He said in one passage (Matthew 11:20–24, NASB), when people rejected him and his message:

> Then He began to reproach the cities in which most of His miracles were done, because they did not repent. "Woe to you, Chorazin! Woe to you, Bethsaida! For if the miracles had occurred in Tyre and Sidon which occurred in you, they would have repented long ago in sackcloth and ashes. Nevertheless I say to you, it shall be more tolerable for Tyre and Sidon in *the* day of judgment than for you. And you,

Capernaum, will not be exalted to heaven, will you? You shall descend to Hades; for if the miracles had occurred in Sodom which occurred in you, it would have remained to this day. Nevertheless I say to you that it shall be more tolerable for the land of Sodom in *the* day of judgment, than for you."

Matthew 23:1–39 is a whole chapter of searing "woes" pronounced upon hypocrites.

**Hex Signs**—Although at one time hex signs were symbols used by witches to invite the power of evil spirits or keep them away, an earlier tradition may be closer to the truth, for hex signs are often used by the very religious Pennsylvania Dutch people on their barns and houses as a means of keeping away evil spirits. The hex was derived by superimposing an I on an X. The I and the X in the Greek alphabet (iota and chi) are the first letters of the names *Jesus* and *Christ* respectively and form a six-sided figure that makes the hex.

**Hippies Looked Like Christ**—Although no one knows what Jesus looked like or whether he had long hair or short, a beard, or a goatee, many of the '60s and '70s hippies who modeled their idea of free love on Jesus' commandments to love the brethren tried to look a little like the classic pictures of Jesus—long hair, beard, scruffy, brown-eyed, and soulful.

**Holly Wreath at Christmas**—There is a legend of a shepherd boy who had nothing to bring to the just-born Jesus but a crown of brown, dried-up leaves. But it didn't look very nice. When he reached the stable in Bethlehem, he began to cry that all he had to present was this wreath. The Christ Child reached out to touch the wreath, and its leaves turned a brilliant green. The boy's tears turned into rich red berries on the crown.

**Holy Grail: Indiana Jones' Version**—The name "Indiana Jones" has spawned three mega-hit movies. Two of them, the first and the third, involve biblical artifacts. The first, *Raiders of the Lost Ark*, is a story of how Jones finds and saves the lost ark, the centerpiece of the Hebrew Temple and faith. To the Jews of the Old Testament, it was God's dwelling place on earth.

The third movie, *The Last Crusade*, goes back to another artifact, the Holy Grail, which is the cup that Jesus used at his last meal with his disciples before his crucifixion. Jesus used the wine in the cup as a symbol of his blood and passed it to each of his disciples to drink. In the movie, Jones is presented with a huge table filled with various "grails." Most are gold or silver and are embedded with gems. After Jones' enemy is destroyed by drinking out of the wrong cup, Indiana stands at the table to make his own selection. He needs the supernatural cup to heal his father, who has been shot in the abdomen. All the grails save one are gemmed masterpieces, but Jones selects the only one that "a poor carpenter" might use—a cup made of fired clay.

It was an appropriate gesture, for Jesus had few dealings with rich people and their possessions and probably would have used something from a common home, rough hewn, crudely made and personal for that final celebration with his disciples.

**Hometown**—Jesus grew up in Nazareth, but lived somewhere else—in Capernaum, near the northwest side of the Sea of Galilee. He moved specifically there to fulfill prophecy (Matt. 4:12–16, NASB):

> Now when He [Jesus] heard that John had been taken into custody, He withdrew into Galilee; and leaving Nazareth, He came and settled in Capernaum, which is by the sea, in the region of Zebulun and Naphtali. This was to fulfill what was spoken through Isaiah the prophet, saying,
> "The Land Of Zebulun and the land of Naphtali, by the way of the sea, beyond the Jordan, Galilee of the Gentiles—the people who were sitting in darkness saw a great light, and to those who were sitting in the land and shadow of death, upon them a light dawned."

**Human: Was Jesus Completely Human?**—Through the ages, theologians have discussed many ways to interpret the identity of Christ. At various times, different errors have frustrated people in determining the truth. One is to exalt Christ to be God but not really human. The other is to make Christ human but not fully God.

An answer to this question (see other entries regarding Christ's divinity under **Incarnation** and **Messiah**) is that Christ was both God and man in one person, completely human and completely divine. In considering here only his human side, what proof do we have that Jesus was truly and completely human? Consider the following evidence:

He was born of a woman (see Luke 2:1–7 and Gal. 4:4).
He grew and developed as a normal human (see Luke 2:52).
He was seen and touched by other people (see 1 John 1:1; Matt. 26:12).

He had a human soul and spirit (see Matt. 26:38 and Luke 23:46).
He went through normal human experiences:
Hunger (Matt. 4:2)
Thirst (John 19:28)
Tiredness and the need for sleep (John 4:6)
The need to pray (Mark 1:35)
Compassion for hurting people (Matt. 9:36)
Affection and concern for lost people (Mark 10:21)
Grief and sorrow (John 11:35)
Testing and tempting (Matt. 4:1–10; Heb. 4:15)
Love for close friends (John 11:5, 21:7)
Betrayal (John 13:21–30)
Experienced being hated and ridiculed (Matt. 27:39–44)
Felt pain and fear (Matt. 26:36–46)
He felt forsaken and rejected by God (Matt. 27:46).
He had human names: "Son of Man"(Luke 19:10); "Jesus"(Matt. 1:21); "Son of David"(Mark 10:47); "Man"(Isa. 53:3; 1 Tim. 2:5).
He was able to die (Matt. 27:45–50).

All this data indicates that Jesus was truly human. The need for this is spelled out in Hebrews 2:17–18: "For this reason he had to be made like his brothers in every way, in order that he might become a merciful and faithful high priest in service to God, and that he might make atonement for the sins of the people. Because he himself suffered when he was tempted, he is able to help those who are being tempted."

If Jesus wasn't entirely human, how could he hope to make his followers want to be like him, to follow him, to trust him, to love him, and to worship him?

**Human Responses to Jesus' Message**—In the parable of the sower, Jesus shows there are basically four ways people respond to his message (see Matt. 13:3–23). He pictures a sower throwing seed on four types of soil: hard, thin, weedy, and good. He tells his listeners that the seed represents God's Word.

When seed falls on the hard soil, birds of the air representing Satan rush down and steal the seed before it can take root. Some people, Jesus shows, hear God's Word, but before they even think about it or try to understand, Satan steals it from their mind and they make no attempt to retrieve it.

The seed on the thin soil does take root, but it dries up in the heat of the sun. Jesus makes the parallel that some people hear God's Word and receive it with joy at first, but when hardships and difficult things come into their lives, they give it up, presumably believing that God has let them down.

The third kind of soil receives the Word, but the soil allows weeds and thorns to grow—it isn't pruned and weeded—and eventually the weeds choke the small planting. Again, the parallel is that some people receive God's Word with joy, but then they turn their eyes to the "pleasures of this world" and, like weeds and thorns, they let those pleasures overrun their obedience to and love for God.

The final kind of soil Jesus calls "good soil," and neither the heat of the sun nor the pleasures and riches of this world deter it from growing. It eventually produces fruit—thirtyfold, sixtyfold, and a hundredfold. This kind of person doesn't give up when trials come, nor does he or she succumb to letting pleasure and riches overrun his or her faith.

Scholars argue as to whether the last three soils are people of faith at different levels, or if only the fourth soil has real faith. Jesus does not give an answer to that question, but in many other passages it is clear that Jesus expects obedience to his words and that his followers will be people who practice godliness, love their neighbors as themselves, and love God with all their heart, soul, mind, and might.

**Humility Was Always Honored**—Jesus always honored people of humility, even when they had done evil things. Such a person was Zacchaeus, a leading tax collector who had made a fortune in his business. He was short of stature, which perhaps gave him a sense of inferiority. On the only occasion he is mentioned in scripture, he develops an interest in Jesus. When he finally gets a chance to see Jesus, Zacchaeus goes to the street where Jesus is approaching. A great crowd gathers, greeting the Savior. Zacchaeus couldn't see over the heads of the people and couldn't push through, so he climbed a sycamore tree and hung there so he could see Jesus. When Jesus spotted him, he walked over to the tree and said, "Zacchaeus, come down immediately. I must stay at your house today" (Luke 19:5).

Zacchaeus slid down and walked with Jesus toward his house. On the way, they talked. Suddenly, Zacchaeus stopped and said to Jesus, "Look, Lord! Here and now I give half of my possessions to the poor, and if I have cheated anybody out of anything, I will pay back four times the amount." Jesus was pleased and replied, "Today salvation has come to this house, because this man, too, is a son of Abraham. For the Son of Man came to seek and to save what was lost" (see Luke 19:1–10).

When a person humbles himself or herself before God, God always takes note. The first of Jesus' Beatitudes says, "Blessed are the poor in spirit, for theirs is the kingdom of heaven." To be "poor in spirit" did not mean defective as a cheerleader, but to recognize and admit your need and dependency on God for all the things of life.

**Hypocrisy: The Scathing Jesus**—Jesus could be quite blistering when it came to hypocrisy. Look at his comments to the Pharisees in Matthew 23:2–12:

> "The teachers of the law and the Pharisees sit in Moses' seat. So you must obey them and do everything they tell you. But do not do what they do, for they do not practice what they preach. They tie up heavy loads and put them on men's shoulders, but they themselves are not willing to lift a finger to move them.
>
> "Everything they do is done for men to see: They make their phylacteries wide and the tassels of their prayer shawls long; they love the place of honor at banquets and the most important seats in the synagogues; they love to be greeted in the marketplaces and to have men call them 'Rabbi'.
>
> "But you are not to be called 'Rabbi,' for you have only one Master and you are all brothers. And do not call anyone on earth 'father,' for you have one Father, and he is in heaven. Nor are you to be called 'teacher,' for you have one Teacher, the Christ. The greatest among you will be your servant. For whoever exalts himself will be humbled, and whoever humbles himself will be exalted."

**Hypocrisy the Greatest Sin?**—Jesus often pointed out hypocrisy in some of his enemies as their biggest fault. He pointed out how hypocrites try to show how religious they are by making their religion a public ritual. An example is from the Sermon on the Mount (Matt. 6:1–8), where he scathingly zeroes in on their giving and prayer habits:

> "Be careful not to do your 'acts of righteousness' before men, to be seen by them. If you do, you will have no reward from your Father in heaven.
>
> "So when you give to the needy, do not announce it with trumpets, as the hypocrites do in the synagogues and on the streets, to be honored by men. I tell you the truth, they have received their reward in full. But when you give to the needy, do not let your left hand know

what your right hand is doing, so that your giving may be in secret. Then your Father, who sees what is done in secret, will reward you.

"But when you pray, do not be like the hypocrites, for they love to pray standing in the synagogues and on the street corners to be seen by men. I tell you the truth, they have received their reward in full. When you pray, go into your room, close the door and pray to your Father, who is unseen. Then your Father, who sees what is done in secret, will reward you."

# I

**Icons: The Jesus of the Tortilla**—The *Chicago Tribune* reported the story of a woman in New Mexico who was frying tortillas. One of the tortillas got burned in an unusual way, and when she studied it, she realized it looked like a picture of Jesus. She took it to all her friends and relatives. They also agreed it looked like Jesus, so she took it to her local parish, where she asked the priest to bless it. He was reluctant at first, but when she testified as to how the Jesus tortilla had changed her life—made her more compassionate, gentle, easier to get along with—he went through with it.

Taking it home, she enclosed the tortilla in glass, setting it on a bed of cotton. Then she opened a shrine to which visitors could come and see the "Jesus of the Tortilla." In time, nearly eight thousand people visited the shrine. All agreed the tortilla's burn marks looked like Jesus, except one reporter who said instead they resembled the face of the heavyweight boxer, Leon Spinks.

**Identity: Who or What Did Jesus Say He Was?**—There are seven "I am" statements in the Bible in which Jesus graphically states his identity. From them we gain an insight into his character and also the depth of his greatness. They are all from the Book of John:

*John 6:35:* "I am the bread of life. He who comes to me will never go hungry, and he who believes in me will never be thirsty."

*John 8:12:* "I am the light of the world. Whoever follows me will never walk in darkness, but will have the light of life."

*John 10:9:* "I am the gate; whoever enters through me will be saved. He will come in and go out, and find pasture."

*John 10:11:* "I am the good shepherd. The good shepherd lays down his life for the sheep."

*John 11:25:* "I am the resurrection and the life. He who believes in me will live, even though he dies."

*John 14:6:* "I am the way and the truth and the life. No one comes to the Father except through me."

*John 15:5:* "I am the vine; you are the branches. If a man remains in me and I in him, he will bear much fruit; apart from me you can do nothing."

**Identity: Who People Said Jesus Was**—Even in his own day, it was debated among the people who Jesus really was. Some said Elijah, some said John the Baptist, and some said one of the prophets. On one occasion (Matt. 16:13–17), Jesus confronted his disciples about who they believed he was. They answered similarly, until Peter made a final statement of faith and understanding:

> When Jesus came to the region of Caesarea Philippi, he asked his disciples, "Who do people say the Son of Man is?"
> They replied, "Some say John the Baptist; others say Elijah; and still others, Jeremiah or one of the prophets."
> "But what about you?" he asked. "Who do you say I am?"
> Simon Peter answered, "You are the Christ, the Son of the living God."
> Jesus replied, "Blessed are you, Simon son of Jonah, for this was not revealed to you by man, but by my Father in heaven."

**Identity: Who Was Jesus?**—C.S. Lewis, the patron saint of modern Christianity and a stalwart and eloquent defender of the faith, often used a special paradigm to describe the options he felt Christ left us as to his identity. Scholars today have called Jesus everything from the incarnation of God, to a prophet and teacher and good man, to a blasphemer of the worst sort. But Lewis, having studied the texts we have of Jesus' life and words, summed up the realistic options more precisely with these words:

> A man who was merely a man and said the sort of things Jesus said wouldn't be a great moral teacher. He'd be either a lunatic—on a level with a man who says he's a poached egg—or else he'd be the devil of hell. You must make your choice. Either this man was and is the Son of

God, or else a madman or something worse. . . . But don't let us come up with any patronizing nonsense about his being a great human teacher. He hasn't left that open to us. He didn't intend to.

**Impeccability of Christ: Could Jesus Sin?**—Could Jesus have committed a sin if he had wanted to? Could he have been tempted and given in, as movies like *The Last Temptation of Christ* have tried to show?

A doctrine called the "impeccability of Christ" is the answer to this question. "Impeccability" comes from the French terms *in* and *peccare*. The word means to be incapable of sin, to be entirely without fault. This means Christ not only was *able not* to sin, but was also *not able* to sin in any form. The idea of the doctrine comes from the following scriptures:

*Habakkuk 1:13:* "Your eyes are too pure to look on evil; you cannot tolerate wrong."

*2 Corinthians 5:21:* "God made him who had no sin to be sin for us, so that in him we might become the righteousness of God."

*Hebrews 4:15:* "For we do not have a high priest who is unable to sympathize with our weaknesses, but we have one who has been tempted in every way, just as we are—yet was without sin."

*James 1:13:* "When tempted, no one should say, 'God is tempting me.' For God cannot be tempted by evil, nor does he tempt anyone."

*1 John 1:5:* "This is the message we have heard from him and declare to you: God is light; in him there is no darkness at all."

*1 John 3:5:* "But you know that he appeared so that he might take away our sins. And in him is no sin."

From these scriptures we see that not only was Jesus sinless in that he never committed sin, but he was also incapable of committing sin. The problem some have with this is that if Christ could not sin, he also could not truly be tempted. If so, then how can he be an example to us of one who has faced temptation and triumphed? If he could not sin, it was a closed issue. He cannot really understand what we face during temptation, nor can we learn from him as an example of one who can defeat temptation.

From passages like Matthew 4:1–10, where Satan "tempted" Jesus in the wilderness, we find no evidence that Jesus was not truly tempted. Certainly, Satan believed he could make Jesus fall or he would not have tried. In other passages (Heb. 2:17–18 and 4:15–16), we learn that Jesus was tempted "in every way, just as we are—yet was without sin." How then can these two ideas—being incapable of sinning and yet being truly tempted to sin—be reconciled?

It is the idea of "testing" and "tempting" that must be understood. The Greek word *peirasmos* can mean either "testing" or "tempting." When something is tested, two results are possible: success or failure. Someone may be tested over and over with success every time, but the test remains real in each situation. A successful test proves that a person or thing can stand the pressure. Achieving success every time does not mean the pressure wasn't there or that the test was somehow bogus.

Thus, although Jesus was tested completely and always met success, every test was real and put pressure on him that he had to withstand. Because he always met with success, Jesus knows how to help people at any stage in the process—those undergoing an easy test, a moderate test, a difficult test, or an excruciating test. He knows how to succeed in all situations and thus can help people in all situations.

But, some may ask, didn't Jesus ever experience guilt, failure, frustration, or the agony of defeat?

Yes, on the cross he experienced all the emotions, feelings, psychological ramifications, and agonies of complete failure before God. When Jesus hung on the cross, the sin of the world was placed on him in some mystical way by God the Father, and Jesus experienced the full impact of sinful humanity. He became spiritually separated from the Father; he went to the place of eternal damnation; and he knew all the agonies of what it is to commit sin in the eyes of a holy God. Such scriptures as these confirm this:

Separation from God through the experience of personal guilt and sin through the sins of the world being laid on him: *Matthew 27:46:* "About the ninth hour Jesus cried out in a loud voice, '*Eloi, Eloi, lama sabachthani?*'—which means, 'My God, my God, why have you forsaken me?'"

All the results of sin, suffering, disease, and pain through humankind's sin being laid on him: *Isaiah 53:12:* "Therefore I will give him a portion among the great, and he will divide the spoils with the strong, because he poured out his life unto death, and was numbered with the transgressors. For he bore the sin of many, and made intercession for the transgressors."

And *Matthew 8:17:* "This was to fulfill what was spoken through the prophet Isaiah: 'He took up our infirmities and carried our diseases.'"

The agonies of hell: *1 Peter 3:18–19:* "For Christ died for sins once for all, the righteous for the unrighteous, to bring you to God. He was put to death in the body but made alive by the Spirit, through whom also he went and preached to the spirits in prison who disobeyed long ago when God waited patiently in the days of Noah while the ark was being built."

Although in many ways what happened to Christ on the cross remains a mystery that only study in eternity will enable us to fathom fully, the truth remains that Jesus experienced all the depths, deceptions, tricks, and tribulations of true testing and tempting. When we go to him, we can be sure we will find a sympathetic, informed, helpful, and empowering Savior.

**Impostors: Booked as Jesus**—When Charles Manson was booked by police for the murders of Sharon Tate and several others, he wrote himself in as "Manson, Charles M., a.k.a. Jesus Christ, God." Manson believed we're all part of a much greater whole and in such a sense we are one. As a result, there is no such thing as death. He came to the conclusion that killing isn't wrong.

Jesus predicted that such impostors would come, especially in the end times: "For many will come in my name, claiming, 'I am the Christ,' and will deceive many" (Matt. 24:5).

**Incarnation: Was Jesus God in Human Flesh?**—"Incarnation," from the Latin *in carne*, or "in flesh," means Christ being God in human flesh. The argument has raged for centuries as to whether Jesus was really God in human flesh. Although the Old Testament does not clearly delineate the coming of God in human flesh, except in Isaiah 7:14, where the son born of the virgin is called "Immanuel," which means "God with us," the New Testament has many strong statements of Christ being God in human flesh. Among them are these:

*John 1:1–3, 14, 18:* "In the beginning was the Word, and the Word was with God, and the Word was God. He was with God in the beginning. Through him all things were made; without him nothing was made that has been made. . . . The Word became flesh and lived for a while among us. We have seen his glory, the glory of the one and only Son, who came from the Father, full of grace and truth. . . . No one has ever seen God, but God the only Son, who is at the Father's side, has made him known."

*Philippians 2:5–11:* "Your attitude should be the same as that of Christ Jesus: Who, being in very nature God, did not consider equality with God something to be grasped, but made himself nothing, taking the very nature of a servant, being made in human likeness. And being found in appearance as a man, he humbled himself and became obedient to death—even death on a cross! Therefore God exalted him to the highest place and gave him the name that is above every name, that at the name of Jesus every knee should bow, in heaven and on earth and under the earth, and every tongue confess that Jesus Christ is Lord, to the glory of God the Father."

*Colossians 1:15–17:* "He is the image of the invisible God, the first-born over all creation. For by him all things were created: things in heaven and on earth, visible and invisible, whether thrones or powers or rulers or authorities; all things were created by him and for him. He is before all things, and in him all things hold together."

*Hebrews 1:1–3:* "In the past God spoke to our forefathers through the prophets at many times and in various ways, but in these last days he has spoken to us by his Son, whom he appointed heir of all things, and through whom he made the universe. The Son is the radiance of God's glory and the exact representation of his being, sustaining all things by his powerful word. After he had provided purification for sins, he sat down at the right hand of the Majesty in heaven."

*2 Peter 1:1–3:* "Simon Peter, a servant and apostle of Jesus Christ, To those who through the righteousness of our God and Savior Jesus Christ have received a faith as precious as ours: Grace and peace be yours in abundance through the knowledge of God and of Jesus our Lord. His divine power has given us everything we need for life and godliness through our knowledge of him who called us by his own glory and goodness."

*Revelation 19:11–16:* "I saw heaven standing open and there before me was a white horse, whose rider is called Faithful and True. With justice he judges and makes war. His eyes are like blazing fire, and on his head are many crowns. He has a name written on him that no one knows but he himself knows. He is dressed in a robe dipped in blood, and his name is the Word of God. The armies of heaven were follow-ing him, riding on white horses and dressed in fine linen, white and clean. Out of his mouth comes a sharp sword with which to strike down the nations. 'He will rule them with an iron scepter.' He treads the winepress of the fury of the wrath of God Almighty. On his robe and on his thigh he has this name written: KING OF KINGS AND LORD OF LORDS."

Although one may opt for other answers to the question, Who was Jesus?—great teacher, leader, charlatan, fraud—it's plain from these scriptures that the people closest to Jesus—Peter, the apostle Paul, and John—have written that they saw him as God in human flesh.

**Inn Was Probably a Caravansary**—What was the inn that turned away the parents of Jesus the day before Christmas when they sought lodging in Bethlehem? It was probably a "caravansary," which was usually a compound built around a water supply that housed traveling merchants, soldiers, pilgrims, and others. Thus, the inn that turned away Joseph and Mary was probably such a caravansary where camel drivers and muleteers would have gathered to swap stories, drink, tell jokes, and spend the night revelling. Maybe being born in a stable was better!

**Isaac: Prophetic Picture of Things to Come**—In the Old Testament, God told Abraham to sacrifice his son Isaac on Mt. Moriah. This was to be a blood sacrifice; that is, Isaac would be killed as a special sacrifice to God. Abraham probably did not understand all the ramifications of what God was doing, but in Hebrews 11:19 it is revealed that "Abraham reasoned that God could raise the dead, and figuratively speaking, he did receive Isaac back from death." Thus Abraham decided to go through with the sacrifice on that basis.

When he reached Mt. Moriah and actually prepared to offer up Isaac, however, the "angel of the Lord" stopped him, saying, "Do not lay a hand on the boy. . . . Do not do anything to him. Now I know that you fear God, because you have not withheld your son, your only son" (Gen. 22:12). Obviously, this was something of a picture of what would happen to Jesus Christ, where God sacrificed God's Son for the world. But the sacrifice of Isaac goes beyond that. First, it demonstrated Abraham's true faith and willingness to obey God even when he didn't understand why God might make such a weird and lethal command. Second, Abraham, being the first Jew, becomes a picture of God beginning a whole new way of dealing with people, as God did in Jesus Christ. Third, it reveals the first person who believed that God could raise the dead. Fourth, it is a picture, according to the passage in Hebrews 11:19, of God raising God's own Son from the dead. There are many such "pictures" or "types" in scripture that fortell the events of Christ's life or other coming events through examples.

# J

**Jefferson's Bible**—Thomas Jefferson, a deist, had Congress issue a special edition of the Bible in which the Founding Father, concentrating only on Jesus' moral teachings, had taken out all references to the supernatural. The last words of this Bible were: "There laid they Jesus and rolled a great stone at the mouth of the sepulchre and departed."

**Jerusalem: City of Great Religions**—All three of the world's great monotheistic (belief in one God) religions—Judaism, Christianity, and Islam—regard Jerusalem as a holy city. Jesus prophesied that it would be flattened, not "one stone upon another," shortly after his death and resurrection. It happened in A.D. 70, a dark hour for Jews especially.

**Jesuits: Don't Call Me That!**—Jesuits, ordained members of the Society of Jesus, are known the world over for their compassion and teachings. They are known as Jesuits to almost everyone. However, they have never officially adopted the term, nor does the Roman Catholic Church ever call them that.

**Jesus: If He Lived Today, a Portrait**—What would Jesus be like if he walked among us today?

Many have tried to show such a Jesus. One of the most successful renditions is Father Joseph Girzone's novel *Joshua*. In his version, Joshua, who portrays Jesus, is a young carpenter who comes to a small town and after several weeks has quite a following. Children have seen him do "magical" tricks, people have been healed, and a wonderful wood-carved statue of Moses has been donated to the local synagogue. Eventually, Joshua's fame grows until the pope in Rome summons him for a review of his beliefs, which many consider heretical. After convincing the pope himself that he is real, Joshua disappears. But he leaves a grand legacy of love and hope behind him, as well as a mass of so-called religious authorities who have been outraged and are calling for Joshua's head!

**Jesus Seminar**—A gathering of a number of biblical and other scholars called "The Jesus Seminar" has in the last few years worked at identifying what is authentic and what isn't authentic in the biblical accounts of Jesus' life. What they have come up with are only a few statements and almost nothing of the actual history. They systematically study each statement, event, or story from Jesus' life and then vote as to whether they think it's authentic.

**Jonah**—Jonah was a Hebrew prophet living around 760 B.C. who ministered to the northern half of the nation of Israel, which was actually called Israel (the southern kingdom was called Judah, after the name of the primary tribe that occupied it). God told Jonah to travel eastward to the city of Nineveh and prophecy against it. Instead, Jonah, not wanting to warn Nineveh, an enemy of the Jews, about impending disaster and possibly lead them to repent and seek God's mercy, fled to

Tarshish in the opposite direction. He boarded a ship at the seaport of Joppa, hid in the hold, and tried to wait out God's call. God decided to stop the prophet by sending a huge storm on the sea that almost sank the ship. When the sailors discovered that Jonah's disobedience was the cause of the storm, they tried to fix things, but in the end they threw Jonah overboard. Immediately, about to drown, Jonah called out to God for mercy and was swallowed by a "great fish" (not necessarily a whale). Jonah remained in the fish for three days and nights, perhaps because it took that long to get him to land. There, the fish vomited him up, and Jonah obeyed God's orders from that point and went to Nineveh. Jesus used this event as a picture of what would happen to him. Just as Jonah spent three days and nights in the belly of the giant fish, so Jesus would spend that length of time dead before he would be resurrected (see Matt. 12:39–41). This reference also indicates that Jesus believed that Jonah's experience really happened!

**Josephus: The First Outside-the-New-Testament Thoughts on Jesus**—Flavius Josephus's books written early in the second century offer some interesting thoughts on Jesus as a worker of wonders, but also as much more than a normal man. Josephus wrote: "About this time lived Jesus, a wise man, if it be proper to call him a man, for he was a doer of wonderful works—a teacher of such men as receive the truth with pleasure. He drew over to him both many of the Jews and many of the Greeks. He was the Christ. And when Pilate, at the instigation of the principal men among us, had condemned him to the cross, those who had loved him at first did not forsake him. For he appeared to them alive again on the third day, the divine prophets having foretold these and many other wonderful things concerning him. And the sect of Christians, so named after him, are not extinct to this day." Josephus was a Jew and not a convert to Christianity.

**Judas Iscariot: Jesus Knew Judas Would Betray Him**—From the early days of his ministry, Jesus knew that Judas Iscariot would betray him. He speaks of the fact that Judas was a devil in John 6:70–71. On Jesus' last night with his disciples before his resurrection, he celebrated the Passover in the upper room of a house in Jerusalem. There he instituted the rite of the Lord's Supper or Eucharist. At one point, he told the disciples that one person would betray him. John 13:26–27 (NASB) says:

> Jesus therefore answered, "That is the one for whom I
> shall dip the morsel and give it to him." So when He

had dipped the morsel, He took and gave it to Judas, *the son* of Simon Iscariot. After the morsel, Satan then entered into him.

Jesus Therefore said to him, "What you do, do quickly."

An interesting detail of this is that Jesus washed Judas's feet earlier, as he did with all the other disciples, and he even allowed Judas to participate in the Lord's Supper. Moreover, he warned Judas several times of the impending betrayal, perhaps even trying to stop him, and he allowed Judas to leave and go to the priests without having the others hold him. From this it's clear that Jesus not only tried to keep Judas from disaster, but even bore him no malice or hatred.

**Judas Iscariot: Judas Tried to Give the Money Back**—Judas, after betraying Jesus for thirty pieces of silver, felt remorse and conviction about it after Jesus was executed. Matthew 27:3–5 (NASB) records the event:

> Then when Judas, who had betrayed Him, saw that He had been condemned, he felt remorse and returned the thirty pieces of silver to the chief priests and elders, saying, "I have sinned by betraying innocent blood." But they said, "What is that to us? See *to that* yourself!" And he threw the pieces of silver into the sanctuary and departed; and he went away and hanged himself.

Perhaps when Judas decided to betray Jesus, he did not believe that the chief priests would actually have Jesus executed. Maybe he thought Jesus would only be rebuked or even censured. But this had already happened many times to Jesus in his relationship with the leading Jews.

Strangely enough, these events were prophesied in the Old Testament, matters that were quite beyond Judas's control. The payment of thirty pieces of silver and the priests' using it (after Judas threw it into the temple) to buy a potter's field were prophesied in Zechariah 11:12–13 (NASB):

> And I said to them, "If it is good in your sight, give *me* my wages; but if not, never mind!" So they weighed out thirty *shekels* of silver as my wages.
> Then the LORD said to me, "Throw it to the potter, *that* magnificent price at which I was valued by them." So I took the thirty *shekels* of silver and threw them to the potter in the house of the Lord.

**Judas Iscariot: The Odds Are On**—H.L. Mencken, who lampooned Jesus every chance he got and claimed to be an atheist, wasn't one to gamble. But he put odds on Judas Iscariot over Jesus this way: "Courtroom: A place where Jesus Christ and Judas Iscariot would be equals, with the betting odds in favor of Judas."

**Judas Iscariot: The Straw That Broke Judas's Back**—What turned Judas against Jesus? There is no clear indication in scripture of what precisely it was, but one event stands out. In Matthew 26:6–15, a woman comes to the house of Simon the Leper where Jesus was dining and anointed Jesus' feet with expensive perfume. We know that this woman was Mary, the sister of Lazarus (see John 12:1–11), a strong believer in Jesus. Judas witnessed this "waste" (he is referred to in the John passage), and Matthew says, "Then one of the Twelve—the one called Judas Iscariot—went to the chief priests and asked, 'What are you willing to give me to hand him over to you?'" Perhaps this was the issue that broke Judas. Scripture is silent on the matter, so any reason offered is pure speculation. It was known, though, that Judas was a thief; he was the treasurer of Jesus' disciples and took money from the kitty for his own use (see John 12:6). Jesus also called him a "devil" (John 6:70–71), so presumably Jesus understood Judas's true nature. Whatever the reason for his defection, it was probably not, as some have suggested in recent days, because he was trying to push Jesus into bringing in the kingdom of God. If that was his purpose, there are many ways he might have "helped" Jesus, including (1) talking to him about it; (2) convincing Jesus that now was the right time; and (3) getting the disciples on his side about it. Instead, he chose to sell Jesus out for thirty pieces of silver, which goes along with his character as a thief, a person concerned only about money.

**Judging Others: Jesus Forbade Judging Others, Yet He Is Known as the Judge of All**—Several times in scripture, Jesus warns people not to judge others. The best passage is from the Sermon on the Mount (Matt. 7:1–5, NASB):

> "Do not judge lest you be judged. For in the way you
>    judge, you will be judged; and by your standard of mea-
>    sure, it will be measured to you.
> "And why do you look at the speck that is in your
>    brother's eye, but do not notice the log that is in your
>    own eye? Or how can you say to your brother, 'Let me
>    take the speck out of your eye,' and behold, the log is

in your own eye? You hypocrite, first take the log out
of your own eye, and then you will see clearly to take
the speck out of your brother's eye."

Here, Jesus was pointing out the hypocritical, pharisaical practice of condemning and judging others for minor things like their dress, their failure to keep up with certain "traditions," their prayer habits, their race, and many other things. Judging people about character traits, race, nationality, idiosyncrasies, small infractions, and personality is wrong in God's eyes.

**Kenosis: The Emptying of Christ**—In Christian theology, one will soon run across the doctrine of the kenosis, a Greek word that means "emptying." The idea of the kenosis is found in Philippians 2:5–8: "Your attitude should be the same as that of Christ Jesus: Who, being in very nature God, did not consider equality with God something to be grasped, but made himself nothing, taking the very nature of a servant, being made in human likeness. And being found in appearance as a man, he humbled himself and became obedient to death—even death on a cross!"

The idea that Jesus "made himself nothing" is the essence of the kenosis, but what does it mean? Does it mean Jesus shed his divinity to become a human being? Does it mean he was not truly divine, but something far above human though not quite God-like?

The essence of the kenosis is this:

1. As the God-man, Jesus' glory as God was "veiled," or purposely hidden, from his observers. That is, when the disciples looked at Jesus, they saw a person just like themselves, with flesh, organs, a body and face like any other whole person. Through the kenosis, Jesus did not demand that people bow in worship to him, nor did he expect them to understand fully who he really was. This is brought out in Philippians 2:5 where it says that Jesus, "being in very nature God, did not consider equality with God something to be grasped."

2. As the God-man, Jesus took on human flesh with all its normal functions, needs, desires, and frailties, short of being sinful. Jesus took on complete humanity through the kenosis, an act tantamount to a human becoming an ant in order to communicate with ants. This is

brought out in Philippians 2:6: He "made himself nothing, taking the very nature of a servant, being made in human likeness."

3. As the God-man, Jesus voluntarily chose not to use all of his divine abilities (omnipotence, omniscience) at certain times in order to communicate clearly and squarely with people. Thus, setting aside his eternality, he subjected himself to pain and death. Setting aside his omniscience, he experienced separation from his Father. Setting aside his omnipotence, he chose not to try to save himself. This is brought out again in Philippians 2:8, where it is written, "And being found in appearance as a man, he humbled himself and became obedient to death—even death on a cross!"

The kenosis is what ultimately makes possible the reality of believers being able to identify with, trust, and know Christ personally.

**Kingdom That Lasts a Thousand Years**—The doctrine known as premillennialism states that Jesus will return and reign on earth for a thousand years, establishing the perfect kingdom. At the end, Satan will be freed from his chains and allowed to lead a final rebellion, which, when defeated, ushers in eternity (see Revelation 20).

**Kneeling in Prayer**—Jesus was the first to kneel in prayer. He often did it when he prayed in the Garden of Gethsemane. The tradition of kneeling while praying is built on his example there (see Luke 22:41).

**Knock on Wood**—This practice, found even today, goes back hundreds of years. It was derived from the idea of touching or knocking on the cross of Christ. This symbolized faith in Christ and a desire for the blessing that comes through belief.

**Lamb and Lion**—In the New Testament, Jesus is called both the Lamb of God and the Lion of the tribe of Judah (see John 1:29 and Rev. 5:5). How can he be a lamb—meek, mild, tame, small, innocent, pure, helpless—and a lion—strong, ferocious, large, majestic, courageous, untamed? Scripture often joins such seemingly contradictory ideas together, painting a full portrait of Christ rather than limiting him in a single symbol. As the lamb, Jesus pictured the sacrifice that Jews brought to the Temple so that they could be forgiven for their sins.

The lamb was the most common sacrificial animal among those who could afford it. It was centrally featured in the Passover, the greatest rite of the Jewish people. Jesus, thus, was the sacrificial lamb who would take away the sins of the world, as John the Baptist said in John 1:29.

As the lion from the tribe of Judah, Isaiah 31:4 says, "This is what the LORD says to me: 'As a lion growls, a great lion over his prey—and though a whole band of shepherds is called together against him, he is not frightened by their shouts or disturbed by their clamor—so the LORD Almighty will come down to do battle on Mount Zion and on its heights.'" As a lion, Jesus is a defender of the downtrodden and a warrior for those who are oppressed. When he comes back to earth, he will reign over the nations and rule them "with a rod of iron" (Rev. 2:27). Thus, he is called these two seemingly contradictory beasts because he is both, and neither alone is a great enough image for all of his character.

**Language: Jesus Spoke the Language of the People**—What language did Jesus speak? From various passages in the New Testament where he is quoted, Jesus apparently spoke Aramaic, a derivative of Hebrew that was the common language of the Jews. Some examples (from NASB):

*Mark 5:41:* "And taking the child by the hand, He said to her, 'Talitha kum!' (which translated means, 'Little girl, I say to you, arise!')."

*Mark 15:34:* "And at the ninth hour Jesus cried out with a loud voice, 'Eloi, Eloi, lama sabachthani?' which is translated, 'My God, My God, why hast thou forsaken me?'"

*John 1:38:* "And Jesus turned, and beheld them following, and said to them, 'What do you seek?' And they said to Him, 'Rabbi (which translated means Teacher), where are You staying?'"

*John 1:41:* "He found first his own brother Simon and said to him, 'We have found the Messiah' (which translated means Christ)."

*John 1:42:* "He brought him to Jesus. Jesus looked at him, and said, 'You are Simon the son of John; you shall be called Cephas' (which translated means Peter)."

It's possible that Jesus knew other languages, perhaps Koine Greek, which was the most common language of the world at that time and the language of diplomacy (just as English today is the common language of the world). But there is no clear indication that he did.

**Last Name**—"Christ" wasn't Jesus' last name. The name "Jesus Christ" means "Jesus the Messiah" in Greek. It would be similar to other expressions many have used to identify people throughout history, such as "Attila the Hun," "Peter the Great," and "William the

Conqueror." Normally, Jesus would have been known as Joshua ben Joseph, meaning Jesus, legal son of Joseph.

**Last Supper: House**—The Church of St. Mary of Zion in Jerusalem is supposedly the site of the house where Jesus celebrated the Last Supper with his disciples. It was built during the Crusades.

**Last Words**: Jesus' final word to his disciples was that they were to go into all the world and preach the gospel. Versions of this are found in all four of the Gospels (NASB):

*Matthew 28:18–20:* "And Jesus came up and spoke to them, saying, 'All authority has been given to Me in heaven and on earth. Go therefore and make disciples of all the nations, baptizing them in the name of the Father and the Son and the Holy Spirit, teaching them to observe all that I commanded you; and lo, I am with you always, even to the end of the age.'"

*Mark 16: 15–16:* "And He said to them, 'Go into all the world and preach the gospel to all creation. He who has believed and has been baptized shall be saved; but he who has disbelieved shall be condemned.'"

*Luke 24:46–49:* "He said to them, 'Thus it is written, that the Christ should suffer and rise again from the dead the third day, and that repentance for forgiveness of sins should be proclaimed in His name to all the nations, beginning from Jerusalem. You are witnesses of these things. And behold, I am sending forth the promise of My Father upon you; but you are to stay in the city until you are clothed with power from on high.'"

*John 20:21–23:* "Jesus therefore said to them again, 'Peace *be* with you; as the Father has sent Me, I also send you.' And when He had said this, He breathed on them and said to them, 'Receive the Holy Spirit. If you forgive the sins of any, *their sins* have been forgiven them; if you retain the *sins* of any, they have been retained.'"

Acts also records this version of the Great Commission:

*Acts 1:8:* "'You will receive power when the Holy Spirit comes on you; and you will be my witnesses in Jerusalem, and in all Judea and Samaria, and to the ends of the earth.'"

**Last Words of Jesus on the Cross**—The following are the last words Jesus spoke from the cross:

To the Roman soldiers and the crowd gathered to watch him die: "Father, forgive them, for they do not know what they are doing" (Luke 23:34).

To the repentant thief crucified on the cross next to Jesus: "Today you will be with me in paradise" (Luke 23:43).

To his mother Mary and his disciple John: "Dear woman, here is your son. . . . Here is your mother" (John 19:26–27).

To God, his Father: "My God, my God, why have you forsaken me?" (Matt. 27:46).

To the Roman soldiers: "I am thirsty" (John 19:28).

To the crowd: "It is finished" (John 19:30), the words written across a prisoner's sentence posted to his cell door in Roman prisons when his sentence was concluded.

To his Father: "Father, into your hands I commit my spirit" (Luke 23:46).

**Laughter**—Jesus wept, became angry, and showed many other emotions, but the Bible never records him as laughing. He used wit frequently (see **Wit**), but there is no indication that Jesus laughed or even smiled. It would be hard to believe, however, that he could have been a complete, whole person without showing these two kinds of emotion. Apparently, it just wasn't important enough to the writers of the New Testament to mention it.

**Law: Jesus Made the Hebrew Law Even Harder**—The Jews of Jesus' day, especially the Pharisees, discovered all sorts of ways to increase the requirements of the Mosaic Law on the people. Behavior on the Sabbath was a big issue, because God had said in the Ten Commandments (see Exodus 20) that no work was to be performed. The Pharisees interpreted this provision in some bizarre ways. For instance, pharisaical rules for the Sabbath included not being allowed to spit on the Sabbath because someone might step on the spit, leave a small furrow in the dirt, and be guilty of "plowing." Or the spit might water a seed in the soil and the person would be considered "farming" or "planting." One couldn't walk on grass on the Sabbath because one might dislodge a seed and be guilty of "sowing." A woman was prohibited from looking into a mirror on the Sabbath because she might spot a gray hair and pluck it.

These might seem trivial, but to the pious Jew it was all part of serving and obeying God. The problem was that many Jews, in their zeal to keep the Sabbath, overlooked other more important considerations. Thus, in the Sermon on the Mount, Jesus laid out several interpretations of the Law that were extraordinarily difficult to obey. In Matthew 5:21–26, Jesus qualified the commandment against murder by saying that being angry with someone was tantamount to committing murder, calling someone an "empty head" invited judgment, and labeling some-one a "fool" could lead to sentencing to eternal hell.

In the next passage, Jesus lays out his interpretation of the com-mandment against adultery. This time he says that looking on a woman and lusting after her was as much adultery as actually lying with her.

He goes on to cite the Pharisees' tendency to make lofty but false vows (Matt. 5:33–37), taking revenge on those who have hurt you (Matt. 5:38–42), and loving your enemies (Matt. 5:42–48). In effect, Jesus laid out far more stringent demands on people on the basis of Moses' Law than ever before. But his interpretations were strictly spir-itual, not like the legalistic demands of the Pharisees. Why? Perhaps to show his listeners how far they were from being able, in their own strength, to make themselves worthy of heaven.

**Leaders: Fall Down and Worship?**—Napoleon Bonaparte said, "If Socrates should enter the room, we would all rise and do him honor. But if Jesus Christ came into the room, we would all fall down and wor-ship him."

**Leaders: Invite Him to Dinner?**—Thomas Carlyle (1795–1881) called for "hero-rulers," strong, just men who came to power not by election but by the force of their character. He didn't seem to know what to do with Jesus, meek and mild Savior of the world. But perhaps he understood all too well how Jesus would be treated if he came today: "If Jesus Christ were to come today people would not crucify him. They would ask him to dinner and hear what he had to say, and make fun of it."

**Legacy: Benjamin Franklin's Final Opinion**—In a letter to Ezra Stiles, president of Yale College, shortly before Franklin's death, the statesman wrote that he believed Jesus' system of morals and religion to be "the best the world ever saw or is likely to see." He wasn't sure about the divinity of Christ, "having never studied it," but because he was near death he said that such a study was needless "when I expect soon to have an opportunity of knowing the truth with less trouble." He saw no harm, though, in believing in Jesus' deity, for it would make "his doctrines more respected and better observed."

**Lepers Healed and Touched**—One of the small gestures Jesus often made when healing lepers was to touch them with his hand. Lepers were required to stay outside of the town in areas sequestered and inhabited only by other lepers. They couldn't come into town or near people without shouting, "Unclean! Unclean!" to announce their presence. Thus, most lepers were solitary, rejected sorts who rarely received pleasant words or a touch. When Jesus healed lepers, he touched them while they were still lepers as a sign of compassion and love. A modern example of such astounding compassion occurred when Princess Diana reached out to children with AIDS, cuddling them and seating them on her lap.

**Letter from Heaven: A Letter Written by Jesus from Heaven—**
The letter supposedly written by Jesus was found eighteen miles from Iconium, fifty-three years after Jesus' crucifixion. It was originally said to be found under a large stone at the foot of the cross. The stone was engraved with the words "Blessed are they that shall turn me over." On the letter was written, "The Commandments of Jesus Christ. Signed by the Angel Gabriel, seventy-four years after our Savior's birth." Here are some excerpts from the letter:

> Whoever worketh on the Sabbath shall be accursed. I command you to go to church and keep the Lord's Day holy, without any manner of work. . . . I advise you to fast five days in the year, beginning with Good Friday and continuing the four Fridays following. . . . You shall diligently and peaceably labour in your respective callings wherein it has pleased God to call you. . . . He that hath given to the poor shall not be unprofited. . . . He that hath a copy of the letter, written with my own hand and spoken with my own mouth, and keepeth it without publishing it to others, shall not prosper, but he that publisheth it to others shall be blessed of me. . . . Whosoever shall have a copy of this letter and keep it in their house, nothing shall hurt them, and if any woman be in childbirth and put her trust in me, she shall be delivered of her child. You shall hear no more of me but by the Holy Spirit until the Day of Judgment.

This letter, according to Professor Robert Priebsch of London, was written first in Latin toward the end of the sixth century in Ebusa, one of the Balearic Islands in the Mediterranean Sea near Spain. It was given to the bishop Vincentius, who accepted it and passed it on to his people. He sent a copy of it to Licinianus, bishop of Cathagena, who denounced it. Over the years it has surfaced repeatedly and been denounced by most scholars.

**Liar, Lunatic, Legend, or Lord?**—When people argue over who Jesus was, they come at it in different ways, but the classic argument is that there are four options: One, he is a lunatic. Two, he is a liar. Three, he is a legend made up by his followers. Four, he is truly Lord.

Dealing with the first three is fairly simple. No lunatic could speak the words, do the deeds, and solve the problems that Christ did, let alone fulfill ancient prophecy, conquer death, and save the world from sin.

If Jesus was a liar, he was also a fool, because the Jews and Romans crucified him not for his deeds or words, but because he claimed to be the Messiah.

He couldn't have been a legend, because his story was told repeatedly during the lifetimes of those who knew him and witnessed his acts. Multitudes of manuscripts, both secular and Christian, tell his story. A legend must begin centuries after a man's life, when no one is around to contradict the story.

If he is not a liar, lunatic, or legend, what other option is there besides Lord?

**Liberated Man**—Jesus qualifies as a truly liberated man by the way he treated women. In Jesus' day, men regarded women as possessions, even as beasts, not equal to men before God. A favorite prayer of a Pharisee was to say, "Thank you, God, that I am not a Gentile, a tax-gatherer, or a woman." Women didn't receive the right to an education, and if they failed to bear children, kept an untidy house, made unsavory meals, or in any way displeased their husbands, they could be divorced merely at the signing of a certificate.

Jesus changed all that. He called the Jewish practice of divorce "hardness of heart"(see Matt. 19:3–9) and allowed for divorce only in the case of adultery. When a woman was caught in the act of adultery and dumped at his feet to see what he would do with her, Jesus protected the woman from stoning, assured her he didn't condemn her, and told her only to "leave your life of sin" (see John 8:2–11). He treated women with dignity by healing them and defending their right to come to him. He received their love and worship, and commended them for their commitment, which exceeded the commitment of his own disciples (see John 12:1–8). He became close friends with a number of women, as evidenced by the fact that a group of women were the first to return to his grave after his death (see Luke 24:1–7). One of Jesus' best followers was Mary Magdalene, a woman out of whom Jesus cast seven demons (Luke 8:2). Plainly, Jesus appreciated women and valued them far above the norm in his culture, paving the way for women's rights and other movements that have come into play in modern times.

**Listening to Him: Jesus Considered Being Listened to More Important Than Being Waited on!**—In the story of Martha the Servant and Mary the Student in Luke 10:38–42 (NASB), Jesus finds himself at their house enjoying a meal and teaching the people present. Martha took on the work of serving, but when her sister Mary decided not to help but to sit at Jesus' feet listening to his teaching, Martha complained to Jesus, saying, "Lord, do You not care that my sister has left me to do all the serving alone? Then tell her to help me." Jesus refused, countering, "Martha, Martha, you are worried and bothered about so many things; but *only* a few things are necessary, really *only* one, for Mary has chosen the good part, which shall not be taken away from her."

**Literature: Christ in Literature**—Jesus has been featured as both a bit player and a major figure in the work of such greats as Victor Hugo (*Les Miserables* is largely about a man's conversion in harsh circumstances and how his faith in Christ leads him to victory over oppression), William Faulkner (*As I Lay Dying* and others offer a look at faith in the South), Flannery O'Connor (renowned for the "Christ-figures" in her short stories), Graham Greene (whose *The Power and the Glory* is an amazing picture of faith in the midst of sin), Taylor Caldwell (such classics as *Dear and Glorious Physician* and *Great Lion of God* portray the lives of Luke and Paul, two of Jesus' second-generation disciples), Chaim Potok (a Jewish writer who shows how fanaticism among Jews "crucified" a boy's parents in *My Name Is Asher Lev* and nearly destroyed an artistic genius), Evelyn Waugh (*Brideshead Revisited* is a study of Roman Catholics dealing with their faith in Christ), and Walker Percy (whose *Second Coming* is an excellent look at a man who seeks a Christ who speaks today).

**Lord's Prayer: Did Jesus Pray It?**—Contrary to popular belief, Jesus did not give his disciples what is called The Lord's Prayer to be repeated verbatim but as a model or template to follow in prayer. It covers a number of topics important in any prayer:

*Praise and worship:* "Our Father who is in heaven, Hallowed be your name."

*Admission of priorities:* "Your kingdom come. Your will be done on earth as it is in heaven."

*Request for food and sustenance:* "Give us this day our daily bread."

*Request for forgiveness:* "And forgive us our debts, as we also have forgiven our debtors."

*Request for guidance:* "And do not lead us into temptation, but deliver us from evil."

*Affirmation of God's position and power:* "For yours is the kingdom and the power and the glory forever. Amen." (Matt. 6:9–13)

If Jesus had meant this prayer to be repeated over and over without thought and meditation, he contradicted himself, for just two verses before he gave this prayer as a model, he said, "And when you pray, do not keep on babbling like pagans, for they think they will be heard because of their many words."

Although it's wise to know this prayer and to memorize it, its purpose was that the prayer be used as a guide for general prayer and supplication.

**Lord's Prayers**—Matthew and Luke record two different versions of basically the same prayer. What is the explanation for the differences? (See Matt. 6:9–13 and Luke 11:2–4.) Matthew contains the prayer we know as The Lord's Prayer, which is quoted in the previous entry above. Luke's version records these words: "Father, hallowed be your name, your kingdom come. Give us each day our daily bread. Forgive us our sins, for we also forgive everyone who sins against us. And lead us not into temptation."

Luke obviously leaves out a number of elements that Matthew includes. The reason for the difference is probably that Jesus repeated the basic outline of this prayer many times during his ministry on earth. Matthew records what he said in the Sermon on the Mount. Luke refers to an occasion when the disciples actually sat down with Jesus and asked him to teach them to pray. Undoubtedly, Jesus used this prayer template on a number of occasions, fitting it to the circumstances rather than offering a prayer to be repeated verbatim.

**Lord's Supper: Next Time in Heaven!**—Jesus celebrated the Lord's Supper only once, the night before he was crucified. After completing the rite, he told his disciples, "I tell you, I will not drink of this fruit of the vine from now on until that day when I drink it anew with you in my Father's kingdom" (Matt. 26:29). The Lord's Supper was to be a remembrance of what Jesus did on the cross, pouring out his blood and giving his body for the sins of the world.

**Lord's Supper: Weird Uses of the Host from the Lord's Supper**—In the Middle Ages, there were many weird beliefs about the host (the consecrated wafer that is called "Christ's body"). Some said it had magical power, could cure swine fever, make one potent, protect criminals from discovery, and so on. John Lake (1624–1689), bishop of Chicester, said the practices of stealing the blessed host from churches was common among "witches, sorcerers, charmers, enchanters, dreamers, soothsayers, necromancers, conjurers, cross-diggers, devil-raisers, miracle-doers, dog-leeches, and bawds."

**Love: To Illustrate, Jesus Chose Someone Truly Hated**—When Jesus had an opportunity to tell a story about what it means to love one's neighbor, he told the parable of the good Samaritan (Luke 10:30–37). In it Jesus used two very respectable persons in the eyes of the Jews, a priest and a Levite. These two, Jesus said, did not help the man who had fallen among robbers and was beaten. Then Jesus chose a third person, a Samaritan, as the character who helped the beaten man and showed neighborly love. Samaritans were hated by "pure Jews" because they were considered "half-breeds," having intermarried with Gentiles when their nation was taken into slavery in 722 B.C. by the Assyrians. They lived in an area between Judea (the lower part of the nation) and Galilee (west of the Sea of Galilee in the north).

Jesus went out of his way to befriend and preach to Samaritans, much to the astonishment of his disciples (see John 4, where Jesus ministered to the village of Sychar on his way through Samaria to Galilee). Supposedly pure Jews despised Samaritans so much that when they took trips from Judea to Galilee, they usually crossed over the Jordan River, which flowed between the Sea of Galilee and the Dead Sea, traveled northward on the east side of the Jordan in Perea, a Gentile nation, and then crossed over the Jordan once again when they were north of Samaria. Jews hated Samaritans even more than they hated Gentiles because they considered Samaritans traitors. Gentiles "couldn't help" what they were, but supposedly Samaritans could, even if their "sin" had been committed over seven hundred years before.

Jesus must have used the example of a Samaritan to confront the leaders of the Jews about their hypocrisy and to show that God loved all people, regardless of race or heritage.

**Love: Jesus Appreciated a Loving Gesture**—When a woman was criticized for using up a whole bottle of expensive perfume on Jesus, he defended her actions, saying she had done a good deed for him (Matt. 26:1–16).

**Love: Whom Did Jesus Love?**—"Christ did not love humanity. He never said that he loved humanity. He loved men" (G.K. Chesterton).

**Lowlifes**—Jesus hung out with them. He was known as a glutton and drunkard, and some of his favorite people were sinners and tax gatherers (Matt. 9:9–13). Mary Magdalene, one of his staunchest supporters, had been a sinner. Matthew, the author of the first Gospel, was a tax collector. So was Zacchaeus. The Pharisees greatly resented Jesus' tendency to "hang out" with the so-called low lifes of the world, but Jesus responded to their criticism, according to Matthew 9:10–13, in this way:

> While Jesus was having dinner at Matthew's house, many tax collectors and "sinners" came and ate with him and his disciples. When the Pharisees saw this, they asked his disciples, "Why does your teacher eat with tax collectors and 'sinners'?"
>
> On hearing this, Jesus said, "It is not the healthy who need a doctor, but the sick. But go and learn what this means: 'I desire mercy, not sacrifice.' For I have not come to call the righteous, but sinners."

From this we can see that Jesus' purpose was to minister to those who desired it, not those who already considered themselves "good" and "righteous." It's not that Jesus considered the latter truly good in the eyes of God, but that *they* thought they were good, which was the source of their pride and their hypocrisy.

**Lunch After Resurrection**—On one of Jesus' resurrection appearances, he didn't give a lecture; he gave his disciples lunch! We find in John 21:1–14 a story in which the disciples had gone fishing with Peter, perhaps to get their minds off the events of Jesus' death and resurrection. They fished all night and caught nothing. Jesus appeared on the shore and told them to throw the net out onto the right side of the boat. They did so, caught 153 fish, and then realized the person on shore must be Jesus. Peter dove off the boat to swim in while the others rowed for shore in the boat. When they got there, the text says, "They saw a fire of burning coals there with fish on it, and some bread." Apparently, Jesus had prepared lunch for them.

It's an interesting gesture, because it shows that the disciples were being faithless and disobedient by going fishing (they were supposed to wait for Jesus in Galilee). However, Jesus didn't hold it against them; and perhaps to show that he didn't, he provided this small gesture as a token of his love and encouragement.

**Lying: Colson's Argument About Lies**—Charles Colson, at one time Richard Nixon's "hatchet man," was imprisoned for his involvement in

Watergate, but he became a Christian in the process. He talks about how hard it is to maintain a lie under pressure, especially legal pressure. When Nixon's lies about Watergate were exposed, all the president's men ran for the hills and legal cover. But when Jesus' disciples were accused of lying about his resurrection appearances and identity, all of them went to execution rather than deny their conviction that Jesus was the Christ. It's an interesting contrast, because if the resurrection was a lie and if the disciples had conjured the whole story, it would make sense for them to recant in the face of death. None of them did.

**Madame Tussaud's Rates Christ**—London's famed waxworks conducted a survey in the 1970s to see which of their wax figures was most loved and most hated. Ahead of Jesus as most loved was Winston Churchill. Most hated was Hitler, well ahead of Mao Tse-tung and Richard Nixon.

**Magazines: Jesus on the Cover of *Time* and *Newsweek*—**Recent issues have addressed the person and work of Jesus, raising the question of who he was and what he came to do. *Time* recently featured Jesus on the cover of the December 6, 1999, issue. The inside article by Reynolds Price states unequivocally: "It would require much exotic calculation, however, to deny that the single most powerful figure—not merely in these two millenniums but in all human history—has been Jesus of Nazareth. Not only is the prevalent system of denoting the years based on an erroneous 6th century calculation of the date of his birth, but a serious argument can be made that no one else's life has proved remotely as powerful and as enduring as that of Jesus. It's an astonishing conclusion in light of the fact that Jesus was a man who lived a short life in a rural backwater of the Roman Empire, who died in agony as a convicted criminal, and who may never have intended so much as a small portion of the effects worked in his name" (*Time*, 6 December 1999, 86).

**Marriage: Celibate, Living with, or Married?**—Was Jesus celibate, contrary to the portrayal in *The Last Temptation of Christ*? Did he ever have conjugal relations?

There is no evidence that Jesus had anything other than platonic relationships with women. To have done otherwise would have invited a tremendous dichotomy and possibly a cosmic problem, for being fully divine and fully human, his mating with a woman would have produced a—what? Would such a child have had his powers of healing and miracles? And what of later generations? How would they figure into the equation? Would they have been hunted down by the leading religious leaders or the Romans? Would they have had the power to never die?

It appears that Jesus avoided any possible conflict by not marrying or mating in his lifetime.

**Maundy Thursday**—Maundy Thursday, celebrated on the Thursday before Easter Sunday, recalls the events of John 13 in which Jesus took off his outer clothes, accepted the role of a common slave, and washed his disciples' feet. This stupendous act, made even more amazing when you consider who Jesus was and who his disciples were, became an example to follow. Especially in the Middle Ages, the event was commemorated by noblemen, kings, and bishops. These lords and royals went out into the streets and washed the feet of the poor in imitation of Christ.

In 1572, Queen Elizabeth I performed this deed to thirty-nine poor people at Greenwich Palace. James II, however, was the last English monarch to follow the practice in person, though as late as the eighteenth century the Archbishop of York was still washing the feet of the poor on Maundy Thursday.

Today, a practice is still maintained by the monarchy. Silver coins, minted especially for Maundy Thursday, are put into white leather purses with red thongs and are distributed to the poor. The Queen walks the length of the choir in Westminster Abbey and presents the gifts in the nave. At the same time, she carries a bouquet of flowers for protection against the plague, a tradition passed down from the Dark Ages.

**Messiah: Was Jesus the Anointed One?**—In Jewish tradition and in the Old Testament, the Spirit of God repeatedly predicted the coming of the Messiah, or the "anointed one," the person whom God would use to rescue Israel from all its troubles and make it the primary government of the world.

For centuries, Jews and Christians alike have argued whether Jesus could be the Messiah. Jews expected a political, kingly, ruling Savior. Jesus was meek and mild, a sacrificial Savior and one who died an ignominious death on a Roman cross, a horror to most Jews.

The problem is solved, at least for Christians, with an understanding of God's real predictions. In effect, the Spirit of God prophesied the coming of one Messiah but in two different capacities: one as a suffering Savior, and a second as a reigning King. For the former, we find the following kinds of prophecies attached to his coming:

He would destroy the power of Satan, who had caused the casting out of Adam and Eve from the perfect environment, the Garden of Eden. *Genesis 3:15:* "And I will put enmity between you and the woman, and between your offspring and hers; he will crush your head, and you will strike his heel."

He would be a descendant of Abraham and a blessing to the whole world. *Genesis 12:2–3:* "I will make you into a great nation and I will bless you; I will make your name great, and you will be a blessing. I will bless those who bless you, and whoever curses you I will curse; and all peoples on earth will be blessed through you."

He would be a prophet like Moses, doing miracles and changing forever the way Israel lived and served God. *Deuteronomy 18:15:* "The LORD your God will raise up for you a prophet like me from among your own brothers. You must listen to him."

He would be "cut off" approximately 483 prophetic years (a 360-day year) after a decree by Persian King Artaxerxes to rebuild the destroyed Jerusalem (this occurred around 445 B.C.). This puts the "cutting off" of the Messiah about A.D. 30, where most scholars date the death of Christ. *Daniel 9:25–26:* "Know and understand this: From the issuing of the decree to restore and rebuild Jerusalem until the Anointed One, the ruler, comes, there will be seven 'sevens,' and sixty-two 'sevens.' It will be rebuilt with streets and a trench, but in times of trouble. After the sixty-two 'sevens,' the Anointed One will be cut off and will have nothing."

He would be born of a virgin and called Immanuel, "God with us." *Isaiah 7:14:* "Therefore the Lord himself will give you a sign: 'The virgin will be with child and will give birth to a son, and will call him Immanuel.'"

He would be born in Bethlehem of Judea, a small city that was also the birthplace of King David. *Micah 5:2:* "But you, Bethlehem Ephrathah, though you are small among the clans of Judah, out of you will come for me one who will be ruler over Israel, whose origins are from of old, from ancient times."

He would come into Jerusalem as a coming king, riding on a donkey's colt. *Zechariah 9:9:* "Rejoice greatly, O Daughter of Zion! Shout, daughter of Jerusalem! See, your king comes to you, righteous and having salvation, gentle and riding on a donkey, on a colt, the foal of a donkey."

He would be betrayed by a close friend. *Psalm 41:9:* "Even my close friend, whom I trusted, he who shared my bread, has lifted up his heel against me."

He would be betrayed for thirty pieces of silver. *Zechariah 11:12–13:* "I told them, 'If you think it best, give me my pay; but if not, keep it.' So they paid me thirty pieces of silver. And the LORD said to me, 'Throw it to the potter'—the handsome price at which they priced me! So I took the thirty pieces of silver and threw them into the house of the LORD to the potter."

He would be rejected by his people. *Isaiah 53:3:* "He was despised and rejected by men, a man of sorrows, and familiar with suffering. Like one from whom men hide their faces he was despised, and we esteemed him not."

He would not defend himself to his accusers. *Isaiah 53:7:* "He was oppressed and afflicted, yet he did not open his mouth; he was led like a lamb to the slaughter, and as a sheep before her shearers is silent, so he did not open his mouth."

He would pay for the sins of the world through a sacrificial death. *Isaiah 53:5:* "But he was pierced for our transgressions, he was crushed for our iniquities; the punishment that brought us peace was upon him, and by his wounds we are healed."

His means of death would be crucifixion. *Psalm 22:14–17:* "I am poured out like water, and all my bones are out of joint. My heart has turned to wax; it has melted away within me. My strength is dried up like a potsherd, and my tongue sticks to the roof of my mouth; you lay me in the dust of death. Dogs have surrounded me; a band of evil men has encircled me, they have pierced my hands and my feet. I can count all my bones; people stare and gloat over me."

His garments would be divided up among his executioners, and they would cast lots for them. *Psalm 22:18:* "They divide my garments among them and cast lots for my clothing."

He would die with wicked people, but be buried in a rich man's tomb. *Isaiah 53:9:* "He was assigned a grave with the wicked, and with the rich in his death, though he had done no violence, nor was any deceit in his mouth."

He would rise from the dead. *Isaiah 53:11:* "After the suffering of his soul, he will see the light of life and be satisfied; by his knowledge my righteous servant will justify many, and he will bear their iniquities."

He would not see permanent decay. *Psalm 16:9–10:* "Therefore my heart is glad and my tongue rejoices; my body also will rest secure, because you will not abandon me to the grave, nor will you let your Holy One see decay."

He would be great throughout the world. *Isaiah 53:12:* "Therefore I will give him a portion among the great, and he will divide the spoils with the strong, because he poured out his life unto death, and was numbered with the transgressors. For he bore the sin of many, and made intercession for the transgressors."

He would reign in glory forever. *Isaiah 9:6–7:* "For to us a child is born, to us a son is given, and the government will be on his shoulders. And he will be called Wonderful Counselor, Mighty God, Everlasting Father, Prince of Peace. Of the increase of his government and peace there will be no end. He will reign on David's throne and over his kingdom, establishing and upholding it with justice and righteousness from that time on and forever. The zeal of the LORD Almighty will accomplish this."

These prophecies are not exhaustive. There are many others relating to Jesus' first coming. Although acceptance of Christ as the Messiah remains a difficult issue, it is hard to argue with the evidence of these specific prophecies that many believe could only have been fulfilled by Christ.

**Michelangelo's Greatest Sculpture**—The *Pieta*, considered Michelangelo's greatest work of sculpture, depicts the Virgin Mary holding the body of the dead Jesus after being taken from the cross.

**Millennium**—Millennium, which means "a thousand," is taken from Revelation 20:1–4, which states that Christ will bind Satan and reign for a thousand years. Many believed that Jesus would come again at the end of the first millennium (the first thousand years after Christ's death), or around A.D. 1032, and many awaited his return at that time. More recently, the Y2K celebration invited belief in the possibility of Jesus' returning around that time. Apparently, so far he hasn't.

The biblical teaching of the millennium is based on Revelation 20:4–8 where we find these words:

> I saw thrones on which were seated those who had been given authority to judge. And I saw the souls of those who had been beheaded because of their testimony for Jesus and because of the word of God. They had not worshiped the beast or his image and had not received his mark on their foreheads or their hands. They came to life and reigned with Christ a thousand years. (The rest of the dead did not come to life until the thousand years were ended.) This is the first resurrection. Blessed

and holy are those who have part in the first resurrection. The second death has no power over them, but they will be priests of God and of Christ and will reign with him for a thousand years.

When the thousand years are over, Satan will be released from his prison and will go out to deceive the nations in the four corners of the earth—Gog and Magog—to gather them for battle. In number they are like the sand on the seashore.

Apparently, the disciples expected Jesus to set up Israel's kingdom on earth sometime in their future, for they asked him in Acts 1:6–8:

So when they met together, they asked him, "Lord, are you at this time going to restore the kingdom to Israel?"

He said to them: "It is not for you to know the times or dates the Father has set by his own authority. But you will receive power when the Holy Spirit comes on you; and you will be my witnesses in Jerusalem, and in all Judea and Samaria, and to the ends of the earth."

It is not clear how much Jesus taught his disciples about the millennium or of his reign on earth, but from many other passages they expected to reign with him and to cause Israel to rise to a point of supremacy over all other nations. Jesus neither accepts nor repudiates their idea, but merely tells them to get on with the primary work of taking the gospel to the world.

Nonetheless, this idea of a reign of the Messiah is found all through the Old Testament in the promises of God to Israel that a descendant of David the king would sit on his throne and reign forever and ever. It would be a time of peace, justice, prosperity, and glory, according to such prophetic passages as these:

*Isaiah 2:2–4:* "In the last days the mountain of the LORD's temple will be established as chief among the mountains; it will be raised above the hills, and all nations will stream to it. Many peoples will come and say, 'Come, let us go up to the mountain of the LORD, to the house of the God of Jacob. He will teach us his ways, so that we may walk in his paths.' The law will go out from Zion, the word of the LORD from Jerusalem. He will judge between the nations and will settle disputes for many peoples. They will beat their swords into ploughshares and their spears into pruning hooks. Nation will not take up sword against nation, nor will they train for war anymore."

*Isaiah 11:2–9:* "The Spirit of the LORD will rest on him—the Spirit of wisdom and of understanding, the Spirit of counsel and of power, the Spirit of knowledge and of the fear of the LORD—and he will delight in the fear of the LORD. He will not judge by what he sees with his eyes, or decide by what he hears with his ears; but with righteousness he will judge the needy, with justice he will give decisions for the poor of the earth. He will strike the earth with the rod of his mouth; with the breath of his lips he will slay the wicked. Righteousness will be his belt and faithfulness the sash around his waist. The wolf will live with the lamb, the leopard will lie down with the goat, the calf and the lion and the yearling together; and a little child will lead them. The cow will feed with the bear, their young will lie down together, and the lion will eat straw like the ox. The infant will play near the hole of the cobra, and the young child put his hand into the viper's nest. They will neither harm nor destroy on all my holy mountain, for the earth will be full of the knowledge of the LORD as the waters cover the sea."

*Isaiah 35:3–10:* "Strengthen the feeble hands, steady the knees that give way; say to those with fearful hearts, 'Be strong, do not fear; your God will come, he will come with vengeance; with divine retribution he will come to save you.' Then will the eyes of the blind be opened and the ears of the deaf unstopped. Then will the lame leap like a deer, and the tongue of the dumb shout for joy. Water will gush forth in the wilderness and streams in the desert. The burning sand will become a pool, the thirsty ground bubbling springs. In the haunts where jackals once lay, grass and reeds and papyrus will grow. And a highway will be there; it will be called the Way of Holiness. The unclean will not journey on it; it will be for those who walk in that Way; wicked fools will not go about on it. No lion will be there, nor will any ferocious beast get up on it; they will not be found there. But only the redeemed will walk there, and the ransomed of the LORD will return. They will enter Zion with singing; everlasting joy will crown their heads. Gladness and joy will overtake them, and sorrow and sighing will flee away."

There are several different views of the millennium that were popular at different times in church history:

*Amillennialism*—Popularized by St. Augustine, this view says that Christ will return at the end of the Church Age, and there is no earthly thousand-year reign. Rather, the present reign of Christ in heaven is the millennium John spoke of in Revelation 20. This is the most widely accepted view of Last Things in the Roman Catholic Church and many Protestant denominations.

*Postmillennialism*—This view states that Christ will come after the millennium, which will be a thousand-year period of prosperity and peace brought in through the efforts of the church. This view was popular in the late nineteenth century before World War I, when a Golden Age of economic prosperity at that time was thought to be the sign that the millennium was beginning. The many wars of the twentieth century have derailed much talk of postmillennialism.

*Premillennialism*—This view states that Christ will return before the millennium and then will reign for a thousand years with the nation of Israel as a focal point of his reign. After the thousand years, which will be a time of great prosperity and justice, God will create the "new heavens and the new earth," and eternity will begin. This view is held by many "evangelical" believers and has been made popular by such authors as Hal Lindsey in his book *The Late Great Planet Earth* and by Tim LaHaye and Jerry Jenkins with their fictional Left Behind series of novels.

Much debate reigns among believers about this doctrine. The primary truth that must emerge is that at the end of time, Christ will reign forever and will certainly bring in an era of peace, abundance, justice, and goodness like the world has never seen.

**Miracle in Two Stages**—On one occasion, when Jesus healed a blind man, the blind man was not completely healed initially. The following passage in Mark 8:22–25 indicates that the blind man's sight was only partially returned. Jesus had to do it again!

> They came to Bethsaida, and some people brought a blind man and begged Jesus to touch him. He took the blind man by the hand and led him outside the village. When he had spit on the man's eyes and put his hands on him, Jesus asked, "Do you see anything?"
> He looked up and said, "I see people; they look like trees walking around."
> Once more Jesus put his hands on the man's eyes. Then his eyes were opened, his sight was restored, and he saw everything clearly.

Was Jesus' healing power defective here, or was something else going on? Obviously, the scripture doesn't say. Speculating, one could conclude that it was included in the Gospels to demonstrate that Jesus' miracles were performed on a case-by-case basis and that he was willing to help until the job was done. It also shows that Jesus was personally involved with the people he healed. He was not just a miracle worker who kept a hands-off perspective, or who went from miracle to miracle without thinking about the results and the effects on his patients.

**Miracle That Hurt**—The one unfortunate miracle Jesus performed was his cursing the fig tree (Matt. 21:18–19).

**Miracles: Jesus Stymied**—There were occasions when Jesus could not perform miracles or was greatly limited. In Mark 6:1–6 we find:

> Jesus left there and went to his home town, accompanied by his disciples. When the Sabbath came, he began to teach in the synagogue, and many who heard him were amazed.
>
> "Where did this man get these things?" they asked. "What's this wisdom that has been given him, that he even does miracles! Isn't this the carpenter? Isn't this Mary's son and the brother of James, Joses, Judas and Simon? Aren't his sisters here with us?" And they took offence at him.
>
> Jesus said to them, "Only in his home town, among his relatives and in his own house is a prophet without honor." He could not do any miracles there, except lay his hands on a few sick people and heal them. And he was amazed at their lack of faith.
>
> Then Jesus went around teaching from village to village.

Apparently, when such a lack of faith and such monumental criticism was leveled at Jesus, he either refused or felt compelled not to perform miracles. We know he could perform miracles even when faith wasn't present; we know this from the many healings he performed on people who did not even ask for them. But when a group of people exhibit disdain, he apparently refused to force on them something they didn't need or want.

**Miracles: Jesus Unleashed**—Many people wonder what might have happened had Jesus indiscriminately used his miraculous powers. The "apocryphal" gospels, those written in the second and third centuries that are not regarded as authentic, show us. In them, Jesus made clay sparrows, threw them into the air, and turned them into birds. Dried fish were thrown into water and turned into real fish. When his playmates irritated him, Jesus turned them into goats. He healed blind and deaf people just to see the results.

The problem with such so-called miracles is that they run counter to the whole purpose of the miracles. Jesus never did things for show, but to help, heal, and authenticate his ministry.

**Miracles and Jesus' Identity**—Why did Jesus do miracles? It's plain he did them primarily to minister to hurting people. Over and over we see his personal concern for those who were broken, even when it meant criticism and attacks from his enemies.

A second reason was to authenticate himself as God's Son. In one situation, people brought him a paralytic on a pallet. In Matthew 9:2–7, we read:

> Some men brought to him a paralytic, lying on a mat. When Jesus saw their faith, he said to the paralytic, "Take heart, son; your sins are forgiven."
>
> At this, some of the teachers of the law said to themselves, "This fellow is blaspheming!"
>
> Knowing their thoughts, Jesus said, "Why do you entertain evil thoughts in your hearts? Which is easier: to say, 'Your sins are forgiven,' or to say, 'Get up and walk'? But so that you may know that the Son of Man has authority on earth to forgive sins. . . ." Then he said to the paralytic, "Get up, take your mat and go home." And the man got up and went home.

From this passage, we can see that Jesus specifically authenticated his ministry on the basis of the miracles. His power proved he was the Son of God, the Messiah.

On another occasion, talking with his disciples, Jesus told them that seeing him was the equivalent of seeing the Father. Philip, one of the Twelve, wanted Jesus to show them the Father then and there. But Jesus answered, "Believe me when I say that I am in the Father and the Father is in me; or at least believe on the evidence of the miracles themselves"(John 14:11). The miracles in this case were meant to authenticate everything else he said. In another passage Jesus says, "I did tell you, but you do not believe. The miracles I do in my Father's name speak for me"(John 10:25).

On still another occasion, when the Pharisees accused Jesus of performing miracles by the power of Satan, Jesus said, "How can Satan drive out Satan? If a kingdom is divided against itself, that kingdom cannot stand. If a house is divided against itself, that house cannot stand. And if Satan opposes himself and is divided, he cannot stand; his end has come"(Mark 3:23–26).

One final reason for his miracles was to move people to repentance. Jesus said in Luke 10:13: "Woe to you, Korazin! Woe to you, Bethsaida! For if the miracles that were performed in you had been performed in Tyre and Sidon, they would have repented long ago, sitting in sackcloth and ashes."

**Miracles on Demand**—Jesus refused to perform miracles on demand. Every one of the miracles he performed had a specific purpose—to help, to heal, to fix a bad situation. He never did miracles as a performance. In fact, when he had opportunities to stun his onlookers with some work of power, he refused. In Matthew 12:38–39, we read:

> Then some of the Pharisees and teachers of the law said to
>    him, "Teacher, we want to see a miraculous sign from
>    you."
> He answered, "A wicked and adulterous generation asks
>    for a miraculous sign! But none will be given it except
>    the sign of the prophet Jonah."

Herod Antipas also longed to see a work of power performed in his presence. Jesus appeared before the governor at one of his trials on the night before his crucifixion. Luke 23:8–11 records this scene:

> When Herod saw Jesus, he was greatly pleased, because
>    for a long time he had been wanting to see him. From
>    what he had heard about him, he hoped to see him per-
>    form some miracle. He plied him with many questions,
>    but Jesus gave him no answer. The chief priests and the
>    teachers of the law were standing there, vehemently
>    accusing him. Then Herod and his soldiers ridiculed
>    and mocked him. Dressing him in an elegant robe, they
>    sent him back to Pilate.

**Miraculous Power to His Disciples**—Jesus gave his disciples the power to cast out demons, to heal, and to raise the dead, according to Matthew 10:5–8:

> These twelve Jesus sent out with the following instruc-
>    tions: "Do not go among the Gentiles or enter any
>    town of the Samaritans. Go rather to the lost sheep of
>    Israel. As you go, preach this message: 'The kingdom
>    of heaven is near.' Heal the sick, raise the dead, cleanse
>    those who have leprosy, drive out demons. Freely you
>    have received, freely give."

However, there is not much recorded about the disciples' using these powers. The Book of Acts, however, does contain numerous miracles performed by the disciples and apostles after Jesus' ascension.

**Missions**—In 1873, a Belgian Roman Catholic priest named Joseph Damien De Veuster was sent to minister to lepers on the Hawaiian Island of Molokai. When he arrived, he immediately began to meet each one of the lepers in the colony in hopes of building a friendship. But wherever he turned, people shunned him. It seemed as though every door was closed. He poured his life into his work, erecting a chapel, beginning worship services, and pouring out his heart to the lepers. But it was to no avail! No one responded to his ministry.

After twelve years, Father Damien made the decision to leave. Dejectedly, he made his way to the docks to board a ship to take him back to Belgium. As he stood on the dock, he wrung his hands nervously as he recounted his futile ministry among the lepers. As he looked down at his hands, he noticed some mysterious white spots and felt some numbness. Almost immediately he knew what was happening to his body. He had contracted leprosy! It was then that he knew what he had to do. He returned to the leper colony and to his work. Quickly the word about his disease spread through the colony. Within a matter of hours everyone knew. Hundreds of them gathered outside his hut; they understood his pain, fear, and uncertainty about the future. But the biggest surprise occurred on the following Sunday. As Father Damien arrived at the chapel, he found hundreds of worshipers there. By the time the service began, there were many more, with standing room only and many gathered outside the chapel. His ministry became enormously successful. The reason? He was one of them. He understood and empathized with them.

**Missions: Long Distance Preaching**—Francis Asbury (1745–1816), Methodist missionary to America, traveled nearly 300,000 miles by horseback to plant Methodism in the United States. Although often sick, he preached to thousands of the risen Christ and left a membership in the Methodist church of over 200,000. He preached anywhere and everywhere—in camp meetings, church pulpits, riverboats, bordellos, and saloons.

**Monasteries: Skull Piles**—At St. Catherine's Greek Orthodox Monastery at the foot of Mt. Sinai in Arabia (where Moses received the Ten Commandments) is a huge pile of skulls from the monks who have prayed, lived, and worshiped there. Even today, many monks and others upon their deaths have their heads sent to St. Catherine's to be added to the pile. And you thought cremation was the way to go!

**Moral Code: Has Christ's Way Been Tried?**—Not according to G.K. Chesterton (1874–1936), English man of letters and mystery writer (the Father Brown series). He put it this way: "The Christian ideal has not been tried and found wanting. It has been found difficult, and left untried."

**Mormons**—They are known as the Church of Jesus Christ of Latter Day Saints because they believe they are a revival of true faith in Christ that would occur in the "latter days."

**Most Quoted Line of Jesus: The Golden Rule**—Found in Matthew 7:12, it reads in the King James Version: "Therefore all things whatsoever ye would that men should do to you, do ye even so to them: for this is the law and the prophets."

The phrase "Do unto others as you would have them do unto you" is a simplified derivative of that verse whose origin is unknown.

Confucius (551–479 B.C.) said something similar, "What you do not want others to do to you, do not do to others."

Jesus' "golden rule," though, is proactive, advising us to take good action regardless of what the other person has done or not done. That idea had never been heard before.

**Mother Given to John's Care**—On the cross, Jesus entrusted the care of his mother to his disciple John. This was the scene from John 19:25–27:

> Near the cross of Jesus stood his mother, his mother's sis-
> ter, Mary the wife of Clopas, and Mary of Magdala.
> When Jesus saw his mother there, and the disciple
> whom he loved standing nearby, he said to his mother,
> "Dear woman, here is your son," and to the disciple,
> "Here is your mother." From that time on, this disciple
> took her into his home.

**Mother Teresa's Doctrine for Living**—Mother Teresa won the Nobel Peace Prize in 1979. She was born in Yugoslavia, and at age 17 went to India to work with lepers and the homeless, in Calcutta. In 1948, she left the convent and founded her own order, the Missionaries of Charity, who minister throughout the world to orphans, widows, lepers, the homeless, and the sick. Her code of conduct may be summed up in her words, taking her lead from Matthew 25:

> Feeding the hungry Christ.
> > Clothing the naked Christ.
> > Visiting the sick Christ.
> > Giving shelter to the homeless Christ.
> > Teaching the ignorant Christ.
> > We all long for heaven where God is, but we have it in our power to be in heaven with Him right now—to be happy with Him at this very moment. But being happy with Him now means loving like He loves, helping like He helps, giving as He gives, serving as He serves, rescuing as He rescues, being with Him twenty-four hours a day—touching Him in His distressing disguise.

**Movies: First Film About Jesus' Life**—In 1912, the silent picture *From the Manger to the Cross* appeared in which Robert Henderson played the Savior. Cecil B. DeMille's epic *King of Kings* hit the theaters in 1927 with H.B. Warner playing Jesus. Amazingly, the crucifixion scene was in color. *The Greatest Story Ever Told*, produced by George Stevens, featured Max von Sydow as Jesus and John Wayne as the Roman centurion who, seeing the way Jesus died, proclaimed, "Aw! He truly was the Son of God." Two movies tried to shatter Hollywood's fascination with the Jesus story—Monty Python's *Life of Brian* and Martin Scorsese's *The Last Temptation of Christ*. Both films were boycotted by fundamentalists (especially *Last Temptation*), which ended up being very good publicity for the latter. Critics agree, however, that one of the greatest and most moving renditions was Pier Palo Pasolini's Italian version (with English subtitles), *The Gospel According to St. Matthew* (1964).

**Murder: Jesus Was Almost Murdered, Several Times**—King Herod tried hard, to the point of having every male under two years old killed in Bethlehem. In Matthew 2:16–18, we find the narrative:

> When Herod realized that he had been outwitted by the
> > Magi, he was furious, and he gave orders to kill all the
> > boys in Bethlehem and its vicinity who were two years
> > old and under, in accordance with the time he had
> > learned from the Magi. Then what was said through
> > the prophet Jeremiah was fulfilled: "A voice is heard in
> > Ramah, weeping and great mourning, Rachel weeping

> for her children and refusing to be comforted, because
> they are no more."

Also, when he visited his hometown of Nazareth, Jesus read from a scroll. This is the situation that resulted in Luke 4:16–30:

> He went to Nazareth, where he had been brought up, and
> on the Sabbath day he went into the synagogue, as was
> his custom. And he stood up to read. The scroll of the
> prophet Isaiah was handed to him. Unrolling it, he
> found the place where it is written: "The Spirit of the
> Lord is on me, because he has anointed me to preach
> good news to the poor. He has sent me to proclaim
> freedom for the prisoners and recovery of sight for the
> blind, to release the oppressed, to proclaim the year of
> the Lord's favor."
> Then he rolled up the scroll, gave it back to the attendant
> and sat down. The eyes of everyone in the synagogue
> were fastened on him, and he said to them, "Today this
> scripture is fulfilled in your hearing."
> All spoke well of him and were amazed at the gracious
> words that came from his lips. "Isn't this Joseph's son?"
> they asked.
> Jesus said to them, "Surely you will quote this proverb to
> me: 'Physician, heal yourself! Do here in your home
> town what we have heard that you did in Capernaum.'
> "I tell you the truth," he continued, "no prophet is
> accepted in his home town. I assure you that there were
> many widows in Israel in Elijah's time, when the sky
> was shut for three and a half years and there was a
> severe famine throughout the land. Yet Elijah was not
> sent to any of them, but to a widow in Zarephath in the
> region of Sidon. And there were many in Israel with
> leprosy in the time of Elisha the prophet, yet not one
> of them was cleansed—only Naaman the Syrian."
> All the people in the synagogue were furious when they
> heard this. They got up, drove him out of the town,
> and took him to the brow of the hill on which the town
> was built, in order to throw him down the cliff. But he
> walked right through the crowd and went on his way.

Obviously, the people were incensed that he was saying they were little different from the people living in the days of ancient Israel when God healed only Gentiles.

**Music: A Beer Drinking Song**—One of Martin Luther's primary concerns in leading the Protestant tradition away from Roman Catholic influences was to establish some popular music to be sung in church worship. His most famous hymn, "A Mighty Fortress Is Our God," a great anthem of praise to Christ and God, was written to the tune of a beer-drinking song Luther sang when he sat at table with his cronies celebrating the goodness of God with a great stein of German beer. Maybe today Luther would have us singing in church to the tunes of the Beatles and BeeGees.

**Music: Bob Dylan and Jesus**—For a while in the 1970s and 1980s, Bob Dylan professed faith in Christ. Such albums as *Slow Train Coming* and *Shot of Love* lyricized what he believed Christ would say to our decadent culture. In recent days, Dylan has returned to his Jewish roots but still professes belief in Christ. Of course, who knows what Dylan really thinks; one need only read his pantheon of songs to become completely confused!

**Music: Compelled to Stand, Compelled to Give**—When King George II heard the "Hallelujah Chorus" from Handel's *Messiah* performed for the first time in 1742, he was so moved by the music in praise of Christ that he involuntarily stood in reverence and awe. The audience immediately rose to their feet in obedience to the principle that no one sits when the king is standing. The tradition has been carried on to this day.

A not so well-known tradition was the fact that George Fredrich Handel, because of the great success of *Messiah* and his own faith in Christ, gave all the proceeds as a donation to buy bread to feed the poor. As a result, whenever *Messiah* was performed, many of the poor of the cities of England would gather to hear, knowing that afterward they would receive bread.

**Music: Greater than Jesus**—John Lennon (1940–1980), famed Beatle, composer, and musician, said in an interview, "Christianity will go. It will vanish and shrink. I needn't argue about that; I'm right and I will be proved right. We're more popular than Jesus now; I don't know which will go first—rock 'n' roll or Christianity."

**Music: He Loved Her More than She Would Ever Know**—Paul Simon's song "Mrs. Robinson," featured in the movie *The Graduate*, posited, "Here's to you, Mrs. Robinson, Jesus loves you more than you will know."

**Music: I Thought He Wanted Me for a Disciple**—No, according to Nellie Talbot, hymnwriter, "Jesus wants me for a sunbeam," the title of her only known hymn.

**Music: Jesus Is Just Alright with Them**—The Doobie Brothers have a song in which they sing, "I don't care what they may say, I don't care what they may do, Jesus is just all right with me, Jesus is just all right." The last line is repeated four times.

Apparently, Jesus is all right by the Doobie Brothers' standards!

**Music: Rock Idols Who Idolize Jesus**—The popular Irish rock band, U2, has made no bones about its faith in Christ. Three of the members—Bono, The Edge, and Larry Mullen Jr.—are Christians. Many of their songs contain allusions to scripture. Two of their most famous songs mention their commitment to Christ. "Sunday Bloody Sunday," in which the band shows its grief at a terrorist bombing in Ireland, concludes with the words "The battle's yet begun, to claim the victory Jesus won." And in their 1987 Grammy-winning song "I Still Haven't Found What I'm Looking For," Bono says, "I believe in the Kingdom Come. . . . You broke the bonds, You loosed the chains, You carried the cross, And my shame. . . . You know I believe it."

**Music: Unrecognized in His Day**—Johann Sebastian Bach (1685–1750), considered the greatest composer for the organ ever, was not well known in his day. Musical tastes did not revere his churchly chorales, toccatas, cantatas, preludes, and fugues. But a small band of admirers, pupils (he was cantor at the Thomasschule in Leipzig, Germany), and connoisseurs collected and preserved his works until a later day when he became recognized as one of the greatest of all composers. He was a Lutheran, and his faith in Christ propelled him to produce such grand works as *Mass in B Minor* and *St. Matthew Passion*. Mozart, Beethoven, and Haydn all studied his music and owe him a debt for his spiritual and grandly ecclesiastic works.

**Mysteries: A Stunning Contradiction**—Jesus often turned scripture on its head and knocked over his listeners with a mystery. In Matthew 22:41–46, we find these words:

> While the Pharisees were gathered together, Jesus asked them, "What do you think about the Christ? Whose son is he?"

"The son of David," they replied.

He said to them, "How is it then that David, speaking by the Spirit, calls him 'Lord'? For he says, 'The Lord said to my Lord: "Sit at my right hand until I put your enemies under your feet."' If then David calls him 'Lord,' how can he be his son?" No one could say a word in reply, and from that day on no one dared to ask him any more questions.

Nothing irritated the Pharisees more than being asked a biblical question and not having an immediate answer. They could never be sure what Jesus would say next, so they decided to avoid questioning him completely. In the passage above, obviously Jesus was referring to the fact that not only was he David's son genealogically, but he was also David's Lord, being the Lord of all, King of Kings and Lord of Lords.

Another such instance is found in Matthew 21:23–27, where the Pharisees question Jesus about where he received his authority. The scene unfolds as follows:

Jesus entered the temple courts, and, while he was teaching, the chief priests and the elders of the people came to him. "By what authority are you doing these things?" they asked. "And who gave you this authority?"

Jesus replied, "I will also ask you one question. If you answer me, I will tell you by what authority I am doing these things. John's baptism—where did it come from? Was it from heaven, or from men?"

They discussed it among themselves and said, "If we say, 'From heaven,' he will ask, 'Then why didn't you believe him?' But if we say, 'From men'—we are afraid of the people, for they all hold that John was a prophet."

So they answered Jesus, "We don't know."

Then he said, "Neither will I tell you by what authority I am doing these things."

**Mystics: Lord, What a Talker!**—St. Mary-Magdalen dei Pazzi (1566–1607), a Carmelite nun and Florentine mystic, often spoke of her beloved Lord while in ecstacy. She required six secretaries who recorded her words sometimes for days straight.

**Naked Worshipers**—Adamites were a sect at various times in history whose members worshiped naked. They were promiscuous and believed that Christ was best and most purely worshiped in the nude.

**Names**—There are some 265 names for Christ in the Bible by which he can be called, according to Billy Graham. Among them: Jesus, Lord, Savior, Friend, Good Shepherd, Life, Way, Truth, Resurrection, Light, Bread of Life, King of Kings, Lord of Lords, Master, Son of God, Son of Man, Wonderful Counselor, Mighty God, Everlasting Father, and Prince of Peace.

**Names: Famous People with Christ in Their Last Name**—Dame Agatha Christie; Christina, queen of Sweden (1626–1689); Javachef Christo (sculptor); Petrus Christus (Flemish painter); Edwin P. Christy (minstrel show performer); Fletcher Christian (from the mutiny on H.M.S. Bounty).

**Names: Naming Our Children**—Here are some of the many first names derived from Christ that we name our children: Christopher, Christine, Christian, Christoph, Christina, Kriss, Kris, and Kristine.

**Newspapers: What If Jesus Edited the *Daily News*?**—Many today have argued that the news media—TV, radio, and newspapers—have capitulated to our sensation-seeking culture. But what might happen if Jesus did edit our programming and our newspapers?

Well, it happened, at least figuratively, in 1900. Dr. Charles M. Sheldon, a minister who wrote the best-selling book of all time (after the Bible and Shakespeare) *In His Steps*, challenged the *Topeka Capital* editor, Frederick O. Popenoe, to let him edit the paper for one week and to publish only edifying and helpful news, not sensational "garbage."

When Sheldon took over, he banned smoking, drinking, and profanity from the pressroom. Certain ads—for tobacco, patent medicines, and other bilk-the-public items—were also refused. Stories of good and decency were played up, and sensational stories, still reported, were greatly cut back. By the end of five days, the paper had soared in circulation from 11,223 to 362,684.

Many later disputed that the experiment had been a success, saying it was the result of novelty and clever publicity. Sheldon returned to his pulpit, but the editing bug never left him. In 1920 he went on to edit the magazine *Christian Herald* for four years.

**Nicknames**—In the Bible, God often changed people's names to indicate some great change in their character or destiny. Abram ("father") was changed to Abraham ("father of nations"). Jacob, which means "cheat" or "supplanter," was changed to Israel, which means "one who contends or wrestles with God."

Jesus also changed several of his disciples' names. In John 1:41–42, we find this exchange:

> The first thing Andrew did was to find his brother Simon and tell him, "We have found the Messiah" (that is, the Christ).
> Then he brought Simon to Jesus, who looked at him and said, "You are Simon son of John. You will be called Cephas" (which, when translated, is Peter).

"Peter" is Greek for "rock" or "stone." The choice of this name was perhaps to indicate that Peter would become a true founding stone of Jesus' mission in the world.

Jesus also gave James and John the nickname "Sons of Thunder" on the basis of this experience in Mark 9:38–40:

> "Teacher," said John, "we saw a man driving out demons in your name and we told him to stop, because he was not one of us."
> "Do not stop him," Jesus said. "No one who does a miracle in my name can in the next moment say anything bad about me, for whoever is not against us is for us."

Another passage is even more graphic, Luke 9:51–56:

> As the time approached for him to be taken up to heaven, Jesus resolutely set out for Jerusalem, and he sent messengers on ahead. They went into a Samaritan village to get things ready for him, but the people there did not welcome him, because he was heading for Jerusalem. When the disciples James and John saw this, they asked, "Lord, do you want us to call fire down from heaven to destroy them?" But Jesus turned and rebuked them, and they went to another village.

**Novels: Christmas Story Every Year**—Charles Dickens wrote *A Christmas Carol* while in need of money and on a hard deadline. He wanted to show the impact of Christian love upon a man who had none. Of course, he had no idea it would succeed as well as it did. When it was first published, sales were magnificent, so much so that Dickens undertook to write a Christmas story for every Christmas. But only this one has "gone down in history."

**Novels: The Conversion of the Jews**—Philip Roth, noted Jewish author, in his first book of short stories, *Goodbye, Columbus*, tells a hilarious story he calls the conversion of the Jews. In it, Ozzie and his friend Itzie discuss the events at their local Hebrew school, where the rabbi has told the children that Jesus could not have been born of a virgin because for a woman to have a baby she had to have intercourse with a man. The class is astonished that the rabbi has actually used the word "intercourse," and Roth masterfully raises the humor a notch. But then he has Ozzie ask the rabbi a question: "If God could create heaven and earth in six days . . . why couldn't he let a woman have a baby without having intercourse?" Of course, the rabbi hems and haws and goes into various explanations, none of which satisfy Ozzie.

In the end, when Ozzie is forced to apologize for accusing the rabbi of not knowing real answers to his questions, Ozzie climbs up to the top of the synagogue, crawls out to the edge of the roof, and threatens to jump. As a crowd gathers and firemen arrive, they all try to get him to come down. Ozzie refuses until, when all the Jews in the neighborhood are gathered, he makes them recite the words "God can make a child without intercourse!" Once he gets them all to say that, then he makes them all say they believe in Jesus Christ. Only then does he leap off the building into the safety of the net the fireman have laid out for him.

**Obedience: Jesus Obeyed His Father**—In Hebrews 5:8, the writer says that Jesus "learned obedience from what he suffered." Some consider Jesus the ultimate "free" man, but repeatedly in the Bible Jesus is said to be "in submission" to the Father. One such passage is from

Jesus himself, speaking of his "modus operandi." He said in John 14:28–31:

> "You heard me say, 'I am going away and I am coming back to you.' If you loved me, you would be glad that I am going to the Father, for the Father is greater than I. I have told you now before it happens, so that when it does happen you will believe. I will not speak with you much longer, for the prince of this world is coming. He has no hold on me, but the world must learn that I love the Father and that I do exactly what my Father has commanded me."

**Oldest Prediction of Jesus' First Coming**—The oldest prediction of Jesus' first coming is found in Genesis 3:14–15, where God speaks to the serpent after he tempted Adam and Eve and had them eat of the forbidden fruit, which led to them being ejected from the Garden of Eden:

> So the LORD God said to the serpent, "Because you have done this, Cursed are you above all the livestock and all the wild animals! You will crawl on your belly and you will eat dust all the days of your life. And I will put enmity between you and the woman, and between your offspring and hers; he will crush your head, and you will strike his heel."

The curse on the serpent (the animal) was that it would become a snake. Previously, it had been a majestic creature in the Garden, perhaps even able to talk. The second part of the curse was upon Satan, who had possessed the serpent. It was fourfold: (1) God would put particular enmity between him and the woman. (2) God would put enmity between the serpent's "offspring" and the woman's "offspring," which is interesting in that he refers to a "woman's" offspring and not a "man and woman's" offspring. Some take this to be a reference to Jesus' being born of the Virgin Mary, in which there was no physical human father. (3) This "offspring," referring to Jesus, "would crush the serpent's head," meaning he would be destroyed by Christ. (4) The serpent would "strike Jesus' heel," presumably through the crucifixion.

For many centuries, this was the only real bit of hope humankind had that God would bring good out of bad, stop the power of evil, and send a Savior.

**Painting: A Great Subject Requires Great Artists**—Most of the great artists of history have contributed something to the collection of scenes from Christ's life. They include Rembrandt (1609–1669), Diego Velasquez (1599–1660), El Greco (1541–1614), Giotto (13th-14th century). Others include Picasso, Renoir, Paul Klee, and Norman Rockwell.

**Paintings**—When Leonardo da Vinci was forty-three years old, he was asked by the Duke Lucovinco of Milan to paint the last supper of Jesus with his disciples. Da Vinci paid close attention to detail and did everything perfectly, including an exquisite rendition of the holy grail, the cup used for the wine in Jesus' right hand. When he showed it to a friend, the friend exclaimed, "It's wonderful! The cup is so real, I cannot divert my eyes from it!" Immediately, da Vinci took a brush and wiped out the sparkling cup. He said, "Nothing shall detract from the figure of Christ."

**Paintings: All Those Horrible Pictures of Christ on the Cross**—As Michelangelo once walked through several art galleries in the cities of Europe, he was amazed at the number of paintings showing Jesus dying on the cross. He finally asked, "Why are art galleries filled with so many pictures of Christ upon the cross—Christ dying? Why do artists concentrate upon that passing episode, as if that were the last word and the final scene? Christ's dying on the cross lasted for only a few hours. But to the end of unending eternity, Christ is alive! Christ rules and reigns and triumphs!"

**Paintings: Blake, William**—In contrast to da Vinci's *Last Supper*, which shows Jesus and his disciples sitting at a table, Blake (1757–1827) rightly shows Jesus reclining on ground-level couches while sitting around a laid-out cloth.

**Paintings: Raphael's Last Painting**—*The Transfiguration* was never completed; Raphael, who died at age 37, was painting it when he died. His students carried it in his funeral procession as a symbol of how fleeting life is.

**Paintings: Whose Face Is That at the Last Supper?**—Lucas Cranach the Younger, an artist who dedicated a painting of the Last Supper for the Church of St. Mary in Dessau-Mildensee in 1565, portrayed the event as many have, with Jesus in the middle and his disciples sitting around him. However, in this painting, the disciples are dressed as German burghers of the sixteenth century. Also, in the midst of the group are three recognizable faces—those of Martin Luther, Melancthon (Luther's theological colleague), and the Prince of Anhalt. How modern can we get with these portrayals?

**Paintings of Christ: One of the Twelve Greatest Paintings of All Time**—Rubens' *Descent from the Cross* in Antwerp Cathedral pictures Jesus taken down, dead, the brutality of his sacrifice detailed in a way that has never been done before or since.

**Palm Sunday: Jesus Came to Town on a Donkey**—Whenever a king came to town, he came with the greatest entourage imaginable. Romans loved parades, and when a general returned from conquests, he often rode in a chariot at the head of a procession. Behind him were two large groups of people plus soldiers and lower-level commanders. One group was the dancing, joyful men and women whom the Romans had "liberated." They marched and danced and cavorted as a sign of their joy in being conquered. Behind them, in chains and heavily guarded, were the recalcitrant prisoners who would be sold in the slave market to the highest bidders.

When Jesus came into Jerusalem for what is called his "triumphal entry," Matthew 21:1–11 shows his arrival as follows:

> As they approached Jerusalem and came to Bethphage on the Mount of Olives, Jesus sent two disciples, saying to them, "Go to the village ahead of you, and at once you will find a donkey tied there, with her colt by her. Untie them and bring them to me. If anyone says anything to you, tell him that the Lord needs them, and he will send them right away."
> This took place to fulfill what was spoken through the prophet: "Say to the Daughter of Zion, 'See, your king comes to you, gentle and riding on a donkey, on a colt, the foal of a donkey.'"
> The disciples went and did as Jesus had instructed them. They brought the donkey and the colt, placed their cloaks on them, and Jesus sat on them. A very large crowd spread their cloaks on the road, while others cut

branches from the trees and spread them on the road.
The crowds that went ahead of him and those that fol-
lowed shouted, "Hosanna to the Son of David!"
"Blessed is he who comes in the name of the Lord!"
"Hosanna in the highest!"

When Jesus entered Jerusalem, the whole city was stirred
and asked, "Who is this?"

The crowds answered, "This is Jesus, the prophet from
Nazareth in Galilee."

Palm Sunday on the Christian calendar commemorates this event.
Frequently, churches give worshipers palm branches to take home as a
symbol of what happened when Jesus came to town.

**Parables: To Illustrate and to Befuddle**—Strangely enough, Jesus'
parables weren't designed only to make his teachings clear, but sometimes to obscure them! According to Matthew 13:10–17:

The disciples came to him and asked, "Why do you speak
to the people in parables?"

He replied, "The knowledge of the secrets of the kingdom of heaven has been given to you, but not to them.
Whoever has will be given more, and he will have an
abundance. Whoever does not have, even what he has
will be taken from him. This is why I speak to them in
parables: Though seeing, they do not see; though
hearing, they do not hear or understand. In them is
fulfilled the prophecy of Isaiah: 'You will be ever hearing but never understanding; you will be ever seeing
but never perceiving. For this people's heart has
become calloused; they hardly hear with their ears, and
they have closed their eyes. Otherwise they might see
with their eyes, hear with their ears, understand with
their hearts and turn, and I would heal them.' But
blessed are your eyes because they see, and your ears
because they hear. For I tell you the truth, many
prophets and righteous men longed to see what you
see but did not see it, and to hear what you hear but
did not hear it."

**Parables: Why?**—Another reason Jesus told parables was to fulfill
prophecy. According to Matthew 13:34–35, his purpose was as follows:

> Jesus spoke all these things to the crowd in parables; he
> did not say anything to them without using a parable.
> So was fulfilled what was spoken through the prophet:
> "I will open my mouth in parables, I will utter things
> hidden since the creation of the world."

This prophecy is found in Psalm 78:2, which says, "I will open my mouth in parables, I will utter things hidden from of old."

**Passion Play: Attracts World Travelers**—*The Passion Play*, featuring the events surrounding Jesus' trial, death, and resurrection, is celebrated each year in Oberammergau, Germany, at Easter time. It attracts people the world over.

**Peace and Jesus**—Jesus is often called the "Prince of Peace." He made it clear in several passages that he came specifically to bring peace to the hearts of those who would believe. For instance, in John 14:27, he tells his disciples, "Peace I leave with you; my peace I give you. I do not give to you as the world gives. Do not let your hearts be troubled and do not be afraid." In John 16:33, he assured them, "I have told you these things, so that in me you may have peace. In this world you will have trouble. But take heart! I have overcome the world." His birth was announced by angels who promised peace: "Glory to God in the highest, and on earth peace to men on whom his favor rests" (Luke 2:14).

However, Jesus also made it clear in at least one sense that he didn't come to bring peace, but a sword. He says in one of his messages to the disciples about their forays into the world to convert men and women to the truth of the gospel: "Do not suppose that I have come to bring peace to the earth. I did not come to bring peace, but a sword. For I have come to turn a man against his father, a daughter against her mother, a daughter-in-law against her mother-in-law—a man's enemies will be the members of his own household"(Matt. 10:34–36).

Jesus plainly was predicting that his message would bring dissension and argument, and that believing in him could pit a son against a father, a daughter against her mother, and so on. Obviously, this is exactly what happens today in many families.

**Perfection: If Jesus Was Perfect, How Could He Grow in Wisdom?**—Luke 2:52 says, "Jesus grew in wisdom and stature, and in favor with God and men." This verse indicates that Jesus "grew" in four ways: wisdom (mentally and emotionally), stature (physically), in favor with God (spiritually) and men (socially). One might think that because

Jesus was God incarnate ("in the flesh") that he would have been all-knowing with no need for personal growth and development. However, scripture makes it clear that Jesus was fully human and experienced all the elements of being a human. Thus, although he was truly God in human flesh, he was also truly human in God's person. As a result, he had to experience everything we all experience so that he might "help" us in our need. This idea is confirmed by Hebrews 2:17–18, which says, "For this reason he had to be made like his brothers in every way, in order that he might become a merciful and faithful high priest in service to God, and that he might make atonement for the sins of the people. Because he himself suffered when he was tempted, he is able to help those who are being tempted." Hebrews 4:15 expresses a similar idea: "For we do not have a high priest who is unable to sympathize with our weaknesses, but we have one who has been tempted in every way, just as we are—yet was without sin." Also, Hebrews 5:8 says, "Although he was a son, he learned obedience from what he suffered."

Jesus was just like any of us in his basic human feelings, interests, difficulties, and needs. He identifies with everything we could ever face, and thus in him we find the perfect friend, comrade, and guide through the pains and stresses of life.

**Persecution: Would Not Say, Caesar Is Lord**—Polycarp (70–155), one of the early church fathers who was ultimately put to death at the hand of Romans, was asked simply to say "Caesar is Lord" and he would be spared. They asked, "What harm is there in saying 'Caesar is Lord' and offering incense and saving your life?" Polycarp answered, "For eighty-six years I have been the servant of Jesus Christ, and he never did me any injury. How then can I blaspheme my King who saved me?"

**Pharisees: Jesus Scared the Leading Jews to Death**—Jesus' parable of the vinegrowers showed the Jewish leaders that they were in big trouble. Matthew 21:33–46 records a parable with a direct slash to the Pharisaical jugular vein:

> "Listen to another parable: There was a landowner who planted a vineyard. He put a wall around it, dug a winepress in it and built a watchtower. Then he rented the vineyard to some farmers and went away on a journey. When the harvest time approached, he sent his servants to the tenants to collect his fruit.
> "The tenants seized his servants; they beat one, killed another, and stoned a third. Then he sent other ser-

vants to them, more than the first time, and the tenants treated them the same way. Last of all, he sent his son to them. 'They will respect my son,' he said.

"But when the tenants saw the son, they said to each other, 'This is the heir. Come, let's kill him and take his inheritance.' So they took him and threw him out of the vineyard and killed him.

"Therefore, when the owner of the vineyard comes, what will he do to those tenants?"

"He will bring those wretches to a wretched end," they replied, "and he will rent the vineyard to other tenants, who will give him his share of the crop at harvest time."

Jesus said to them, "Have you never read in the Scriptures: 'The stone the builders rejected has become the capstone; the Lord has done this, and it is marvelous in our eyes'?

"Therefore I tell you that the kingdom of God will be taken away from you and given to a people who will produce its fruit. He who falls on this stone will be broken to pieces, but he on whom it falls will be crushed."

When the chief priests and the Pharisees heard Jesus' parables, they knew he was talking about them. They looked for a way to arrest him, but they were afraid of the crowd because the people held that he was a prophet.

**Pilate: Whatever Happened to Pontius Pilate?**—Pilate has been called "tactless, hot-tempered and weak in ruling; to cover his weakness he often resorted to brutal acts" (Dict. of the Christian Church). He ordered a massacre of innocent Galileans (see Luke 13:1), and for this reason the Romans ultimately removed him. When Jesus stood before him, he tried to have the Savior released. His wife even warned him not to touch Jesus because of a dream she had. According to Matthew 27:19: "While Pilate was sitting on the judge's seat, his wife sent him this message: 'Don't have anything to do with that innocent man, for I have suffered a great deal today in a dream because of him.'"

Pilate ultimately "washed his hands" of the whole affair, though, and delivered Jesus up to be crucified. Rather than do what apparently he knew was right, he was swayed by the crowd and their shouting and his fear of displeasing them.

In the end, he was removed from office, returned to Rome, and there committed suicide.

**Poetry:** *The Divine Comedy* **Wasn't Funny**—*The Divine Comedy*, by Dante Alighieri (1265–1321), is in three parts: Inferno (hell, purification); Purgatorio (purgatory, illumination); and Paradiso (Paradise, union with Christ). It has 100 Cantos, over 14,000 lines written in a complex "terza rima" in which groups of three lines all rhyme and are written in iambic pentameter (five "beats" to a line). It pictures the passage of the poet from hell to paradise, led on by Dante's beloved Beatrice. It became the precursor of a huge body of literature that would exalt the spiritual journey of man to God.

**Poetry: From** *The Wasteland* **to** *Ash Wednesday*—T.S. Eliot, perhaps the greatest English poet of the twentieth century, underwent a dramatic conversion between the writing of his famed poem *The Wasteland* (1922) and *Ash Wednesday* (1930), when he declared himself an Anglo-Catholic. Prior to his conversion, he repeatedly depicted the world as a vast wasteland of despair—spiritually and intellectually arid. After his conversion, he broke that tradition with a new series of much more hopeful poems, proclaiming faith as the path to meaning.

**Poetry: Paradise Lost and Regained**—Although *Paradise Lost* by John Milton (1608–1674) chronicles the battle in heaven between Christ and Satan and the temptation in the Garden of Eden as the beginning of all evil on earth, *Paradise Regained* pictures Christ triumphing over Satan in his temptation in the wilderness. Milton wrote the two epic poems while blind, memorizing the verses in the evening and then repeating them to a secretary in the morning for inscription.

**Poetry: Poem for the Birth**—Christina Georgina Rossetti (1830–1894), a Christian poet, with her brother Dante Gabriel Rossetti became one of the Pre-Raphaelites, a movement in art and writing in the nineteenth century. One of her poems, "In the Bleak Midwinter," captures that moment of Jesus' birth in the stable for one who wonders what he could present to the King of kings:

> What can I give him,
>     Poor as I am?
> If I were a shepherd
>     I would bring a lamb;
> If I were a Wise Man
>     I would do my part;
> Yet what I can I give him—
>     Give my heart.

**Politics: Christ's So-called Political Organs**—Though Jesus never got involved in politics while on earth, many of his followers have, both throughout the ages and in recent times in the United States. Few will forget the impact of Jerry Falwell's "Moral Majority" in the 1970s, which wanted to bring Christ's morality back into national focus. More recently, the "Christian Coalition," begun by one-time presidential candidate Pat Robertson, with members in the millions, and "Concerned Women for America," with a membership of over 600,000, have received much attention in the press as the "Christian Right."

**Politics: Jesus Would Not Have Voted for Them**—The Christian Front, an American Nazi, anti-Semitic group, follows the teachings of Hitler and Nazism. It has little to do with true Christianity. Jesus made clear in such passages as the parable of the Good Samaritan (see Luke 10:30–37) and others that hatred, racism, and similar attitudes are evil and not to be tolerated. Perhaps his greatest diatribe against such an outlook is found in Matthew 25:31–46, where Jesus details the judgment of the sheep and the goats:

> "When the Son of Man comes in his glory, and all the angels with him, he will sit on his throne in heavenly glory. All the nations will be gathered before him, and he will separate the people one from another as a shepherd separates the sheep from the goats. He will put the sheep on his right and the goats on his left.
>
> "Then the King will say to those on his right, 'Come, you who are blessed by my Father; take your inheritance, the kingdom prepared for you since the creation of the world. For I was hungry and you gave me something to eat, I was thirsty and you gave me something to drink, I was a stranger and you invited me in, I needed clothes and you clothed me, I was sick and you looked after me, I was in prison and you came to visit me.'
>
> "Then the righteous will answer him, 'Lord, when did we see you hungry and feed you, or thirsty and give you something to drink? When did we see you a stranger and invite you in, or needing clothes and clothe you? When did we see you sick or in prison and go to visit you?'
>
> "The King will reply, 'I tell you the truth, whatever you did for one of the least of these brothers of mine, you did for me.'

"Then he will say to those on his left, 'Depart from me,
you who are cursed, into the eternal fire prepared for
the devil and his angels. For I was hungry and you gave
me nothing to eat, I was thirsty and you gave me nothing to drink, I was a stranger and you did not invite me
in, I needed clothes and you did not clothe me, I was
sick and in prison and you did not look after me.'
"They also will answer, 'Lord, when did we see you hungry or thirsty or a stranger or needing clothes or sick or
in prison, and did not help you?'
"He will reply, 'I tell you the truth, whatever you did not
do for one of the least of these, you did not do for me.'
"Then they will go away to eternal punishment, but the
righteous to eternal life."

**Pool of Bethesda: Where Angels Tread**—The Pool of Bethesda, at
which Jesus healed a man who had been paralyzed for thirty-eight
years, has been excavated in Jerusalem. It has five porticoes, or porches.
At the time of Jesus' ministry, it was believed that an angel would "stir
up" the water, and whoever first plummeted into the pool at that
moment would be healed.

**Pouch to Hold the Messiah**—On Crete, Muslims still wear an old
costume, with trousers tight below the knee but voluminous above with
a large pouch. The pouch was to accommodate the Messiah, who was
to be born of a man!

**Pray with Perseverance**—Jesus used the parable of the unjust judge
to illustrate the need to pray with perseverance and even to "bug" God.
In Luke 18:2–8, Jesus says:

"In a certain town there was a judge who neither feared
God nor cared about men. And there was a widow in
that town who kept coming to him with the plea,
'Grant me justice against my adversary.'
"For some time he refused. But finally he said to himself,
'Even though I don't fear God or care about men, yet
because this widow keeps bothering me, I will see that
she gets justice, so that she won't eventually wear me
out with her coming!'"
And the Lord said, "Listen to what the unjust judge says.
And will not God bring about justice for his chosen
ones, who cry out to him day and night? Will he keep

putting them off? I tell you, he will see that they get justice, and quickly."

**Prejudice: Was Jesus a Bigot?**—When a Syrophoenician asked for her daughter's healing, Jesus said something that has befuddled scholars for centuries. The exchange is as follows, from Matthew 15:21–28:

> Leaving that place, Jesus withdrew to the region of Tyre and Sidon. A Canaanite woman from that vicinity came to him, crying out, "Lord, Son of David, have mercy on me! My daughter is suffering terribly from demon-possession."
> Jesus did not answer a word. So his disciples came to him and urged him, "Send her away, for she keeps crying out after us."
> He answered, "I was sent only to the lost sheep of Israel."
> The woman came and knelt before him. "Lord, help me!" she said.
> He replied, "It is not right to take the children's bread and toss it to their dogs."
> "Yes, Lord," she said, "but even the dogs eat the crumbs that fall from their masters' table."
> Then Jesus answered, "Woman, you have great faith! Your request is granted." And her daughter was healed from that very hour.

Some interpret this passage to mean that Jesus had narrow and even bigoted ideas against non-Jews. A closer inspection of the story, however, indicates something Jesus often did with his disciples: to suggest to them the thinking of the day, see what their response was, and then do what he intended all along. You find this technique in such passages as Matthew 14:15–16, in which he "tested" his disciples:

> As evening approached, the disciples came to him and said, "This is a remote place, and it's already getting late. Send the crowds away, so they can go to the villages and buy themselves some food."
> Jesus replied, "They do not need to go away. You give them something to eat."

Clearly, Jesus intended to feed the people all along, but he must have wanted to see what kind of thinking his disciples would exhibit in such a situation.

A second example happened when Jesus stilled a storm on the sea. This is recorded in Matthew 8:24–26:

> Without warning, a furious storm came up on the lake, so that the waves swept over the boat. But Jesus was sleeping. The disciples went and woke him, saying, "Lord, save us! We're going to drown!"
> He replied, "You of little faith, why are you so afraid?" Then he got up and rebuked the winds and the waves, and it was completely calm.

One more instance occurred in Matthew 9:2–6, where a paralytic is brought to Jesus for healing:

> Some men brought to him a paralytic, lying on a mat. When Jesus saw their faith, he said to the paralytic, "Take heart, son; your sins are forgiven."
> At this, some of the teachers of the law said to themselves, "This fellow is blaspheming!"
> Knowing their thoughts, Jesus said, "Why do you entertain evil thoughts in your hearts? Which is easier: to say, 'Your sins are forgiven,' or to say, 'Get up and walk'? But so that you may know that the Son of Man has authority on earth to forgive sins. . . ." Then he said to the paralytic, "Get up, take your mat and go home."

As the wise and confident teacher, Jesus often chose the instructive route rather than simply doing whatever others asked.

**Presidents: How to Live**—Jimmy Carter, former president of the United States, taught a Bible class in Plains, Georgia, and exhorted them with the words, "We should live our lives as though Christ were coming this afternoon." Or this evening. Or the next minute, maybe?

**Priest: What Kind of Priest Was Jesus?**—How could Jesus be a Hebrew priest? Priests had to be descended from Levi, one of Jacob's twelve sons. No other tribe was designated to function as priests. Jesus was descended from Judah. Thus, the question many Jews asked from early on was, "How could Jesus offer up his own self as a sacrifice if he wasn't descended from Levi?"

The writer to the Hebrews had the answer. In Hebrews 5:10, it's written that Jesus "was designated by God to be high priest in the order of Melchizedek."

Later, in Hebrews 7:1–7 the writer explains the situation as follows:

> This Melchizedek was king of Salem and priest of God
> Most High. He met Abraham returning from the defeat
> of the kings and blessed him, and Abraham gave him a
> tenth of everything. First, his name means "king of
> righteousness"; then also, "king of Salem" means "king
> of peace." Without father or mother, without geneal-
> ogy, without beginning of days or end of life, like the
> Son of God he remains a priest forever.
> Just think how great he was: Even the patriarch Abraham
> gave him a tenth of the plunder! Now the law requires
> the descendants of Levi who become priests to collect a
> tenth from the people—that is, their brothers—even
> though their brothers are descended from Abraham.
> This man, however, did not trace his descent from
> Levi, yet he collected a tenth from Abraham and
> blessed him who had the promises. And without doubt
> the lesser person is blessed by the greater.

The story of Melchizedek is found in only one place in the Bible,
Genesis 14:17–20:

> After Abram returned from defeating Kedorlaomer and
> the kings allied with him, the king of Sodom came out
> to meet him in the Valley of Shaveh (that is, the King's
> Valley).
> Then Melchizedek king of Salem brought out bread and
> wine. He was priest of God Most High, and he blessed
> Abram, saying, "Blessed be Abram by God Most High,
> Creator of heaven and earth. And blessed be God Most
> High, who delivered your enemies into your hand."
> Then Abram gave him a tenth of everything.

This is all we know about this person from the Bible. Many scholars believe Melchizedek was an early incarnation of Christ, who
appeared at times in Israel's history as an "angel" or even a human, as
in this case. Hebrews 7:11–16 goes on to say:

> If perfection could have been attained through the Levitical
> priesthood (for on the basis of it the law was given to the
> people), why was there still need for another priest to
> come—one in the order of Melchizedek, not in the order

of Aaron? For when there is a change of the priesthood,
there must also be a change of the law. He of whom
these things are said belonged to a different tribe, and no
one from that tribe has ever served at the altar. For it is
clear that our Lord descended from Judah, and in regard
to that tribe Moses said nothing about priests. And what
we have said is even more clear if another priest like
Melchizedek appears, one who has become a priest not
on the basis of a regulation as to his ancestry but on the
basis of the power of an indestructible life.

What the writer is saying is that Jesus could not have been a priest
in the order of Levi (or Aaron, as above) because God instituted something different when Christ came. Melchizedek functioned as a priest
who would never die and who instituted the rite of "bread and wine" as
Jesus himself did.

**Prophecy of Jesus' Birthplace in 700 B.C.**—Micah predicts that the
Messiah will be born in Bethlehem, with these words: "But you, Bethlehem Ephrathah, though you are small among the clans of Judah, out
of you will come for me one who will be ruler over Israel, whose origins are from of old, from ancient times"(Mic. 5:2).

The leaders of the Jews understood this to be true, for when the
Magi arrived from the east because they'd seen a "star" that they
believed indicated the birth of the Jewish Messiah, the priests and
scribes talked to Herod about the situation. The incident is recorded in
Matthew 2:1–6:

After Jesus was born in Bethlehem in Judea, during the
time of King Herod, Magi from the east came to
Jerusalem and asked, "Where is the one who has been
born king of the Jews? We saw his star in the east and
have come to worship him."
When King Herod heard this he was disturbed, and all
Jerusalem with him. When he had called together all
the people's chief priests and teachers of the law, he
asked them where the Christ was to be born. "In Bethlehem in Judea," they replied, "for this is what the
prophet has written: 'But you, Bethlehem, in the land
of Judah, are by no means least among the rulers of
Judah; for out of you will come a ruler who will be the
shepherd of my people Israel.'"

**Prophesying His Death**—Jesus warned his disciples that he would die and be raised three days later. Such passages as the following indicate his plans:

*Matthew 16:21:* "From that time on Jesus began to explain to his disciples that he must go to Jerusalem and suffer many things at the hands of the elders, chief priests and teachers of the law, and that he must be killed and on the third day be raised to life."

*Matthew 17:22–23:* "When they came together in Galilee, he said to them, 'The Son of Man is going to be betrayed into the hands of men. They will kill him, and on the third day he will be raised to life.' And the disciples were filled with grief."

*Luke 18:31–34:* "Jesus took the Twelve aside and told them, 'We are going up to Jerusalem, and everything that is written by the prophets about the Son of Man will be fulfilled. He will be handed over to the Gentiles. They will mock him, insult him, spit on him, flog him and kill him. On the third day he will rise again.' The disciples did not understand any of this. Its meaning was hidden from them, and they did not know what he was talking about."

**Prophetic Description of Jesus**—The only description we have of what Jesus looked like is found in the Book of Revelation. In Revelation 1:12–16 we read:

> I turned around to see the voice that was speaking to me. And when I turned I saw seven golden lampstands, and among the lampstands was someone "like a son of man," dressed in a robe reaching down to his feet and with a golden sash around his chest. His head and hair were white like wool, as white as snow, and his eyes were like blazing fire. His feet were like bronze glowing in a furnace, and his voice was like the sound of rushing waters. In his right hand he held seven stars, and out of his mouth came a sharp double-edged sword. His face was like the sun shining in all its brilliance.

This description, however, was not of Jesus as he appeared in his earthly guise during his life on earth, but as he was after he was resurrected, a glorified and eternal version of the original.

**Prophetic Description of Jesus' Suffering**—Jesus' suffering on the cross was foretold in several places in scripture. One, from David in Psalm 22:11–18, is a precise description of crucifixion:

> Do not be far from me, for trouble is near and there is no
>    one to help.
> Many bulls surround me; strong bulls of Bashan encircle
>    me. Roaring lions tearing their prey open their mouths
>    wide against me. I am poured out like water, and all my
>    bones are out of joint. My heart has turned to wax; it
>    has melted away within me. My strength is dried up
>    like a potsherd, and my tongue sticks to the roof of my
>    mouth; you lay me in the dust of death. Dogs have sur-
>    rounded me; a band of evil men has encircled me, they
>    have pierced my hands and my feet. I can count all my
>    bones; people stare and gloat over me. They divide my
>    garments among them and cast lots for my clothing.

A second passage (Isa. 53:2–9) is a bit less graphic, but also tells similar details of Christ's purpose to suffer and die:

> He grew up before him like a tender shoot, and like a root
>    out of dry ground. He had no beauty or majesty to
>    attract us to him, nothing in his appearance that we
>    should desire him. He was despised and rejected by
>    men, a man of sorrows, and familiar with suffering.
>    Like one from whom men hide their faces he was
>    despised, and we esteemed him not.
> Surely he took up our infirmities and carried our sorrows,
>    yet we considered him stricken by God, smitten by
>    him, and afflicted. But he was pierced for our transgres-
>    sions, he was crushed for our iniquities; the punishment
>    that brought us peace was upon him, and by his wounds
>    we are healed. We all, like sheep, have gone astray,
>    each of us has turned to his own way; and the LORD has
>    laid on him the iniquity of us all.
> He was oppressed and afflicted, yet he did not open his
>    mouth; he was led like a lamb to the slaughter, and as a
>    sheep before her shearers is silent, so he did not open his
>    mouth. By oppression and judgment, he was taken away.
>    And who can speak of his descendants? For he was cut
>    off from the land of the living; for the transgression of
>    my people he was stricken. He was assigned a grave with
>    the wicked, and with the rich in his death, though he had
>    done no violence, nor was any deceit in his mouth.

David wrote about 950 B.C. and Isaiah about 700 B.C. Both wrote
long before crucifixion was even invented.

**Prophetic Picture: The Passover Lamb a Premonition**—At Passover, a celebration of the Jews reminding them of how God delivered them from their slavery in Egypt, Jews would slay a lamb as part of the feast. In the original event, they painted the lamb's blood on the lintels of the door—at the top and on the sides. This was to indicate to the "angel of the Lord" who came to slay the Egyptians that believers lived in the blood-spattered house and the angel should "pass over" them.

The lamb was a prophetic picture of Jesus, called "the Lamb of God" by John the Baptist (John 1:29). According to Matthew 26:28, Jesus' blood was poured out for the forgiveness of sins. When spiritually applied to the believer's heart, Jesus' blood tells God to "pass over" that person in the judgment for sins.

**Psalm Singing**—The Acoemetae ("sleepless ones") were a monastic order in the fifth century who were divided into choirs and practiced round-the-clock singing without intermission the whole year round. Perhaps the first all-night radio station?

**Psychiatrist: Could Jesus Have Been One?**—Jesus might have made a fine psychiatrist or written a book to help people not to worry. Consider his prescription in Matthew 6:25–34 for the problem of worry and fear:

> "Therefore I tell you, do not worry about your life, what you will eat or drink; or about your body, what you will wear. Is not life more important than food, and the body more important than clothes? Look at the birds of the air; they do not sow or reap or store away in barns, and yet your heavenly Father feeds them. Are you not much more valuable than they? Who of you by worrying can add a single hour to his life?
> "And why do you worry about clothes? See how the lilies of the field grow. They do not labor or spin. Yet I tell you that not even Solomon in all his splendor was dressed like one of these. If that is how God clothes the grass of the field, which is here today and tomorrow is thrown into the fire, will he not much more clothe you, O you of little faith? So do not worry, saying, 'What shall we eat?' or 'What shall we drink?' or 'What shall we wear?' For the pagans run after all these things, and your heavenly Father knows that you need them. But seek first his kingdom and his righteousness, and all

these things will be given to you as well. Therefore do
not worry about tomorrow, for tomorrow will worry
about itself. Each day has enough trouble of its own."

**Psychiatrist: Jesus?**—Rollo May, famed author and psychologist, saw
Jesus as uniquely gifted to help hurting people. He said, "Jesus Christ
is the therapist for humanity."

**Questions: Sometimes Jesus Dodged a Question with a Question**—When asked by what authority he taught and did miracles, Jesus
didn't answer but asked another question, as done in Matthew
21:23–27:

Jesus entered the temple courts, and, while he was teaching, the chief priests and the elders of the people came
to him. "By what authority are you doing these things?"
they asked. "And who gave you this authority?"
Jesus replied, "I will also ask you one question. If you
answer me, I will tell you by what authority I am doing
these things. John's baptism—where did it come from?
Was it from heaven, or from men?"
They discussed it among themselves and said, "If we say,
'From heaven,' he will ask, 'Then why didn't you believe
him?' But if we say, 'From men'—we are afraid of the
people, for they all hold that John was a prophet."
So they answered Jesus, "We don't know."
Then he said, "Neither will I tell you by what authority I
am doing these things."

**Quickie Miracle**—When Peter lopped off a slave's ear, Jesus picked it
up and healed it on the spot. This is what happened: "When Jesus' followers saw what was going to happen, they said, 'Lord, should we strike
with our swords?' And one of them struck the servant of the high priest,
cutting off his right ear. But Jesus answered, 'No more of this!' And he
touched the man's ear and healed him" (Luke 22:49–51).

From other related passages we know that the person who swung
the sword was Peter, and the name of the man whose ear was cut off
was Malchus (John 18:10).

**Quitting: Jesus Once Asked His Disciples After a Bad Day if They Wanted to Quit**—On this occasion, Jesus experienced some major defections from his following. Apparently, his listeners didn't like his earlier words about feeding on him as the bread of life. The Jews must have interpreted this almost as a kind of cannibalism, or perhaps they were simply incensed because Jesus refused to become their kind and create bread whenever they wanted it. But the biggest issue occurred when Jesus said, "This is why I told you that no one can come to me unless the Father has enabled him"(John 6:65). This idea of God's sovereignty and power to choose his follower before the follower chose him was repugnant to many Jews, who felt that they had the power to please God and win God's approval on their own.

As many began to depart, grumbling to themselves, Jesus turned to the disciples. This is what happened, according to John 6:67–71:

> "You do not want to leave too, do you?" Jesus asked the Twelve.
> Simon Peter answered him, "Lord, to whom shall we go? You have the words of eternal life. We believe and know that you are the Holy One of God."
> Then Jesus replied, "Have I not chosen you, the Twelve? Yet one of you is a devil!" (He meant Judas, the son of Simon Iscariot, who, though one of the Twelve, was later to betray him.)

**Quotes**—Jesus is the most quoted individual in history, yet *Bartlett's Familiar Quotations* doesn't even list him. Some of his best-known quotes, in addition to those listed under "Wit," are these:

*On being salt in the world:* "You are the salt of the earth. But if the salt loses its saltiness, how can it be made salty again? It is no longer good for anything, except to be thrown out and trampled by men" (Matt. 5:13).

*On being insulted:* "Do not resist an evil person. If someone strikes you on the right cheek, turn to him the other also" (Matt. 5:39).

*On trying to serve God and money:* "No one can serve two masters. Either he will hate the one and love the other, or he will be devoted to the one and despise the other. You cannot serve both God and Money" (Matt. 6:24).

*On seeking wealth and riches:* "But seek first his kingdom and his righteousness, and all these things will be given to you as well" (Matt. 6:33).

*On worry:* "Therefore do not worry about tomorrow, for tomorrow will worry about itself. Each day has enough trouble of its own" (Matt. 6:34).

*On his mission:* "It is not the healthy who need a doctor, but the sick" (Matt. 9:12).

*On evangelism:* "I am sending you out like sheep among wolves. Therefore be as shrewd as snakes and as innocent as doves" (Matt. 10:16).

*On discipleship:* "Come, follow me, and I will make you fishers of men" (Mark 1:17).

*On his purpose:* "For the Son of Man came to seek and to save what was lost" (Luke 19:10).

*On taxes:* "Give to Caesar what is Caesar's, and to God what is God's" (Luke 20:25).

*On God's love:* "For God so loved the world that he gave his one and only Son, that whoever believes in him shall not perish but have eternal life"(John 3:16).

*On worship:* "God is spirit, and his worshipers must worship in spirit and in truth" (John 4:24).

*On coming back:* "Do not let your hearts be troubled. Trust in God; trust also in me. In my Father's house are many rooms; if it were not so, I would have told you. I am going there to prepare a place for you" (John 14:1–2).

*On peace:* "Peace I leave with you; my peace I give you. I do not give to you as the world gives. Do not let your hearts be troubled and do not be afraid" (John 14:27).

*On God's word:* "Sanctify them by the truth; your word is truth" (John 17:17).

**Rapture of the Saints: What Is That All About?**—The "Rapture," or "catching up," of the saints to meet Christ in heaven is found in several passages of scripture. "Rapture" comes from the Latin *raptus*, meaning "to be carried away" by some force, either your own emotion or something else.

Theologically, the Rapture is a technical term sometimes called the "blessed hope" (from Titus 2:13) that Christians will be spared a time of trouble and tribulation at the end of time by being rescued out of the world by Christ himself. The doctrine is based largely on two passages from the writings of Paul:

*1 Corinthians 15:51–53:* "Listen, I tell you a mystery: We will not all sleep, but we will all be changed—in a flash, in the twinkling of an eye, at the last trumpet. For the trumpet will sound, the dead will be raised imperishable, and we will be changed. For the perishable must clothe itself with the imperishable, and the mortal with immortality."

*1 Thessalonians 4:13–18:* "Brothers, we do not want you to be ignorant about those who fall asleep, or to grieve like the rest of men, who have no hope. We believe that Jesus died and rose again and so we believe that God will bring with Jesus those who have fallen asleep in him. According to the Lord's own word, we tell you that we who are still alive, who are left till the coming of the Lord, will certainly not precede those who have fallen asleep. For the Lord himself will come down from heaven, with a loud command, with the voice of the archangel and with the trumpet call of God, and the dead in Christ will rise first. After that, we who are still alive and are left will be caught up together with them in the clouds to meet the Lord in the air. And so we will be with the Lord forever. Therefore encourage each other with these words."

There is much debate in scholarly circles as to the timing of the Rapture, whether it's before a so-called time of tribulation, in the middle of it, or after, and whether it precedes a thousand-year reign of Christ (see "Millennium") or whether it happens at the end of time. Scholars are agreed on a number of elements of the Rapture:

1. Christ will come unexpectedly, without warning or sign, like a "thief in the night." Thus, Christians are always to be ready for that coming by practicing godly, wholesome habits in their lives.

2. All the saints from all time will "meet the Lord in the air." This includes Old Testament believers, such as Abraham, David, and Moses, and all those who have believed since Christ appeared the first time.

3. At that moment, all the saints will be "changed" and be given a supernatural, spiritual body that is immortal, unchangeable, and without taint—utterly perfect.

4. A "trumpet" will sound that all the world will hear, including unbelievers; this will herald the Rapture itself.

Whatever the details of when, where, why, and how the Rapture occurs, scripture has not provided answers. The main idea of the Rapture, though, is that it is a "blessed hope," something all Christians have hoped for since the days of Christ—that we will not all die, but some, at the end of time, will be "translated" into that perfect body without going through death or tribulation. Thus, it is meant to be a great encouragement to Christians everywhere.

**Reason He Came: To Make Life Easier**—In the days of Jesus, one of the greatest problems for believing Jews who wanted to keep the Law was the sheer number of laws to obey. The Pharisees magnified the laws God gave (613 of them) and added to them all sorts of traditions and requirements that became a monstrous burden. Jesus understood the problem. One of the first things he began telling people about his purpose in coming to the world is found in Matthew 11:28–30. There, he says: "Come to me, all you who are weary and burdened, and I will give you rest. Take my yoke upon you and learn from me, for I am gentle and humble in heart, and you will find rest for your souls. For my yoke is easy and my burden is light."

Jesus promised spiritual "rest" to those who would come to him and follow him. Taking "his yoke" meant a yoke for two oxen used during plowing season. Jesus' idea seems to be that he would take one side and the believer the other. Thus, together they would walk in tandem. He would teach that person gently and humbly. Jesus concluded that his yoke was "easy" and his burden was "light," meaning that he would not cause people to live by rules but through grace.

**Red Cross**—The healing organization was the idea of Jean Henry Dunant, a Swiss citizen who had witnessed the suffering of soldiers during the battle of Solferino (1859). In 1864, the Geneva Convention adopted the symbol of the red cross on a white background first as an opposite of the Swiss flag and also as a symbol of Christ's compassion for the hurting. The Red Cross established itself as a health organization for soldiers, refugees, and all who had no other help.

**References Outside the Bible**—A number of nonbiblical authors mentioned Christ in their writings, authenticating some of the facts of his ministry and also his existence, which some scholars have disputed over the years. Among the authors are the following:

*Tacitus*, a Roman historian born around A.D. 52, was Governor of Asia, son-in-law of Julius Agricola (Governor of Britain from A.D. 80–84). He wrote much of what we know of the reign of Nero and mentions Jesus as well as the existence of Christians in Rome. He wrote this around A.D. 112:

> But not all the relief that could come from man, not all the bounties that the prince could bestow, nor all the atone-

ments which could be presented to the gods, availed to relieve Nero from the infamy of being believed to have ordered the conflagration, the fire of Rome. Hence to suppress the rumor, he falsely charged with the guilt, and punished with the most exquisite tortures, the persons commonly called Christians, who were hated for their enormities. Christus, the founder of the name, was put to death by Pontius Pilate, procurator of Judea in the reign of Tiberius; but the pernicious superstition, represented for a time broke out again, not only through Judea, where the mischief originated, but through the city of Rome also.

*Lucian of Samosota*, a satirist of the second century who scorned Christ and his followers, alluded to Christ when he wrote: "the man who was crucified in Palestine because he introduced this new cult into the world. . . . Furthermore, their first lawgiver persuaded them that they were all brothers one of another after they have transgressed once for all by denying the Greek gods and by worshiping that crucified sophist himself and living under his laws."

*Suetonius*, court official and historian under Hadrian, annalist of the Imperial House, wrote around A.D. 120, "As the Jews were making constant disturbances at the instigation of Chrestus, he expelled them from Rome."

*Pliny the Younger*, Governor of Bithynia in Asia Minor in A.D. 112, wrote to Emperor Trajan asking for counsel on how to deal with Christians. He explained how he had been persecuting and killing Christians and "made them curse Christ, which a genuine Christian cannot be induced to do." In the same letter, he says, "They affirmed, however, that the whole of their guilt, or their error, was, that they were in the habit of meeting on a certain fixed day before it was light, when they sang in alternate verse a hymn to Christ as to a god, and bound themselves to a solemn oath, not to any wicked deeds, but never to commit any fraud, theft, adultery, never to falsify their word, not to deny a trust when they should be called upon to deliver it up."

*Thallus*, a Samaritan-born historian, wrote in A.D. 52 about Christ. His writings have vanished, but he is quoted in *Julius Africanus*, a Christian writer, around A.D. 221, speaking of the darkness that covered Judea during Christ's crucifixion, saying, "Thallus, in the third book of his histories, explains away this darkness as an eclipse of the sun—unreasonably, as it seems to me (unreasonably, of course, because a solar eclipse could not take place at the time of the full moon), and it was at the season of the Paschal full moon that Christ died."

A letter from a man named *Mara Bar-Serphon*, preserved in the British Museum and written some time after A.D. 73, mentions that men of wisdom were often persecuted. He says, "What advantage did the Athenians gain from putting Socrates to death? Famine and plague came upon them as a judgment for their crime. What advantage did the men of Samos gain from burning Pythagoras? In a moment their land was covered with sand. What advantage did the Jews gain from executing their wise King? It was just after that that their kingdom was abolished. God justly avenged these three wise men: the Athenians died of hunger; the Samians were overwhelmed by the sea; the Jews, ruined and driven from their land, live in complete dispersion. But Socrates did not die for good; he lived on in the teaching of Plato. Pythagoras did not die for good; he lived on in the statue of Hera. Nor did the wise King die for good; He lived on in the teaching which He had given."

Of course, there are many references to Christ in the writings of the men known as the church fathers: Tertullian, Origen, Justin Martyr, the Shepherd of Hermas, the Letter of Barnabas, and many others. Josephus also wrote about Jesus (see entry under **Josephus**).

**Referrals: How Jesus Made Disciples**—Jesus used a method in gathering his disciples that many people use in finding clients—referrals. Look how this passage progresses, and you can see his methodology, from John 1:35–51:

*Step One:* John the Baptist points Jesus out to two of the former's disciples:

> The next day John was there again with two of his disciples. When he saw Jesus passing by, he said, "Look, the Lamb of God!"
> When the two disciples heard him say this, they followed Jesus.

*Step Two:* Jesus met them and invited them to his home:

> Turning round, Jesus saw them following and asked, "What do you want?"
> They said, "Rabbi" (which means Teacher), "where are you staying?"
> "Come," he replied, "and you will see."
> So they went and saw where he was staying, and spent that day with him. It was about the tenth hour.

Andrew, Simon Peter's brother, was one of the two who heard what John had said and who had followed Jesus.

*Step Three:* Andrew went to his brother Simon and told him about Jesus:

The first thing Andrew did was to find his brother Simon and tell him, "We have found the Messiah" (that is, the Christ).

Then he brought Simon to Jesus, who looked at him and said, "You are Simon son of John. You will be called Cephas" (which, when translated, is Peter).

*Step Four:* Jesus found another person the next day from the same town:

The next day Jesus decided to leave for Galilee. Finding Philip, he said to him, "Follow me."

Philip, like Andrew and Peter, was from the town of Bethsaida.

*Step Five:* Philip went to Nathanael and told him about Jesus:

Philip found Nathanael and told him, "We have found the one Moses wrote about in the Law, and about whom the prophets also wrote—Jesus of Nazareth, the son of Joseph."

"Nazareth! Can anything good come from there?" Nathanael asked.

"Come and see," said Philip.

When Jesus saw Nathanael approaching, he said of him, "Here is a true Israelite, in whom there is nothing false."

"How do you know me?" Nathanael asked.

Jesus answered, "I saw you while you were still under the fig tree before Philip called you."

Then Nathanael declared, "Rabbi, you are the Son of God; you are the King of Israel."

Jesus said, "You believe because I told you I saw you under the fig tree. You shall see greater things than that." He then added, "I tell you the truth, you shall see heaven open, and the angels of God ascending and descending on the Son of Man."

**Rejection: Does Jesus Reject Anyone? No, Jesus Always Reached Out to Everyone**—As illustrated by the parable of the great feast, Jesus excludes no one from his kingdom. Whoever wants to come may come to him. Any excluding is done by the one who rejects Jesus, not the other way around. Consider Jesus' words in Luke 14:16–24:

> "A certain man was preparing a great banquet and invited many guests. At the time of the banquet he sent his servant to tell those who had been invited, 'Come, for everything is now ready.'
>
> "But they all alike began to make excuses. The first said, 'I have just bought a field, and I must go and see it. Please excuse me.'
>
> "Another said, 'I have just bought five yoke of oxen, and I'm on my way to try them out. Please excuse me.'
>
> "Still another said, 'I have just got married, so I can't come.'
>
> "The servant came back and reported this to his master. Then the owner of the house became angry and ordered his servant, 'Go out quickly into the streets and alleys of the town and bring in the poor, the crippled, the blind and the lame.'
>
> "'Sir,' the servant said, 'what you ordered has been done, but there is still room.'
>
> "Then the master told his servant, 'Go out to the roads and country lanes and make them come in, so that my house will be full. I tell you, not one of those men who were invited will get a taste of my banquet.'"

**Relics: What About All Those Old Bones Laying Around?**—A relic is the "material remains" of a saint. In Roman Catholic tradition, relics are venerated because they once belonged to members of the church in whom the Holy Spirit resided. God is believed to use the relics to perform miracles and also answer prayer. The biblical basis for the veneration and use of relics is from Acts 19:12, where handkerchiefs touched by the apostles were used for healing. In the Old Testament, other miracles occurred through touching Elijah's mantle (2 Kings 2:14) and Elisha's bones (2 Kings 13:21).

A letter from Smyrna about A.D. 156 is the earliest known reference to relics. In that letter, which describes the death of Polycarp, an early church saint and father, the writers say, "We took up his bones, which are more valuable than precious and finer than refined gold, and laid them in a suitable place, where the Lord will permit us to gather ourselves together, as we are able, in gladness and joy, and to celebrate the birthday of his martyrdom." The Crusaders contributed much to the gathering of relics, bringing back many such "trophies" from the Holy Land. In the Eastern Church, some practiced the actual dismemberment of a saint, to have his limbs and organs distributed among the churches. The Council of Nicaea in 787 decreed that all churches were to be established only through the presence of relics. Numerous relics of all sorts are found throughout Europe and Eastern churches, among them:

*The Head of St. Andrew*—In one of the piers that support St. Peter's dome.

*The Lance that Pierced Jesus' Side on the Cross*—In one of the piers that support St. Peter's dome.

*Last Supper Bathing Basin*—The "Holy Basin" Jesus used to wash the disciples' feet before the Last Supper is in the Cathedral of St. Lorenzo at Genoa.

*Mary's Hair*—Supposed actual locks of the Virgin's hair are kept at churches in Naples and Rome.

*Mary's Holy Girdle*—In a church in Prato, Italy.

*Mary's Milk*—In the church of San Gaudioso e Patrizio in Naples and at St. Mary of the People at Rome.

*Mary's Wedding Ring*—In Cathedral Perugia.

**Religious Leaders of the World: How Do We Know Who the True God Is?**—Through the ages, religious leaders have appeared and disappeared. How does Jesus stack up against them? Should they be given equal authority? Should they be considered as having a greater or lesser grasp of truth than Jesus?

The best way to solve the problem is to study each of those leaders and come to your own conclusions. For me, the following story tells the tale:

Several of the great religious leaders of history were gathered at a table arguing about who was the true Messiah to humankind. Each had his say, and it went like this:

*Moses (1400s B.C.):* "Through me, the people of Israel found life and hope. I gave the world the Ten Commandments and God's own word."

*Buddha (563–483 B.C.):* "As the great teacher, I renounced my great wealth and place as son of a king. Through meditation I achieved enlightenment. Those who will follow my Four Noble Truths and the Eightfold Path will reach Nirvana, break the law of Karma, and become one with the true infinity."

*Confucius (551–479 B.C.):* "I told my people how to live well and build peace, truth, and goodness in their government. If you use my teachings about "jen" (goodheartedness), you will become citizens who will make their government proud. Following my system of ethics and goodness will bring in world justice."

*Jesus Christ (4 B.C.–A.D. 32):* "I am the way, the truth, and the life; he who comes to me shall never die, but shall have eternal life."

*Muhammad (A.D. 570–632):* "There is one God, Allah, and I am his prophet. I have shown the world the one true way. Those who practice the teachings of Allah's book, the Koran, will be rewarded with heaven and everlasting life."

*Mohandas Gandhi (1869–1948):* "Through trial and error, I have combined Christian, Muslim, and Hindu teachings. My new system will bring in true justice and goodness in the world. Follow my path and you will achieve true salvation and harmony with the universe."

After each of these men finished, someone in the listening audience said, "But how do we know who is the true Savior of the world?"

A person in the wings stood. He said, "Gentlemen, there is a simple solution: will the real Savior please rise—from the dead?"

The thing that sets Jesus apart from all other world religious leaders is this one: He rose from the dead. No one else has ever done such a thing in the convincing way Jesus did. It is the resurrection on which all of Christianity stands or falls, for as Paul said in 1 Corinthians 15:14–19: "And if Christ has not been raised, our preaching is useless and so is your faith. More than that, we are then found to be false witnesses about God, for we have testified about God that he raised Christ from the dead. But he did not raise him if in fact the dead are not raised. For if the dead are not raised, then Christ has not been raised either. And if Christ has not been raised, your faith is futile; you are still in your sins. Then those also who have fallen asleep in Christ are lost. If only for this life we have hope in Christ, we are to be pitied more than all men."

**Repartee: Did Jesus Ever Use Wit and Wisdom to Silence His Enemies?**—Jesus had many enemies who would eventually kill him. Before the cross, though, these enemies often plotted to catch him in a theological trap. They thought if they could only get him to contradict a great teaching of Moses' Law or one of the prophets, the people would turn against him.

On one occasion, a woman was caught in the act of adultery (see John 8:1–11). The Pharisees, the ultra-religious people of Jesus' day, brought the woman to Jesus and cast her at his feet. They then said that the law of Moses required stoning (capital punishment by hurling large stones at the victim) of such people. "What do you command?" they demanded of Jesus.

The trap was subtle. If Jesus said to let her go, he would be denying Moses' Law, which commanded the people to stone such women. But if he ordered them to stone her, the Romans would take him to prison, because only they could carry out capital punishment.

What could Jesus do? Either way he answered, he was sure to suffer reproach.

Some in the crowd must have stood there in hard-eyed silence as they anticipated Jesus' demise. Others, though, agonized, not wanting their hero and leader to be shamed.

But that's where Jesus pulls out an incredible line that both saves the woman and the truth of the all-powerful law: "Let him who is without sin cast the first stone."

Some must have tightened their grip on their stones as they gleefully prepared to throw them. But Jesus leaned down and wrote in the dust. No one knows what he wrote, but perhaps it was a word like, "Thief," or "Liar," or "Coveter." And after scripting each word, Jesus probably looked up and fixed the very person guilty of such sins with his all-knowing eyes. One by one, the people dropped their stones, and soon no one remained to stone the woman. Jesus had upheld Moses' Law and avoided Roman imprisonment with a single wise word. Then he completed the story by telling the woman, "I don't condemn you either; go and sin no more." He had shown in one deft word that God was both just and compassionate, holy and gracious at the same time.

**Resurrection: People Didn't Always Recognize Jesus After the Resurrection**—After Jesus rose from the dead, it appears that on several occasions his disciples didn't recognize him immediately. For instance, consider the following situations:

1. Jesus appeared to Mary Magdalene in the Garden of the Tomb. She thought he was the gardener, according to John 20:11–18:

> Mary stood outside the tomb crying. As she wept, she bent over to look into the tomb and saw two angels in white, seated where Jesus' body had been, one at the head and the other at the foot.
> They asked her, "Woman, why are you crying?"
> "They have taken my Lord away," she said, "and I don't know where they have put him." At this, she turned around and saw Jesus standing there, but she did not realize that it was Jesus.
> "Woman," he said, "why are you crying? Who is it you are looking for?"

Thinking he was the gardener, she said, "Sir, if you have
carried him away, tell me where you have put him, and
I will get him."

Jesus said to her, "Mary."

She turned toward him and cried out in Aramaic, "Rab-
boni!" (which means Teacher).

Jesus said, "Do not hold on to me, for I have not yet
returned to the Father. Go instead to my brothers and
tell them, 'I am returning to my Father and your
Father, to my God and your God.'"

Mary of Magdala went to the disciples with the news: "I
have seen the Lord!" And she told them that he had
said these things to her.

2. Jesus appears to two disciples walking along the road to Emmaus
and walks with them, according to Luke 24:13–16:

Now that same day two of them were going to a village
called Emmaus, about seven miles from Jerusalem.
They were talking with each other about everything
that had happened. As they talked and discussed these
things with each other, Jesus himself came up and
walked along with them; but they were kept from rec-
ognizing him.

3. When the disciples went fishing, Jesus appeared on the beach to
ask them questions about their luck the night before (John 21:1–7):

Afterward Jesus appeared again to his disciples, by the Sea
of Tiberias. It happened this way: Simon Peter,
Thomas (called Didymus), Nathaniel from Cana in
Galilee, the sons of Zebedee, and two other disciples
were together. "I'm going out to fish," Simon Peter
told them, and they said, "We'll go with you." So they
went out and got into the boat, but that night they
caught nothing. Early in the morning, Jesus stood on
the shore, but the disciples did not realize that it was
Jesus. He called out to them, "Friends, haven't you any
fish?" "No," they answered. He said, "Throw your net
on the right side of the boat and you will find some."
When they did, they were unable to haul the net in
because of the large number of fish. Then the disciple
whom Jesus loved said to Peter, "It is the Lord!" As
soon as Simon Peter heard him say, "It is the Lord," he

> wrapped his outer garment around him (for he had
> taken it off) and jumped into the water.

Skeptics might suggest that this person who appeared to the disciples was not really Jesus, but another person he'd arranged with before his death to put on a hoax. The argument fails, though, in that the disciples repeatedly didn't expect Jesus to rise from the dead, even though he'd told them he would. Also, all of them were rather skeptical; if he did look different after his resurrection, being glorified and in his eternal body, they quickly recognized the personality behind the new guise.

**Resurrection: What Is the Evidence for It?**—How do we know Jesus truly rose? The Bible tells the story. After his crucifixion, Jesus was laid in Joseph of Arimathea's stone tomb. He remained there from Friday night to Sunday morning. Roman guards watched the tomb the whole time because the Jews who had demanded Jesus' death wanted to make sure his body wasn't stolen. They feared that a "resurrection myth," which Jesus talked about to his followers, would be spread abroad and an even worse situation would result. The Romans placed a government seal on the tomb, which warned anyone who might molest the remains that all of Rome was against them. Finally, the authorities rolled a huge stone over the hole to keep the body safe.

Meanwhile, Jesus' disciples had all fled. None of them believed that Jesus would rise from the dead, even though he'd told them over and over he would. They were cowards and had no desire to fight off a Roman guard and steal the body, no matter how much they revered their leader.

But that didn't deter God the Father from raising Jesus. An angel rolled away the stone, scaring the Roman guards out of their wits and sending them in a panic to the Jews who hired them. When several women and then several of Jesus' disciples arrived at the tomb, they found it empty, the grave clothes lying on the stone slab as if a body had simply "passed through" them.

Jesus appeared to his followers over the next forty days. At one point, he appeared to over five hundred believers at once. He ate with his disciples. He allowed them to touch him. He seemed able to pass through the walls of buildings, yet he was as real as the walls he passed through. He was a vision of health, though he bore the scars of the crucifixion. And he so convinced his followers that he had conquered death that they went out and changed the world as a result.

Some say this was a hoax. The book *The Passover Plot*, a best-seller in the late 1960s by Hugh Schonfield, put forward the theory that Jesus planned the crucifixion with his disciples, weaving an uncanny plot never discovered until Schonfield figured it out. Anyone who reads the book, however, finds holes in the theory everywhere. Everything hinges on Jesus' being a fraud from the start, and that itself is preposterous.

Other theories suggest that the disciples went to the wrong tomb or that they "hallucinated" Jesus' appearances because of their great zeal. Another says Jesus "swooned" on the cross and didn't die, but revived later and escaped from the tomb, gathering his disciples and showing them he'd conquered death.

But none of these answers the basic questions:

1. How did Jesus, after enduring torture and massive bodily harm, convince his followers he was the Lord of life? He would have been a sick man for a long time afterward if he did "swoon" or "plot" his way into a counterfeit resurrection. Yet the narrative shows he appeared to them robust and healthy—glorified, in fact—less than forty-eight hours after dying a horrible, agonizing, and physically disabling death.

2. What changed Jesus' disciples? Every one of them ran the night of Jesus' trial. None of them expected to see Jesus alive, in any form. They were losers before the resurrection; afterward, they became lions. If Jesus "faked" his resurrection, how did he convince these men, all of them skeptics and cowards, to go out, face persecution and death, and proclaim a hoax they knew was a hoax?

3. If Jesus didn't rise from the dead, what is Christianity left with? What do Christians proclaim, besides a nice set of ideals few people can keep? The cornerstone of Christianity is the resurrection. If Jesus stayed dead, we are fools, for we have believed a lie worse than death itself.

The great news Christianity announces is: Jesus lived a perfect life, died on the cross for our sins, and was raised from the dead. The resurrection proved three things: Jesus was God; he had conquered death; and the Father had accepted his sacrifice. Without the resurrection, Christianity is nothing more than another set of principles and laws most people ignore.

The resurrection ultimately explains everything:

> Why the Bible seems to have resident "divine" power.
>
> Why the disciples changed from cowards to courageous men of faith.
>
> Why the gospel is so compelling to many people.
>
> Why Christianity has so affected the world.
>
> How people today can "experience" Jesus as a friend and person.
>
> Why Christians have the hope of life after death.

If Jesus did not rise from the dead, then to follow Christ has no point. If Jesus did rise from the dead, to ignore him invites God's displeasure and possible rejection.

**Resurrection Appearances**—Jesus appeared to his followers twelve recorded times after his crucifixion. They are as follows:

1. To Mary Magdalene—John 20:11–18.
2. To the other women—Matthew 28:9–10.
3. To the soldiers who saw the stone rolled away (it is not clear what they saw, so this one is speculative)—Matthew 28:11–15.
4. To Peter—Luke 24:34, 1 Corinthians 15:5.
5. To two disciples traveling to Emmaus—Luke 24:13–32.
6. To ten assembled disciples—Luke 24:36–43; John 20:19–25; 1 Corinthians 15:5.
7. To the eleven assembled disciples—John 20:26–31; 1 Corinthians 15:5.
8. To seven disciples while fishing—John 21:1–25.
9. To the eleven disciples in Galilee—Matthew 28:16–20; 1 Corinthians 15:6.
10. To James, Jesus' half-brother—Luke 24:44–49; 1 Corinthians 15:7.
11. To the disciples in Jerusalem—Luke 24:44–49; Acts 1:3–8.
12. At his ascension—Luke 24:50–53; Acts 1:9–12.

**Resurrection Body: What Was Jesus' Body Like?**—From the story of Jesus' resurrection, many theories have abounded about what his body was like. Several thoughts from scripture help:

1. The disciples perceived that it was a real body. *John 20:19–20:* "On the evening of that first day of the week, when the disciples were together, with the doors locked for fear of the Jews, Jesus came and stood among them and said, 'Peace be with you!' After he said this, he showed them his hands and side. The disciples were overjoyed when they saw the Lord."

2. His body was the same as the one laid in the tomb. *John 20:25–29:* "When the other disciples told [Thomas] that they had seen the Lord, he declared, 'Unless I see the nail marks in his hands and put my finger where the nails were, and put my hand into his side, I will not believe it.' A week later his disciples were in the house again, and Thomas was with them. Though the doors were locked, Jesus came and stood among them and said, 'Peace be with you!' Then he said to Thomas, 'Put your finger here; see my hands. Reach out your hand and put it

into my side. Stop doubting and believe.' Thomas said to him, 'My Lord and my God!' Then Jesus told him, 'Because you have seen me, you have believed; blessed are those who have not seen and yet have believed.'"

3. Jesus did a number of normal things with his body: he ate some fish (Luke 24:42–43); he allowed himself to be seen and touched (Luke 24:39); he spoke to the disciples and walked with them (Luke 24:13–31); he broke bread (24:30); he wore clothing (Luke 24:15); he made a fire and lunch (John 21:9–10).

4. Jesus performed several supernatural things with his body as well: he appeared seemingly out of nowhere in certain places and rooms (John 20:26); he caused a miraculous catch of fish for the disciples (John 21:4–6); he rose bodily before the disciples into heaven (Acts 1:9); he apparently did many other signs that were not written down (John 20:30–31).

There was also one strange detail about Jesus' body revealed through his resurrection appearances: He wasn't always recognized. For more details on this, see the entry "Resurrection: People Didn't Always Recognize Jesus After the Resurrection."

A more specific picture of the supernatural, eternal body is provided by Paul in 1 Corinthians 15:40–44:

> There are also heavenly bodies and there are earthly bod-
> ies; but the splendor of the heavenly bodies is one kind,
> and the splendor of the earthly bodies is another. The
> sun has one kind of splendor, the moon another and
> the stars another; and star differs from star in splendor.
> So will it be with the resurrection of the dead. The body
> that is sown is perishable, it is raised imperishable; it is
> sown in dishonor, it is raised in glory; it is sown in
> weakness, it is raised in power; it is sown a natural
> body, it is raised a spiritual body.
> If there is a natural body, there is also a spiritual body.

This passage reveals six elements of a resurrected body, which is what Jesus' body was like at the time of his appearances:

1. It is heavenly—suited for the climate and environment of heaven;
2. It is splendorous—marvelously capable of doing all that is necessary in the heavenly realm;
3. It is imperishable—unable to decay;
4. It is glorious—incredibly powerful, beautiful, and perfect;

5. It is powerful—imbued with special abilities out of this world;
6. It is spiritual—perfectly conveying the true thoughts and expression of the inner spirit.

Though these details are somewhat sketchy, they are certainly motivating for any of us down here on the planet who are overweight, overwrought, and overwhelmed!

**Resurrection of Jesus: The Disciples Stole the Body!**—When the leaders of the Jews learned that Jesus had been resurrected, they came up with the claim that the disciples stole his body, according to Matthew 28:11–15:

> While the women were on their way, some of the guards went into the city and reported to the chief priests everything that had happened. When the chief priests had met with the elders and devised a plan, they gave the soldiers a large sum of money, telling them, "You are to say, 'His disciples came during the night and stole him away while we were asleep.' If this report gets to the governor, we will satisfy him and keep you out of trouble." So the soldiers took the money and did as they were instructed. And this story has been widely circulated among the Jews to this very day.

This theory continues today, although it has serious problems:

1. If the body had been stolen, an investigation would probably have recovered it. No investigation was ever done.

2. The disciples didn't expect Jesus to rise. All abandoned him. Why would they have perpetrated a plot they didn't even believe in?

3. The tomb was guarded by armed soldiers, trained in war and fighting. If the disciples deserted Jesus when he was on trial, how would they have mustered the courage to face Roman soldiers, move the stone and recover the body, then dispose of it and pass on a tale of resurrection?

4. The Pharisees put a seal on the stone and made the tomb secure, according to Matthew 27:62–66, anticipating that a theft might occur. They were well prepared to stop such a thing, and the disciples didn't have the numbers or the power to pull off a theft.

5. Every one of the disciples and many others, if they made up the story of Christ's resurrection, died for that story. At no time in history have serious numbers of people willingly died to perpetrate a lie when they knew it was a lie.

6. If the body was stolen, the disciples not only did that crime, but

also made up all the resurrection stories, acts that would greatly have militated against their beliefs. The Ten Commandments, the most revered part of the Mosaic Law, forbade such falsehood, saying, "You shall not bear false witness."

The conclusion is that it would be more difficult to believe that the disciples perpetrated this hoax than that Christ actually did rise from the dead.

**Resuscitation: Always Aware of a Need**—Jesus not only resuscitated people from the dead; he also took steps to minister to their physical needs after the resuscitation. After raising Jairus's daughter from the dead, while everyone looked on astonished, Jesus told them to give her something to eat, according to Mark 5:38–43:

> When they came to the home of the synagogue ruler, Jesus saw a commotion, with people crying and wailing loudly. He went in and said to them, "Why all this commotion and wailing? The child is not dead but asleep." But they laughed at him.
> After he put them all out, he took the child's father and mother and the disciples who were with him, and went in where the child was. He took her by the hand and said to her, "*Talitha kom!*" (which means, "Little girl, I say to you, get up!"). Immediately the girl stood up and walked around (she was twelve years old). At this they were completely astonished. He gave strict orders not to let anyone know about this, and told them to give her something to eat.

When Lazarus was raised from the dead, after being in the tomb for four days, Jesus had to tell people what to do when Lazarus came out: "When he had said this, Jesus called in a loud voice, 'Lazarus, come out!' The dead man came out, his hands and feet wrapped with strips of linen, and a cloth around his face. Jesus said to them, 'Take off the grave clothes and let him go'" (John 11:43–44).

**Resuscitations: Whom Did Jesus Raise from the Dead?**—Jesus "resuscitated"(not "resurrected") three people in the Gospels. These were resuscitations because the people later lived normal lives; they did not receive "glorified" spiritual bodies, and they did not live eternally, but died normal deaths. Christ's resurrection was not a resuscitation, because his new body was eternal, glorified, and spiritually attuned. It

was a resurrection, from the Latin *resurrectio*, "to rise from the dead."
The three resuscitations are:

1. Jairus's daughter—Mark 5:21–43.
2. The widow of Nain's son—Luke 7:11–18.
3. Lazarus—John 11:38–44.

**Resuscitations: People Raised When Jesus Died**—When Jesus died
on the cross, strange events occurred in the Temple and in the tombs.
Matthew 27:50–53 records:

> And when Jesus had cried out again in a loud voice, he
> gave up his spirit.
> At that moment the curtain of the temple was torn in two
> from top to bottom. The earth shook and the rocks
> split. The tombs broke open and the bodies of many
> holy people who had died were raised to life. They
> came out of the tombs, and after Jesus' resurrection they
> went into the holy city and appeared to many people.

Believers in Jesus who had died suddenly appeared alive after Jesus'
crucifixion. The veil of the Temple, made of thick fabric that could not
be torn easily, was "rent in two." This signified the fact that God had
opened up the holiest place of the Temple where the ark resided, and
God's presence remained to all seekers and comers. No one was barred
from coming into intimacy with God from that time on.

The resuscitations that apparently occurred are mentioned only by
Matthew. It's possible they did not remain long on earth, were given
glorified bodies, and ascended to heaven, much like the Rapture that
Paul mentions will precede the actual coming of Christ (see 1 Thess.
4:13–18). However, little to nothing more is known about this event.

**Return of Christ: What It Will Look Like**—How will Jesus return?
Two passages offer fairly detailed pictures of how it will happen. Jesus
told his disciples in Matthew 24:24–31:

> "For false Christs and false prophets will appear and per-
> form great signs and miracles to deceive even the
> elect—if that were possible. See, I have told you ahead
> of time.
> "So if anyone tells you, 'There he is, out in the desert,' do
> not go out; or, 'Here he is, in the inner rooms,' do not

believe it. For as the lightning comes from the east and flashes to the west, so will be the coming of the Son of Man. Wherever there is a carcass, there the vultures will gather.

"Immediately after the distress of those days 'the sun will be darkened, and the moon will not give its light; the stars will fall from the sky, and the heavenly bodies will be shaken.'

"At that time the sign of the Son of Man will appear in the sky, and all the nations of the earth will mourn. They will see the Son of Man coming on the clouds of the sky, with power and great glory. And he will send his angels with a loud trumpet call, and they will gather his elect from the four winds, from one end of the heavens to the other."

Revelation 19:11–21 pictures this scene even more graphically:

I saw heaven standing open and there before me was a white horse, whose rider is called Faithful and True. With justice he judges and makes war. His eyes are like blazing fire, and on his head are many crowns. He has a name written on him that no one but he himself knows. He is dressed in a robe dipped in blood, and his name is the Word of God. The armies of heaven were following him, riding on white horses and dressed in fine linen, white and clean. Out of his mouth comes a sharp sword with which to strike down the nations. "He will rule them with an iron scepter." He treads the wine-press of the fury of the wrath of God Almighty. On his robe and on his thigh he has this name written: KING OF KINGS AND LORD OF LORDS.

And I saw an angel standing in the sun, who cried in a loud voice to all the birds flying in midair, "Come, gather together for the great supper of God, so that you may eat the flesh of kings, generals, and mighty men, of horses and their riders, and the flesh of all people, free and slave, small and great."

Then I saw the beast and the kings of the earth and their armies gathered together to make war against the rider on the horse and his army. But the beast was captured, and with him the false prophet who had performed the miraculous signs on his behalf. With these signs he had deluded those who had received the mark of the beast and worshiped his image. The two of them were thrown alive into the fiery lake of burning sulphur. The rest of them were killed with the sword that came out of the mouth of the rider on the horse, and all the birds gorged themselves on their flesh.

**Revolutionary**—One of Jesus' disciples, Simon the Zealot, was a member of a terrorist group, the Zealots, who were bent on the over-throw of Rome. Perhaps Jesus selected Simon not only for his faith, but because of his familiarity with politics, to round out the crew he'd selected, which included fishermen (James, John, Peter, Andrew), a mystic (Nathanael), a skeptic (Thomas), a tax collector (Matthew), an accountant (Philip), and others about whom we know little to nothing. Beyond the immediate Twelve, you also find leading women (Salome, Mary the mother of Clopas), a sinner (Mary Magdalene), family mem-bers (the Virgin Mary), Pharisees (Joseph of Arimathea and Nicode-mus), Greeks and Romans, many people whom Jesus healed and cast demons out of, and over five hundred others whom Paul mentions in 1 Corinthians 15:5–7. Presumably, hundreds if not thousands of others were on the fringes, as indicated by the feeding of the five thousand and the feeding of the four thousand.

**Rich and Poor: Jesus Had Some Strong Opinions About Money and Rich People**—Though Jesus is sometimes criticized for saying, "The poor you always have with you"(see Mark 14:7, NASB: "For the poor you always have with you, and whenever you wish, you can do them good; but you do not always have Me"), this was said in the con-text of a faithful woman anointing his head and feet with an expensive perfume. Jesus saw this as a "good deed" done to him, not as a slam on the poor. Jesus himself had no money or even a place to call home, so he was well-acquainted with what it meant to be poor.

Jesus did have some "hard things" to say about rich people, however, that might give one pause about the value of wealth. In the parable of the rich fool, Jesus pictured a rich farmer who was so wealthy, he had to build bigger barns for all his crops. This is the parable Jesus told in Luke 12:16–21 (NASB):

> "The land of a certain rich man was very productive. And he began reasoning to himself, saying, 'What shall I do, since I have no place to store my crops?'
> "And he said, 'This is what I will do: I will tear down my

barns and build larger ones, and there I will store all
my grain and my goods. And I will say to my soul,
"Soul, you have many goods laid up for many years *to
come*; take your ease, eat, drink *and* be merry."'

"But God said to him, 'You fool! This *very* night your soul
is required of you; and *now* who will own what you
have prepared?'

"So is the man who lays up treasure for himself, and is not
rich toward God."

Jesus' point here is not that it's bad to be wealthy or even to plan
well how to use your wealth, but that a life that excludes consideration
of God and his purposes ends badly.

In another parable, Jesus pictured a poor man named Lazarus and a
rich man at whose door Lazarus used to beg. The parable is found in
Luke 16:19–31 (NASB):

"Now there was a certain rich man, and he habitually
dressed in purple and fine linen, gaily living in splendor
every day. And a certain poor man named Lazarus was
laid at his gate, covered with sores, and longing to be
fed with the *crumbs* which were falling from the rich
man's table; besides, even the dogs were coming and
licking his sores.

"Now it came about that the poor man died and he was
carried away by the angels to Abraham's bosom; and the
rich man also died and was buried. And in Hades he
lifted up his eyes, being in torment, and saw Abraham
far away, and Lazarus in his bosom. And he cried out
and said, 'Father Abraham, have mercy on me, and send
Lazarus, that he may dip the tip of his finger in water
and cool off my tongue; for I am in agony in this flame.'

"But Abraham said, 'Child, remember that during your life
you received your good things, and likewise Lazarus
bad things; but now he is being comforted here, and
you are in agony. And besides all this, between us and
you there is a great chasm fixed, in order that those
who wish to come over from here to you will not be
able, and *that* none may cross over from there to us.'

"And he said, 'Then I beg you, Father, that you send him to
my father's house—for I have five brothers—that he may
warn them, lest they also come to this place of torment.'

"But Abraham said, 'They have Moses and the Prophets;
let them hear them.'

> "But he said, 'No, Father Abraham, but if someone goes
> to them from the dead, they will repent!'
> "But he said to him, 'If they do not listen to Moses and
> the Prophets, neither will they be persuaded if someone
> rises from the dead.'"

Again, Jesus' point was not that it was wrong or sinful to be rich, but that rich people sometimes see no reason to honor God in their lives. Such people, Jesus shows from the parable, will not believe or accept the truth about God and God's creation until it's too late.

Perhaps Jesus' most scathing criticism of the rich occurred when a rich young man came to him with a question. He probably served in the synagogue as an elder or teacher. He possessed all the qualities that in the modern world would make him a true "mover and shaker": wealth, youth, and power. Nonetheless, this is the exchange that takes place between him and Jesus in Matthew 19:16–26 (NASB):

> And behold, one came to Him and said, "Teacher, what
> good thing shall I do that I may obtain eternal life?"
> And He said to him, "Why are you asking Me about what
> is good? There is *only* One who is good; but if you wish
> to enter into life, keep the commandments."
> He said to Him, "Which ones?"
> And Jesus said, "You shall not commit murder; you shall
> not commit adultery; you shall not steal; you shall not
> bear false witness; honor your father and mother; and
> you shall love your neighbor as yourself."
> The young man said to Him, "All these things I have kept;
> what am I still lacking?"
> Jesus said to him, "If you wish to be complete, go *and* sell
> your possessions and give to *the* poor, and you shall
> have treasure in heaven; and come, follow Me."
> But when the young man heard this statement, he went
> away grieved; for he was one who owned much property.
> And Jesus said to His disciples, "Truly I say to you, it is
> hard for a rich man to enter the kingdom of heaven.
> And again I say to you, it is easier for a camel to go
> through the eye of a needle, than for a rich man to
> enter the kingdom of God."
> And when the disciples heard *this*, they were very aston-
> ished and said, "Then who can be saved?"
> And looking upon *them* Jesus said to them, "With men
> this is impossible, but with God all things are possible."

From this story, we can see that Jesus bore no anger or hatred for this rich young man because he was rich or young. He wanted to inherit eternal life, and so far he had not discovered the way to do it. Jesus did not spell out the details of the gospel for him—believe and you shall be saved—but he told him to "follow me," which was the essence of the gospel. In order to see whether the man would follow him, Jesus gave him a little test that involved a specific act of obedience in following him. He told the young man to sell everything he had and to give it to the poor. It is not that this was a requirement for salvation, but scholars believe that Jesus had given him a step to take. Now Jesus would see whether this man would obey it. When the man refused, his real motives were exposed. He didn't want to obey Jesus on this one point because he apparently wasn't willing to give up his wealth. Some suggest that if this man had said to Jesus, "I will do it," Jesus might have said, "Because you are willing, you have inherited eternal life." However, that is an inference from ways that Jesus dealt with others, rather than what Jesus might have done in this case.

In any event, Jesus explains the problem with having riches; having riches makes it difficult for the person to enter God's kingdom. Why? Because the rich person thinks trusting in his riches is better than trusting God. The former makes eternal life impossible.

In the end, though, Jesus makes clear to the disciples that God can reclaim even rich men, for what is impossible with man is possible with God.

The following proverb gives insight into Jesus' possible thinking in this situation: "Two things I ask of you, O LORD; do not refuse me before I die: Keep falsehood and lies far from me; give me neither poverty nor riches, but give me only my daily bread. Otherwise, I may have too much and disown you and say, 'Who is the LORD?' Or I may become poor and steal, and so dishonor the name of my God" (Prov. 30:7–9).

**Riches: Jesus Promised Great Riches to Those Who Followed Him**—To the religious leaders of Jesus' day, riches were the final and ultimate sign of God's blessing. Jesus himself promised great riches to those who would follow him. He said in Matthew 19:23–30:

> Then Jesus said to his disciples, "I tell you the truth, it is hard for a rich man to enter the kingdom of heaven. Again I tell you, it is easier for a camel to go through the eye of a needle than for a rich man to enter the kingdom of God."

> When the disciples heard this, they were greatly aston-
> ished and asked, "Who then can be saved?"
> Jesus looked at them and said, "With man this is impossi-
> ble, but with God all things are possible."
> Peter answered him, "We have left everything to follow
> you! What then will there be for us?"
> Jesus said to them, "I tell you the truth, at the renewal of
> all things, when the Son of Man sits on his glorious
> throne, you who have followed me will also sit on
> twelve thrones, judging the twelve tribes of Israel. And
> everyone who has left houses or brothers or sisters or
> father or mother or children or fields for my sake will
> receive a hundred times as much and will inherit eter-
> nal life. But many who are first will be last, and many
> who are last will be first."

As always, Jesus holds out a carrot, then in a certain sense takes
it back. It is an essential principle of his kingdom: His kingdom is
not of this world; therefore, all that comes with his kingdom is given
in the next world, not this one. The one who accepts this truth by
faith will inherit much wealth ultimately. This, of course, was a teaching with great appeal to the poor and the many slaves in the
Roman Empire at the time of Jesus' life and teaching. Thus it is that
the majority of Christians the world over have been people with
little wealth, power, and prestige. They dedicate their lives to serve
Christ in this world with the hope that the next will prove much more
hospitable.

**Robe**—Lloyd Douglas's novel *The Robe* was a best-seller in its day and
became a classic movie starring Richard Burton. It details the path
Jesus' "seamless" cloak took after the Romans gambled for it at his crucifixion. Marcellus, a Roman centurion, touches the robe that Christ
wore and temporarily loses his mind. Later, he resolves his crisis by
coming to believe in the Christ as the Son of God, and he goes to Israel
to learn more about him. He is greatly troubled by the fact that he was
the one who crucified the Son of God. But when he meets Peter, who
tells Marcellus his own story of sin—denying he even knew Jesus on the
night Jesus was betrayed—Marcellus comes to understand the great
forgiveness there is in Christ. He goes home to Rome a new man and,
in fact, a believer in Christ as the Messiah.

**Robin's Red Breast**—A legend tells the story of a small brown bird
who lived in the stable where Jesus was born. As the robin watched the

events unfold and the birth of the Christ child, it suddenly saw that Joseph, in his concern for his wife and child, had almost let the fire go out, the same fire that kept the Christ child warm. The robin flew down from the rafters and fanned the flames with its wings until they stoked and warmed. As the flames reached even higher, the robin's breast was suddenly turned a bright red as a gift of God. Its breast would remind all who ever looked upon it that God had blessed it even as it had blessed God's son.

This is only a legend, but in it we find a truth: Those who honor the Son of God will be honored by the Son's Father.

**Rules: Jesus Often Went Out of His Way to Break the Rules—** There is a vast difference between God's laws and Man's rules. One of Jesus' greatest conflicts was with the Pharisees over the multitude of rules that they used to make themselves right with God. On several occasions, Jesus specifically broke their rules in order to show that he obeyed a higher law, God's law. Consider the following instances.

In John 4, we see Jesus talking with a Samaritan woman who had been married five times and was now living with a sixth man. The Pharisees had strong rules about associating with unbelievers, women, and prostitutes—they were out of bounds. Thus, Jesus broke three rules when he had a conversation with this woman and befriended her.

On a second occasion, Jesus allowed his disciples to pick and eat some grain while traveling. This was illegal on the Sabbath, according to the Pharisees. This exchange takes place in Matthew 12:1–8:

> At that time Jesus went through the cornfields on the Sab-
> bath. His disciples were hungry and began to pick some
> heads of grain and eat them. When the Pharisees saw
> this, they said to him, "Look! Your disciples are doing
> what is unlawful on the Sabbath."
> He answered, "Haven't you read what David did when he
> and his companions were hungry? He entered the
> house of God, and he and his companions ate the con-
> secrated bread—which was not lawful for them to do,
> but only for the priests. Or haven't you read in the Law
> that on the Sabbath the priests in the temple desecrate
> the day and yet are innocent? I tell you that one greater
> than the temple is here. If you had known what these
> words mean, 'I desire mercy, not sacrifice,' you would
> not have condemned the innocent. For the Son of Man
> is Lord of the Sabbath."

On one level, Jesus was deliberately confronting the Pharisees about their harsh Sabbath rules that kept people from meeting basic needs on the Sabbath. On another level, he was demonstrating to them how they ignore God's laws in order to keep their own rules. In this case, God called for "mercy, not sacrifice," from Hosea 6:6: "For I desire mercy, not sacrifice, and acknowledgment of God rather than burnt offerings." The Pharisees frequently set aside God's laws in favor of their own rules. In Matthew 12:9–14 we read:

> Going on from that place, he went into their synagogue, and a man with a shriveled hand was there. Looking for a reason to accuse Jesus, they asked him, "Is it lawful to heal on the Sabbath?"
>
> He said to them, "If any of you has a sheep and it falls into a pit on the Sabbath, will you not take hold of it and lift it out? How much more valuable is a man than a sheep! Therefore it is lawful to do good on the Sabbath."
>
> Then he said to the man, "Stretch out your hand." So he stretched it out and it was completely restored, just as sound as the other. But the Pharisees went out and plotted how they might kill Jesus.

Jesus' whole approach to Pharisaical rules is summed up in Matthew 23:2–12, where he says:

> "The teachers of the law and the Pharisees sit in Moses' seat. So you must obey them and do everything they tell you. But do not do what they do, for they do not practice what they preach. They tie up heavy loads and put them on men's shoulders, but they themselves are not willing to lift a finger to move them.
>
> "Everything they do is done for men to see: They make their phylacteries wide and the tassels of their prayer shawls long; they love the place of honor at banquets and the most important seats in the synagogues; they love to be greeted in the marketplaces and to have men call them 'Rabbi.'
>
> "But you are not to be called 'Rabbi,' for you have only one Master and you are all brothers. And do not call anyone on earth 'father,' for you have one Father, and he is in heaven. Nor are you to be called 'teacher,' for you have one Teacher, the Christ. The greatest among you will be your servant. For whoever exalts himself

will be humbled, and whoever humbles himself will be exalted."

Perhaps the greatest affront Jesus saw from the Pharisees was the fact that they often gave great sums of money to the Temple while ignoring the needs of their own family. Thus, he says in Mark 7:6–13:

> He replied, "Isaiah was right when he prophesied about you hypocrites; as it is written: 'These people honor me with their lips, but their hearts are far from me. They worship me in vain; their teachings are but rules taught by men.' You have let go of the commands of God and are holding on to the traditions of men."
> And he said to them: "You have a fine way of setting aside the commands of God in order to observe your own traditions! For Moses said, 'Honor your father and mother,' and, 'Anyone who curses his father or mother must be put to death.' But you say that if a man says to his father or mother: 'Whatever help you might otherwise have received from me is Corban' (that is, a gift devoted to God), then you no longer let him do anything for his father or mother. Thus you nullify the word of God by your tradition that you have handed down. And you do many things like that."

This became the primary point of contention between Jesus and the Pharisees, which ultimately led to their conspiring to put him to death. Jesus confronted and rejected their whole way of life, which was based on a system of rules he said was made up by men, not given to them by God. This kind of teaching is today called "legalism." It means keeping certain rules in order to gain eternal life, rather than living by faith in Christ and his truth.

**Rules: Winning Friends and Influencing People**—Dale Carnegie, the master of friendship and influence, took his lead from the greats, including Jesus. He said, "The ideas I stand for are not mine. I borrowed them from Socrates. I swiped them from Chesterfield. I stole them from Jesus. And I put them in a book. If you don't like their rules, whose would you use?"

**Sacred Heart of Jesus**—Marguerite Marie Alacoque (1647–1690) had a vision of the heart of Jesus burning with love for humankind. She was led from there to establish the "Holy Hour" of Communion every Friday, plus the feast of the Sacred Heart on the Friday after the feast of Corpus Christi.

**St. Francis's Way**—St. Francis of Assisi (Italy) was gradually converted from the life of the rich son of a merchant to a life of poverty and preaching the gospel. At first, during prayer, he received a vision of the crucified Christ beckoning him to "take up his cross and follow him." Francis interpreted this at first to mean repairing several churches in his hometown. Later, on February 24, 1209, he received a "word" from Jesus telling him to preach the gospel, taking no gold or silver or copper with him as support. He collected a band of friars who eventually took their preaching throughout the whole world as "Franciscan Friars." They established the Franciscan prayer, "Lord, make me an instrument of your peace."

**St. Patrick: Christ for Every Season**—On his breastplate, St. Patrick wrote and wore a prayer that said this:

> Christ to protect me today
> > against poison, against burning,
> > against drowning, against wounding,
> > so that there may come abundance of reward.
> Christ with me, Christ before me, Christ behind me,
> Christ in me, Christ beneath me, Christ above me,
> Christ on my right, Christ on my left,
> Christ where I lie, Christ where I sit, Christ where I arise,
> Christ in the heart of every man who thinks of me,
> Christ in the mouth of every man who speaks of me,
> Christ to every eye that sees me,
> Christ in every ear that hears me.

**St. Patrick's Time in Ireland**—Captured in Britain at the age of 16 and sold as a slave, Patrick (390–461) was converted during those early years. In time he escaped and returned to Britain, but a vision from God led him to return to Ireland in 431, where he preached and had a strong influence on many of the heathen chieftains who ruled the countryside. Legend says he drove out the snakes, but perhaps he really drove out much of the unbelief, hatred, and sin that makes people into snakes!

**St. Paul's Writhing Christ**—In St. Paul's Cathedral in London is a life-size statue of Jesus writhing in anguish on the cross. The inscription underneath says, "This is how God loved the world!"

**Saints: A Strange Saint**—The thirteenth century Franciscan saint, Margaret of Cortona, sometimes called "the new Magdalene," lived for nine years with her lover. When he died, she had majestic visions that at times rendered her unconscious but still conveyed the "sweetness of Christ." Giovanni Lanfranco commemorates her experiences in "Ecstasy of St. Margaret of Cortona," a magnificent painting done around 1620.

**Salvation: How Much to Pay for It?**—Jesus' parable of the Pearl of great price shows to what lengths a seeker will go to receive salvation. In it he tells this story: "Again, the kingdom of heaven is like a merchant looking for fine pearls. When he found one of great value, he went away and sold everything he had and bought it" (Matt. 13:45–46).

The point of the parable is that when we find what we truly long for, we are willing to pay any price to get it. Salvation, the gift Christ came to offer, comes at the price of full devotion, commitment, and a life dedicated to his kingdom.

**Satan and Jesus: Satan Tried to Get Him Three Times**—There are a number of occasions in which Jesus felt particular pressure from Satan to give in and quit his mission to earth. The first occurs in Matthew 4:1–11, where Jesus is tempted by the devil in the wilderness.

> Then Jesus was led by the Spirit into the desert to be
>    tempted by the devil. After fasting forty days and forty
>    nights, he was hungry. The tempter came to him and
>    said, "If you are the Son of God, tell these stones to
>    become bread."
> Jesus answered, "It is written: 'Man does not live on bread
>    alone, but on every word that comes from the mouth of
>    God.'"
> Then the devil took him to the holy city and had him
>    stand on the highest point of the temple. "If you are
>    the Son of God," he said, "throw yourself down. For it

is written: 'He will command his angels concerning
you, and they will lift you up in their hands, so that you
will not strike your foot against a stone.' "

Jesus answered him, "It is also written: 'Do not put the
Lord your God to the test.' "

Again, the devil took him to a very high mountain and
showed him all the kingdoms of the world and their
splendor. "All this I will give you," he said, "if you will
bow down and worship me."

Jesus said to him, "Away from me, Satan! For it is written:
'Worship the Lord your God, and serve him only.' "

Then the devil left him, and angels came and attended
him.

In this temptation, Satan appears to test Jesus in three areas: (1) whether Jesus would obey the express commands of his Father by fasting and not seeking food until the right time; (2) whether Jesus would not test God to see whether God would really protect and love him if he were to throw himself off the top of the Temple; and (3) whether Jesus would take the easy path to conquest by worshiping Satan in return for becoming master of the whole earth. In all three cases, Jesus chooses obedience over personal satisfaction, trust in God's love over tangible proof of God's love, and commitment to God's plan rather than taking shortcuts, all of which are typical ways in which people are tempted.

**Satire of Jesus**—Lucian of Samosata (A.D. 125–190), a lawyer in Antioch, traveled and lectured throughout Greece. His speeches were rivaled only by those of Aristophanes. They lampooned religious cults, exposed frauds, penetrated mystery cults, and skeptically analyzed all walks of life in his day. Though he was no believer in Christ, he found Christian practices and life to be reverent and even praiseworthy; he accurately detailed their devotions and beliefs in much the same way as did Luke in the Book of Acts.

**Schweitzer Found Jesus a Mirror**—The author of *The Quest of the Historical Jesus* found looking into and studying the life of Christ a profound experience. He wrote, "There is no historical task which so reveals someone's true self as the writing of a *Life of Christ*."

**Science: Originator of Boyle's Law Scared into Believing**—Robert Boyle (1627–1691), English chemist and physicist, became a Christian in 1641 during a violent thunderstorm in Geneva, Switzerland. He believed in two books: the Bible, and science as "God's second book" to the world that showed God's person and power. He believed so fervently that he refused to take certain kinds of oaths or vows that might suppress doubt. Thus, he refused to be ordained or to become president of the Royal Society, which he cofounded. He is considered the Father of Chemistry and in his time was as important to the advance of science as was Isaac Newton, a close friend and fellow believer.

**Second Coming: Will Jesus Come Again?**—Jesus spelled out the details of his second coming in one major passage, Matthew 24:27–31:

> "For as the lightning comes from the east and flashes to the west, so will be the coming of the Son of Man. Wherever there is a carcass, there the vultures will gather.
> "Immediately after the distress of those days 'the sun will be darkened, and the moon will not give its light; the stars will fall from the sky, and the heavenly bodies will be shaken.'
> "At that time the sign of the Son of Man will appear in the sky, and all the nations of the earth will mourn. They will see the Son of Man coming on the clouds of the sky, with power and great glory. And he will send his angels with a loud trumpet call, and they will gather his elect from the four winds, from one end of the heavens to the other."

More details about his coming are provided in several other passages, among them:

*Acts 1:10–11:* "They were looking intently up into the sky as he was going, when suddenly two men dressed in white stood beside them. 'Men of Galilee,' they said, 'why do you stand here looking into the sky? This same Jesus, who has been taken from you into heaven, will come back in the same way you have seen him go into heaven.'"

*Revelation 1:7:* "Look, he is coming with the clouds, and every eye will see him, even those who pierced him; and all the peoples of the earth will mourn because of him. So shall it be! Amen."

*Revelation 19:11–16:* "I saw heaven standing open and there before me was a white horse, whose rider is called Faithful and True. With justice he judges and makes war. His eyes are like blazing fire, and on his head are many crowns. He has a name written on him that no one but he himself knows. He is dressed in a robe dipped in blood, and his name is the Word of God. The armies of heaven were following him, riding on white horses and dressed in fine linen, white and clean. Out of his mouth comes a sharp sword with which to strike down the nations. 'He will rule them with an iron scepter.' He treads the wine-press of the fury of the wrath of God Almighty. On his robe and on his thigh he has this name written: KING OF KINGS AND LORD OF LORDS."

At least these details can be known about the Second Coming of Christ:

1. He will come on a horse with the armies of heaven.
2. Every eye will see him, even those who are dead.
3. As he comes he will gather all his saints together to be with him.
4. He will set up his kingdom and reign forever.

Many people today are asking, Will this happen soon? Jesus himself provided the answer in Matthew 24:32–39:

> "Now learn this lesson from the fig tree: As soon as its twigs get tender and its leaves come out, you know that summer is near. Even so, when you see all these things, you know that it is near, right at the door. I tell you the truth, this generation will certainly not pass away until all these things have happened. Heaven and earth will pass away, but my words will never pass away.
> "No one knows about that day or hour, not even the angels in heaven, nor the Son, but only the Father. As it was in the days of Noah, so it will be at the coming of the Son of Man. For in the days before the flood, people were eating and drinking, marrying and giving in marriage, up to the day Noah entered the ark; and they knew nothing about what would happen until the flood came and took them all away. That is how it will be at the coming of the Son of Man."

Perhaps the best way to finish this entry comes from Jesus' words in Matthew 24:44: "So you also must be ready, because the Son of Man will come at an hour when you do not expect him."

**Sermons in the Gospels**—Jesus gave eight lengthy discourses in scripture, plus many other extended teachings. But the eight are:

**Service and Rewards: How Long You've Served Doesn't Matter**—Jesus' parable of the laborers shows that salvation is for anyone regardless of age or service. In this parable, he pictures people being hired at different stages in the day, but each receives the same wage. This is what Jesus says in Matthew 20:1–16:

> "The kingdom of heaven is like a landowner who went out early in the morning to hire men to work in his vineyard. He agreed to pay them a denarius for the day and sent them into his vineyard.
>
> "About the third hour he went out and saw others standing in the marketplace doing nothing. He told them, 'You also go and work in my vineyard, and I will pay you whatever is right.' So they went.
>
> "He went out again about the sixth hour and the ninth hour and did the same thing. About the eleventh hour he went out and found still others standing around. He asked them, 'Why have you been standing here all day long doing nothing?'
>
> "'Because no one has hired us,' they answered.
>
> "He said to them, 'You also go and work in my vineyard.'
>
> "When evening came, the owner of the vineyard said to his foreman, 'Call the workers and pay them their wages, beginning with the last ones hired and going on to the first.'
>
> "The workers who were hired about the eleventh hour came and each received a denarius. So when those came who were hired first, they expected to receive more. But each one of them also received a denarius. When they received it, they began to grumble against the landowner. 'These men who were hired last worked only one hour,' they said, 'and you have made them equal to us who have borne the burden of the work and the heat of the day.'
>
> "But he answered one of them, 'Friend, I am not being

unfair to you. Didn't you agree to work for a denarius? Take your pay and go. I want to give the man who was hired last the same as I gave you. Don't I have the right to do what I want with my own money? Or are you envious because I am generous?'

"So the last will be first, and the first will be last."

This parable reveals a great truth about the nature of God's gift of salvation in Christ—that all receive the same gift regardless of their station, ability, experience, talents, or deeds. Anyone who believes Christ gains eternal life, an inheritance, God's love and wisdom and kindness, and everything else without any sense of competition with others—Peter, Paul, or anyone!

**Shepherd for All Seasons**—Jesus was called a shepherd in several passages, each one with a qualifier:

*John 10:11:* "'I am the good shepherd. The good shepherd lays down his life for the sheep.'"

*Hebrews 13:20:* "May the God of peace, who through the blood of the eternal covenant brought back from the dead our Lord Jesus, that great Shepherd of the sheep . . ."

*1 Peter 5:4:* "And when the Chief Shepherd appears, you will receive the crown of glory that will never fade away."

These three adjectives—good, great, and chief—reveal three elements of Jesus' "shepherdness." *Good:* He is righteous and a worthy sacrifice for sins. *Great:* He is majestic and worthy of worship. *Chief:* He is the first and foremost, deserving our loyalty, obedience, and love.

**Shroud of Turin**—The Shroud of Turin purports to be Jesus' burial shroud. Though many scientists have examined it, none have been able to explain the origin of the amazing likeness on the shroud as well as the astonishing marks of the hands, feet, sides, and back, where Jesus was nailed to the cross and brutalized before his execution. Some claim it's a fraud, but none have come up with a plausible explanation.

The problems to solve are these:

1. How did the likeness get onto the shroud? Was it imprinted there by some kind of supernatural electricity or something else?

2. Normally a burial shroud would have been wrapped many times around a dead body rather than laid over it (as the shroud appears to be). How does that square with the apparent idea in scripture that Jesus was "wrapped" in burial clothing?

3. In John 20:6–7, the burial shroud is referred to as strips of linen

rather than a single sheet. Also, the part of the sheet that covered the head was folded up and separate: "Then Simon Peter, who was behind him, arrived and went into the tomb. He saw the strips of linen lying there, as well as the burial cloth that had been around Jesus' head" (John 20:6–7).

4. The Shroud of Turin was discovered in 1354 in the hands of a knight named Geoffroi de Charnay, seigneur de Lirey. It first went on exposition in 1389 and is now preserved in the Cathedral of San Giovanni Battista in Turin, Italy, since 1578. The question for historians is, Why wasn't it known of before 1354, and how did the knight gain possession of it? The answers to these questions are not known.

5. Scientific tests of the age, material, and cause of the image on the shroud have proved inconclusive.

Ultimately, it is a matter of faith whether one believes that this is actually the image of Christ, but it has little to do with proof of his resurrection or any other thing about him.

**Signs of the End Times**—Jesus did give his disciples some signs that he said would precede his Second Coming. Among them are the following:

1. People coming in the name of Christ, claiming to be Christ: "For many will come in my name, claiming, 'I am the Christ,' and will deceive many"(Matt. 24:5).

2. Numerous wars and rumors of wars: "You will hear of wars and rumors of wars, but see to it that you are not alarmed. Such things must happen, but the end is still to come. Nation will rise against nation, and kingdom against kingdom"(Matt. 24:6–7a).

3. Famines and earthquakes: "There will be famines and earthquakes in various places. All these are the beginning of birth pains" (Matt. 24:7b–8).

4. Persecution of Christians: "Then you will be handed over to be persecuted and put to death, and you will be hated by all nations because of me" (Matt. 24:9).

5. Apostasy, or the turning away of many from the true faith: "At that time many will turn away from the faith and will betray and hate each other" (Matt. 24:10).

6. False prophets: "And many false prophets will appear and deceive many people" (Matt. 24:11).

7. Love will cease to exist among people: "Because of the increase of wickedness, the love of most will grow cold" (Matt. 24:12).

8. The message of Christ preached in all the world: "And this gospel of the kingdom will be preached in the whole world as a testimony to all nations, and then the end will come" (Matt. 24:14).

9. The Antichrist declaring himself to be God incarnate: "So when you see standing in the holy place 'the abomination that causes desolation,' spoken of through the prophet Daniel—let the reader understand" (Matt. 24:15).

10. A time of great distress: "For then there will be great distress, unequaled from the beginning of the world until now—and never to be equaled again. If those days had not been cut short, no one would survive, but for the sake of the elect those days will be shortened" (Matt. 24:21–22).

This is a complete list of the things Jesus said would happen before he returned to earth as King and Victor.

**Sin: How Much Do YOU Owe?**—When a woman used a whole bottle of expensive perfume on Jesus, some were outraged. The story unfolds as follows in Luke 7:36–50:

> Now one of the Pharisees invited Jesus to have dinner with him, so he went to the Pharisee's house and reclined at the table. When a woman who had lived a sinful life in that town learned that Jesus was eating at the Pharisee's house, she brought an alabaster jar of perfume, and as she stood behind him at his feet weeping, she began to wet his feet with her tears. Then she wiped them with her hair, kissed them and poured perfume on them.
>
> When the Pharisee who had invited him saw this, he said to himself, "If this man were a prophet, he would know who is touching him and what kind of woman she is—that she is a sinner."
>
> Jesus answered him, "Simon, I have something to tell you."
>
> "Tell me, teacher," he said.
>
> "Two men owed money to a certain moneylender. One owed him five hundred denarii, and the other fifty. Neither of them had the money to pay him back, so he canceled the debts of both. Now which of them will love him more?"
>
> Simon replied, "I suppose the one who had the bigger debt canceled."
>
> "You have judged correctly," Jesus said.
>
> Then he turned toward the woman and said to Simon, "Do you see this woman? I came into your house. You did not give me any water for my feet, but she wet my

feet with her tears and wiped them with her hair. You
did not give me a kiss, but this woman, from the time I
entered, has not stopped kissing my feet. You did not
put oil on my head, but she has poured perfume on my
feet. Therefore, I tell you, her many sins have been forgiven—for she loved much. But he who has been forgiven little loves little."

Then Jesus said to her, "Your sins are forgiven."

The other guests began to say among themselves, "Who is
this who even forgives sins?"

Jesus said to the woman, "Your faith has saved you; go in
peace."

Clearly, Jesus was showing that the depth of one's love is often
determined by the depth of one's sin.

**Sin: Jesus Disobeyed His Parents—Or Did He?**—Jesus was sinless,
but when you look at his mischief in Luke 2:41–51, you may wonder!
The passage says:

Every year his parents went to Jerusalem for the Feast of
the Passover. When he was twelve years old, they went
up to the Feast, according to the custom. After the
Feast was over, while his parents were returning home,
the boy Jesus stayed behind in Jerusalem, but they
were unaware of it. Thinking he was in their company,
they traveled on for a day. Then they began looking
for him among their relatives and friends. When they
did not find him, they went back to Jerusalem to look
for him.

After three days they found him in the temple courts, sitting among the teachers, listening to them and asking
them questions. Everyone who heard him was amazed
at his understanding and his answers. When his parents
saw him, they were astonished. His mother said to him,
"Son, why have you treated us like this? Your father
and I have been anxiously searching for you."

"Why were you searching for me?" he asked. "Didn't you
know I had to be in my Father's house?" But they did
not understand what he was saying to them.

Then he went down to Nazareth with them and was obedient to them. But his mother treasured all these things
in her heart.

Did Jesus disobey his parents, or was this more a misunderstanding that occurred as a result of poor information? The latter seems likely, because Jesus, to pay for the sins of the world, had to be sinless. Disobedience would have amounted to a sin for which he would have had to pay himself, rendering him an insufficient and guilty Savior.

**Sin in Business: Jesus' Prescription for Dealing with a Sinful Friend Still Used Today in Business**—The process of "church discipline" as Jesus outlined it is still used today in many businesses and elsewhere. Jesus told his disciples in Matthew 18:15–17 the proper process for dealing with problems between people: "If your brother sins against you, go and show him his fault, just between the two of you. If he listens to you, you have won your brother over. But if he will not listen, take one or two others along, so that 'every matter may be established by the testimony of two or three witnesses.' If he refuses to listen to them, tell it to the church; and if he refuses to listen even to the church, treat him as you would a pagan or a tax collector."

There are four steps to the process of confronting a wrongdoer:

1. Talk to the person in private about the problem. If he or she takes repentant and life-changing action, it's a win-win situation.

2. If the person won't listen, go a second time, taking along one or two others to listen in and try to act as mediators and witnesses. Again, if the problem is confirmed and the "sinner" takes repentant action, it's still a win-win situation.

3. If the person won't listen, take the issue before the whole church or company or organization and explain the situation. At that point, every person in the organization who has contact with this person is supposed to encourage him or her to repent or "change course."

4. If satisfaction is still not gained, it is appropriate to remove the person from the organization as a viable member.

This process is practiced in many organizations today, from the church to small businesses to big companies and other organizations.

**Singing: Jesus Never Sang a Song—Or Did He?**—Matthew 26:30 records this event: "When they had sung a hymn, they went out to the Mount of Olives." What song did they sing? One of the psalms would have been a logical choice. But who knows? Maybe it was something by a local band. The Disciples, perhaps?

**Sins of a Disciple**—Jesus told Peter that he would deny three times that he knew Jesus. The stories unfold in all four Gospels as follows:

*Matthew 26:69–75:* "Now Peter was sitting out in the courtyard, and a servant girl came to him. 'You also were with Jesus of Galilee,' she said. But he denied it before them all. 'I don't know what you're talking about,' he said. Then he went out to the gateway, where another girl saw him and said to the people there, 'This fellow was with Jesus of Nazareth.' He denied it again, with an oath: 'I don't know the man!' After a little while, those standing there went up to Peter and said, 'Surely you are one of them, for your accent gives you away.' Then he began to call down curses on himself and he swore to them, 'I don't know the man!' Immediately a rooster crowed. Then Peter remembered the word Jesus had spoken: 'Before the rooster crows, you will disown me three times.' And he went outside and wept bitterly."

*Mark 14:66–72:* "While Peter was below in the courtyard, one of the servant girls of the high priest came by. When she saw Peter warming himself, she looked closely at him. 'You also were with that Nazarene, Jesus,' she said. But he denied it. 'I don't know or understand what you're talking about,' he said, and went out into the entryway. When the servant girl saw him there, she said again to those standing around, 'This fellow is one of them.' Again he denied it. After a little while, those standing near said to Peter, 'Surely you are one of them, for you are a Galilean.' He began to call down curses on himself, and he swore to them, 'I don't know this man you're talking about.' Immediately the rooster crowed the second time. Then Peter remembered the word Jesus had spoken to him: 'Before the rooster crows twice you will disown me three times.' And he broke down and wept."

*Luke 22:55–62:* "But when they had kindled a fire in the middle of the courtyard and had sat down together, Peter sat down with them. A servant girl saw him seated there in the firelight. She looked closely at him and said, 'This man was with him.' But he denied it. 'Woman, I don't know him,' he said. A little later someone else saw him and said, 'You also are one of them.' 'Man, I am not!' Peter replied. About an hour later another asserted, 'Certainly this fellow was with him, for he is a Galilean.' Peter replied, 'Man, I don't know what you're talking about!' Just as he was speaking, the rooster crowed. The Lord turned and looked straight at Peter. Then Peter remembered the word the Lord had spoken to him: 'Before the rooster crows today, you will disown me three times.' And he went outside and wept bitterly."

*John 18:15–18, 25–27:* "Simon Peter and another disciple were following Jesus. Because this disciple was known to the high priest, he went with Jesus into the high priest's courtyard, but Peter had to wait outside at the door. The other disciple, who was known to the high priest, came back, spoke to the girl on duty there and brought Peter in. 'Surely you are not another of this man's disciples?' the girl at the door asked Peter. He replied, 'I am not.' It was cold, and the servants and officials stood around a fire they had made to keep warm. Peter also was standing with them, warming himself. . . . As Simon Peter stood warming himself, he was asked, 'Surely you are not another of his disciples?' He denied it, saying, 'I am not.' One of the high priest's servants, a relative of the man whose ear Peter had cut off, challenged him, 'Didn't I see you with him in the olive grove?' Again Peter denied it, and at that moment a rooster began to crow."

To unravel the mystery of these passages, look at the following chart:

| Situation | Scripture | Person | Telltale Sign |
|---|---|---|---|
| 1. At door of priest's house | John | Girl at door | "Not one of his disciples" |
| 2. Peter at fire | John | ? | "Not one of his disciples" |
| 3. Peter seated at fire | Luke, Matthew, Mark | Servant girl | "You were with him" |
| 4. Peter in courtyard | Luke | Man | "You are one of them" |
| 5. Peter at gateway | Matthew | Servant girl | "He was with Jesus" |
| 6. Peter at gateway an hour later | Matthew Luke | Several Several | "Accent gives you away" "You are a Galilean" |
| 7. Peter at fire | John 18:26 | Relative of Malchus | "Didn't I see you at olive grove?" |

Although this all looks rather confusing, it must have happened that Peter was at various places during those hours of Jesus' trial before the priests. People from all over were jumping on him and saying he was one of Jesus' disciples. He probably denied Jesus many times, left and right. Jesus said Peter would deny he knew him three times, perhaps for simplicity's sake or even to preserve something of Peter's pride. In reality, Peter probably denied he knew Jesus many times before the rooster crowed.

**Speaking in Tongues**—Many Christians today, known as Pentecostals, Charismatics, Holiness, and other groups, believe that one of the ways Jesus manifests his presence in a believer is by that person's "speaking in tongues." This means he speaks a language he has never heard, learned, or been exposed to, spontaneously and perfectly. Sometimes the "tongue" may be "heavenly" or "earthly." Jesus told his disciples the Spirit would come upon them after he ascended into heaven, and on the Day of Pentecost (fifty days after the first Easter Sunday) it happened: the disciples spoke of the glories of God in other languages. Eventually tongue speaking died out in the first century, only to be revived in the early 1900s when various preachers began to seek to speak in tongues as the disciples did that first Pentecost Sunday.

**Sports: Athletes Who Claim a Relationship with Christ**—Many pro athletes have claimed to be followers of Christ and have spoken of their faith on national television, including pro football players Reggie White, Mike Singletary, and Roger Staubach; baseball players Orel Hershiser, Dave Dravecky, and Paul Molitor; basketballers David Robinson, A.C. Green, and Mark Price; and Olympians Jim Ryun, Jackie Joyner-Kersee, and Carl Lewis.

**Sports: Jesus an Athlete?**—In his book *On God's Squad*, Norm Evans, at one time a Seattle Seahawks defensive tackle, says, "I guarantee you Christ would be the toughest guy who ever played the game. . . . If he were alive today I would picture a 6–6, 260-pound defensive tackle who would always make the big plays and would be hard to keep out of the backfield. . . . I have no doubt he could play in the National Football League. This game is 90 percent desire, and his desire was perhaps his greatest attribute. Yes, he would make it . . . and he would be a star in this league."

Perhaps, but the "meek and mild" Savior of the world would be hard to identify with and be approached by many people if he fit Evans' description.

**Stable of Jesus' Birth**—The stable where Jesus was born may have been a more healthy environment than the average inn! Considering that most inns in those days lodged disease, prostitutes, pickpockets, and all manner of thieves, it might have been providential that Joseph and Mary found a stable to birth Jesus in. The reason history believes it was a stable is because of one word in Luke 2:7: "And she gave birth to her firstborn, a son. She wrapped him in strips of cloth and placed him in a manger, because there was no room for them in the inn." The telltale word here is "manger," a feed-trough for animals. That is the sole piece of evidence that has led to the tradition that Jesus was born in a stable.

**Star Prophecy**—The star that the Magi supposedly saw announcing the birth of Jesus may have been prognosticated by a pagan prophet around 1400 B.C. The prophet Balaam was commissioned by Balak, the king of Moab, to curse the advancing hordes of Israel, fresh from forty years in the wilderness after their escape from slavery in Egypt under the leadership of Moses. Having heard of the many disasters wrought by the God of Israel, Balak tried to get God to curse Israel through Balaam. However, God did not allow Balaam to curse Israel; instead, each time Balaam tried to do so, he pronounced a blessing on Israel. In Numbers 24:17, Balaam said: "I see him, but not now; I behold him, but not near. A star will come out of Jacob; a scepter will rise out of Israel. He will crush the foreheads of Moab, the skulls of all the sons of Sheth."

The "star" in this passage could be a literal star or some kind of shining human light, a ruler or king. However, when Daniel went to Babylon and became leader over the Magi and seers of that nation, he probably told them of prophecies of the Hebrew Messiah. Six hundred years later, the descendants of these Magi still believed and were looking for a star, perhaps based on this prophecy. When they came to Jerusalem in search of the newborn king of Israel, they told Herod and his court that they had seen a star in the East that they interpreted as a sign of the Messiah's arrival.

**Stations of the Cross**—There are fourteen incidents, or "pictures," depicting Jesus' route to the cross in Roman Catholic tradition:

1. Pilate condemns Jesus to death.
2. Christ carries the cross.
3. Christ falls to the ground under the weight of the cross.
4. Christ meets the Virgin Mary en route to Calvary.
5. Simon of Cyrene takes up Jesus' cross.
6. Christ's face is wiped by St. Veronica (see Veil of Veronica).
7. Christ falls a second time.
8. Christ tells the women of Jerusalem to stop weeping for him.
9. Christ falls a third time.
10. Christ is stripped of his clothing.
11. Christ is nailed to the cross.
12. Christ dies on the cross.
13. Christ's body is taken down from the cross.
14. Christ's body is placed in the tomb.

These fourteen scenes are often found along the walls of Anglican and Roman Catholic churches where during Lent believers pray at each station and relive the story. The rite was instituted by the Franciscans. The form of the service was not instituted until the nineteenth century.

**Steal the Body: The High Priests Were Worried**—The priests and Pharisees who had Jesus condemned to death were afraid the disciples would try to steal the body. Matthew is the only one who records the situation (Matthew 27:62–66):

> The next day, the one after Preparation Day, the chief priests and the Pharisees went to Pilate. "Sir," they said, "we remember that while he was still alive that deceiver said, 'After three days I will rise again.' So give the order for the tomb to be made secure until the third day. Otherwise, his disciples may come and steal the body and tell the people that he has been raised from the dead. This last deception will be worse than the first."
> "Take a guard," Pilate answered. "Go, make the tomb as secure as you know how." So they went and made the tomb secure by putting a seal on the stone and posting the guard.

Later, after Jesus did rise from the dead, the soldiers went to the priests to tell them what had happened (Matthew 28:11–15):

> While the women were on their way, some of the guards went into the city and reported to the chief priests everything that had happened. When the chief priests had met with the elders and devised a plan, they gave the soldiers a large sum of money, telling them, "You are to say, 'His disciples came during the night and stole him away while we were asleep.' If this report gets to the governor, we will satisfy him and keep you out of trouble." So the soldiers took the money and did as they were instructed. And this story has been widely circulated among the Jews to this very day.

Church fathers such as Justin Martyr, Tertullian, and St. John Chrysostom all confirm in their writings that this view of the theft of the body was a prominent Jewish teaching on the issue. The problems with it are these:

1. Soldiers who fell asleep while guarding someone would be put to death.

2. If the body was stolen, it could have been found.

3. The disciples, according to the Gospels, didn't even believe or understand that Jesus was to rise from the dead until after it happened. So why would they steal the body?

4. The disciples all deserted or betrayed Jesus at the end. Which of them had the courage to go up against a Roman guard?

5. If the disciples stole the body, they lied about the resurrection in the Gospels. They all paid for their lies by dying horrid deaths because they would not recant. Never in history is it known that so many people were willing to die for a lie, knowing all along it was a lie.

**Stop Him! Plans to Stop Jesus Started Early**—Those who were against Jesus began conferring to find a way to destroy him early on. In Mark 3:1–6, we find the first evidence of opposition to Jesus:

> Another time he went into the synagogue, and a man with a shriveled hand was there. Some of them were looking for a reason to accuse Jesus, so they watched him closely to see if he would heal him on the Sabbath. Jesus said to the man with the shriveled hand, "Stand up in front of everyone."
> Then Jesus asked them, "Which is lawful on the Sabbath: to do good or to do evil, to save life or to kill?" But they remained silent.
> He looked around at them in anger and, deeply distressed at their stubborn hearts, said to the man, "Stretch out your hand." He stretched it out, and his hand was completely restored. Then the Pharisees went out and began to plot with the Herodians how they might kill Jesus.

**Suffering: Jesus Explains Why People Suffer in This World**— There are many explanations by different religions as to why people suffer, from the Law of Karma of the Hindus to the "illusion of suffering and evil" of Christian Science. In two passages Jesus offers two possible explanations of why people suffer. They are, first, John 9:1–5:

> As he went along, he saw a man blind from birth. His disciples asked him, "Rabbi, who sinned, this man or his parents, that he was born blind?"
> "Neither this man nor his parents sinned," said Jesus, "but this happened so that the work of God might be displayed in his life. As long as it is day, we must do the work of him who sent me. Night is coming, when no one can work. While I am in the world, I am the light of the world."

Jesus' explanation here is that this man suffered not because of previous sins, but in order that God might be glorified in his life through the healing that followed. From this, we can deduce that suffering is not necessarily a punishment for sin, but may be an opportunity to glorify God in your life, either through God's performing a miracle or by your living with the suffering in a way that shows God's power and goodness.

The second passage is Luke 13:1–5:

> Now there were some present at that time who told Jesus about the Galileans whose blood Pilate had mixed with their sacrifices. Jesus answered, "Do you think that these Galileans were worse sinners than all the other Galileans because they suffered this way? I tell you, no! But unless you repent, you too will all perish. Or those eighteen who died when the tower in Siloam fell on them—do you think they were more guilty than all the others living in Jerusalem? I tell you, no! But unless you repent, you too will all perish."

From this text we discern that suffering a certain death or fate is no indication of guilt. The real issue is repentance; if we don't repent, we will perish.

**Sunrise Easter Service**—The first Sunrise Easter Service was held in 1909. While staying at Mission Inn at the foot of Mt. Roubidoux in California, Jacob Riis invited the inn owner and nearly a hundred guests to accompany him to the top of the mountain, watch the sun come up on Easter morning, and then have a service.

**SuperBowl: More in Church Than Watching the SuperBowl**—The Princeton Religion Research Center recently released the statistic that 170 million Americans attend church on Easter Sunday, whereas only 128.9 million watched the 1997 SuperBowl. That's great comfort to Christians about the state of our nation, but it's dimmed when we realize that the Oscars have a worldwide audience of over 1 billion.

**Superhuman Savior**—Daniel Webster was once dining with some eloquent men at a banquet, and they talked about Christ. One asked him how he could comprehend that Jesus could be both God and man.

Webster said, "No, sir, I cannot comprehend it. If I could comprehend him, he would be no greater than myself. I feel that I need a superhuman Savior."

**Superstar: The Play, Not the Person**—*Jesus Christ Superstar* is a rock opera in two acts, with music by Andrew Lloyd Webber and lyrics by Tim Rice. It is based on the last seven days in the life of Jesus Christ. In 1972, *Jesus Christ Superstar* exploded onto the West End stage and changed the face of musical theater forever. The first musical ever to incorporate rock music, it was acclaimed by the press and public alike, and launched the careers of the young song-writing duo Tim Rice and Andrew Lloyd Webber. The score, which is one of their best, is packed with hit songs including "I Don't Know How to Love Him," "Could We Start Again Please," and, of course, "Superstar."

Although *Jesus Christ Superstar* is an entertaining and inspiring musical, it leaves out some key details of Jesus' life—namely, his resurrection—and leaves the viewer with the idea that Jesus was nothing more than a mere man who died a horrible death.

**Superstitions: Walk Under a Ladder and Incur God's Wrath?**— The superstition that walking under a ladder brings bad luck stems from a belief that Jesus was taken down from the cross by putting up a ladder. By walking under a ladder, one was somehow desecrating the death and mission of Christ; thus to do so brings bad luck. None of the Gospels mentions such a thing.

**Surprise: Did Anything Ever Surprise Jesus?**—Sometimes people forget that Jesus was just as human as the rest of us. He could weep, be angry, and enjoy a good meal. He could even be surprised!

When a certain centurion (a Roman soldier in command of a hundred legionnaires) came to Jesus to ask that he heal a servant, Jesus agreed to go. But the centurion immediately stopped him, saying, "Lord, I do not deserve to have you come under my roof. But just say the word, and my servant will be healed" (Matt. 8:8).

Jesus was so moved by this demonstration of faith that Matthew says that Jesus "was astonished" and said to the people around him, "I tell you the truth, I have not found anyone in Israel with such great faith" (Matt. 8:10). That included his disciples!

Apparently, the only thing that ever impressed Christ was real faith!

**Tax in the Fish's Mouth**—When Peter asked Jesus about paying taxes, Jesus sent him out to catch a fish (Matt. 17:24–27). Peter was told that he would find two coins in the fish's mouth, one for him to pay his Temple tax and one for Jesus.

Today, there is a fish called St. Peter's Fish, caught in the Sea of Galilee. Because of its large mouth in which it carries its eggs, it might also be able to hold a couple of coins the size of the Temple tax. The normal yearly tax on Jews was equal to about two days' pay in Jesus' time.

**Taxes: Jesus Was for Paying One's Taxes**—When the Pharisees tried to trap him, Jesus revealed he wasn't against taxes, only against not giving to God God's due. This is what happens in Matthew 22:15–22:

> Then the Pharisees went out and laid plans to trap him in
> his words. They sent their disciples to him along with
> the Herodians. "Teacher," they said, "we know you are
> a man of integrity and that you teach the way of God in
> accordance with the truth. You aren't swayed by men,
> because you pay no attention to who they are. Tell us
> then, what is your opinion? Is it right to pay taxes to
> Caesar or not?"
>
> But Jesus, knowing their evil intent, said, "You hypocrites,
> why are you trying to trap me? Show me the coin used
> for paying the tax." They brought him a denarius, and
> he asked them, "Whose portrait is this? And whose
> inscription?"
>
> "Caesar's," they replied.
>
> Then he said to them, "Give to Caesar what is Caesar's,
> and to God what is God's."
>
> When they heard this, they were amazed. So they left him
> and went away.

This trap was subtle. In this situation, the Pharisees partnered with the Herodians. These two groups normally hated one another, but in Jesus they had a common enemy. The Pharisees were against paying taxes to the Romans because they felt they should pay taxes only to God. Also, the Romans worshiped Caesar as a god, which was idolatry. Caesar's image was featured on the coins, and that, to the Pharisees, was a "graven image." So paying taxes broke three cardinal laws of God, in their judgment.

The Herodians on the other hand supported the Romans and were followers of the government of the land, led by Herod Antipas. To them, paying taxes was a sign of loyalty. Only revolutionaries refused to pay taxes. (There were several groups in Israel who fought the Romans about this, among them the Zealots.) Thus, to refuse to pay taxes or even to question it was a sign of insurrection and could cause one to be arrested and crucified.

As a result, Jesus was trapped. If he said, "Yes, pay taxes," he would be against the Pharisees and most other Jews, and his ministry would be compromised. If he said, "No, you don't have to pay taxes," the Herodians would have him brought to trial as a flaming insurrectionist.

What to do? Jesus did something they never expected. He asked for a coin, asked whose picture was on it, and then said, "Give to Caesar what is Caesar's, and to God what is God's." With this simple statement, he effectively quashed all murmurings of insurrection and not upholding the Law of God, much to the amazement of his listeners. And he also showed that it was still okay, even right, to pay taxes to the existing government.

**Taxmen: If Only Jesus Could Affect All Tax Gatherers This Way—**
Several taxmen are featured in Jesus' portfolio. Tax collectors were hated in Israel because they were considered traitors. They also extorted money through the system the Romans had set up. The way taxation worked was to award contracts to the highest bidders for a certain area of authority. The Romans gave a contract for a price, and then the owner of the contract could go into his area and exact as much tax from it as the people could stand. Thus extortion was common, for the tax collectors had the authority of Rome and its army behind them.

Matthew, also known as Levi, was a tax collector and was called by Jesus to follow him. This Matthew did without question, and he ultimately wrote the first Gospel, which goes by his name.

Zacchaeus was also a tax collector (see Luke 19:1–10). When Jesus saw the short man sitting on a branch of a sycamore tree, he invited Zacchaeus to come down, for Jesus planned to eat dinner at his house. Zacchaeus was pleased and, after talking to Jesus, proclaimed, "Look, Lord! Here and now I give half of my possessions to the poor, and if I have cheated anybody out of anything, I will pay back four times the amount."

It is not known whether Zacchaeus or Matthew extorted from their districts, but from this we can see the effect Jesus had on such people. So great was the attraction to the renegade and rejected tax collectors, that Jesus often dined with "tax collectors and sinners," something the Pharisees complained bitterly about (see Matt. 9:10–13).

**Teaching: The Difference Between Jesus and Other Teachers—** One of the primary differences between Jesus and other teachers was this one, found in Mark 1:22: "The people were amazed at his teaching, because he taught them as one who had authority, not as the teachers of the law."

A similar response was evoked after Jesus preached on the Mount: "When Jesus had finished saying these things, the crowds were amazed at his teaching, because he taught as one who had authority, and not as their teachers of the law"(Matt. 7:28–29).

What exactly was the difference? When the Pharisees and scribes taught, they usually quoted the "experts" constantly, citing this rabbi and that rabbi, bouncing opinion off opinion, arguing back and forth, and ultimately leaving the listeners in a state of confusion as to who was right.

Jesus on the other hand did not quibble about opinions or the arguments of various teachers. Instead, this is the format he used in the Sermon on the Mount (from Matt. 5:21–26), a typical passage:

> "You have heard that it was said to the people long ago, 'Do not murder, and anyone who murders will be subject to judgment.' But I tell you that anyone who is angry with his brother will be subject to judgment. Again, anyone who says to his brother, 'Raca,' is answerable to the Sanhedrin. But anyone who says, 'You fool!' will be in danger of the fire of hell.
>
> "Therefore, if you are offering your gift at the altar and there remember that your brother has something against you, leave your gift there in front of the altar. First go and be reconciled to your brother; then come and offer your gift.
>
> "Settle matters quickly with your adversary who is taking you to court. Do it while you are still with him on the way, or he may hand you over to the judge, and the judge may hand you over to the officer, and you may be thrown into prison. I tell you the truth, you will not get out until you have paid the last penny."

The primary difference between the teachers' teaching and Jesus' teaching was that Jesus said, "I tell you," and stated flatly what the meaning of a passage was, rather than marshaling opinions and laying out arguments. This astounded the crowds, partly because it was so new and different, and partly because it was so simple and understandable.

**Telling the Story**—After healing someone, Jesus often asked the peson not to talk about it! You would think Jesus would have wanted people to "spread abroad" what he'd done so that his fame might increase. But in many instances Jesus did just the opposite. For instance, consider this story, from Matthew 8:1–4, when he healed a leper:

> When he came down from the mountainside, large crowds
>     followed him. A man with leprosy came and knelt
>     before him and said, "Lord, if you are willing, you can
>     make me clean."
> Jesus reached out his hand and touched the man. "I am
>     willing," he said. "Be clean!" Immediately he was cured
>     of his leprosy. Then Jesus said to him, "See that you
>     don't tell anyone. But go, show yourself to the priest
>     and offer the gift Moses commanded, as a testimony to
>     them."

Why did Jesus ask the man not to tell anyone? It's not clear; however, what seems to be Jesus' concern with this leper was that he follow the Law as laid out in Leviticus 14:2–7:

> "These are the regulations for the diseased person at the
>     time of his ceremonial cleansing, when he is brought to
>     the priest: The priest is to go outside the camp and
>     examine him. If the person has been healed of his infec-
>     tious skin disease, the priest shall order that two live
>     clean birds and some cedar wood, scarlet yarn and hys-
>     sop be brought for the one to be cleansed. Then the
>     priest shall order that one of the birds be killed over
>     fresh water in a clay pot. He is then to take the live bird
>     and dip it, together with the cedar wood, the scarlet
>     yarn and the hyssop, into the blood of the bird that was
>     killed over the fresh water. Seven times he shall sprin-
>     kle the one to be cleansed of the infectious disease and
>     pronounce him clean. Then he is to release the live
>     bird in the open fields."

Jesus' purpose in this matter was to follow the Law. Perhaps he knew that if the leper began telling his story to anyone and everyone, the man would forget about his sacred duties; then the Pharisees would have one more thing with which to accuse Jesus—that he didn't encourage people to follow the Law. Some have suggested that Jesus was using "reverse psychology" on the man in order to get him to do exactly what Jesus was telling him not to do. This seems foolish at best and not something Jesus ever did in any other situations.

In any case, we don't know what the leper did, but in other situations the person healed or helped went out and spread the news about Jesus abroad!

**Temple: Jesus Drove Out the Money Changers Twice**—The story of Jesus' driving out the money changers from the Temple is a curious one in scripture, but the amazing thing is that it happened twice, once at the beginning of Jesus' work and once at the end. In John 2:12–17 we find this event:

> After this he went down to Capernaum with his mother and brothers and his disciples. There they stayed for a few days.
> When it was almost time for the Jewish Passover, Jesus went up to Jerusalem. In the temple courts he found men selling cattle, sheep and doves, and others sitting at tables exchanging money. So he made a whip out of cords, and drove all from the temple area, both sheep and cattle; he scattered the coins of the money changers and overturned their tables. To those who sold doves he said, "Get these out of here! How dare you turn my Father's house into a market!"
> His disciples remembered that it is written: "Zeal for your house will consume me."

This occurred shortly after Jesus' first miracle at Cana in which he turned water into wine. It certainly incited the Sadducees against him, for they owned and ran most of the concessions in the Temple at the time, which made them all very wealthy.

Nonetheless, a second instance of driving the money changers out of the Temple occurred early in the last week of Jesus' life on earth. You can find the story in Matthew 21:12–13:

> Jesus entered the temple area and drove out all who were buying and selling there. He overturned the tables of

the money changers and the benches of those selling
doves. "It is written," he said to them, "'My house will
be called a house of prayer,' but you are making it a
'den of robbers.'"

These two events provide "bookends" for Jesus' ministry, as if he
was enclosing the three and a half years in which he taught and healed
in Israel with his own stamp.

**Tempted in Every Way**—One might wonder how Jesus, both human
and divine in one person, could possibly understand what it's like to be
completely human, subject to all the frailties and temptations of that
condition. Several passages tell us, though, that Jesus knows exactly
what it's like to be tempted in every area. One is found in Hebrews
2:17–18: "For this reason he had to be made like his brothers in every
way, in order that he might become a merciful and faithful high priest
in service to God, and that he might make atonement for the sins of the
people. Because he himself suffered when he was tempted, he is able to
help those who are being tempted."

An even greater amplification of this is found later in Hebrews
4:15–16: "For we do not have a high priest who is unable to sympathize
with our weaknesses, but we have one who has been tempted in every
way, just as we are—yet was without sin. Let us then approach the
throne of grace with confidence, so that we may receive mercy and find
grace to help us in our time of need."

Presumably, Jesus felt the power and impact of every kind of temptation any person will ever face. In scripture we see him tempted
through the human need for food, shelter, survival, social acceptance,
popularity, money, success, hope, faith, love, friendship, and many
other things each of us faces. There is no mention of his being tempted
sexually, though undoubtedly as a fully human person he knew what it
was to desire sexual contact and relations. The truth is that Jesus,
according to these passages, experienced everything we will ever face;
moreover, he went to the limit in each case, facing the full power of
temptation and not giving in to it at any stage.

**Testing: Jesus' Mission Began with a Test**—The Spirit of God,
understanding that Jesus needed to "prove" himself, led him up immediately after his baptism to be tempted in the wilderness by the devil.
We find the story in Matthew 4:1–11 and Luke 4:1–13. In each case,
Satan put Jesus to three specific tests, all of which covered the most
basic areas in which people are tempted:

| Situation | Need | Result |
| --- | --- | --- |
| 1. Turn stones into bread | Hunger, obedience to God | Jesus quotes scripture and obeys it |
| 2. Leap off Temple and be caught by angels | To see if God will really come through and can be trusted | Jesus quotes scripture and obeys it |
| 3. Worship Satan and gain the whole world | To fulfill God's plan by his own means | Jesus quotes scripture and obeys it |

From each of these cases, we see a basic assault on God's right to Jesus' obedience, trust, love, and worship. In each case, Satan attacks at a point of normal human need: Will God provide for my needs or should I take matters into my own hands (turning stones into bread)? Can I trust that God will help and protect me, or do I need to "test" God in some way to see if God really cares (leaping off Temple)? Should I try to fulfill God's plan for my life by my own methods, or do I follow God's plan, even when it's difficult (worship Satan and gain the world without going to the cross)?

To each temptation, Jesus quoted an appropriate scripture as guidance for how he should deal with it. Such methodology indicates that temptation should normally be combated with understanding and obedience to scripture.

**Thanking Jesus**—There is very little recorded about the gratitude of people whom Jesus healed or helped in some way. A good example is found in Luke 17:11–19, where Jesus heals ten lepers and gets this response:

> Now on his way to Jerusalem, Jesus traveled along the border between Samaria and Galilee. As he was going into a village, ten men who had leprosy met him. They stood at a distance and called out in a loud voice, "Jesus, Master, have pity on us!"
> When he saw them, he said, "Go, show yourselves to the priests." And as they went, they were cleansed.
> One of them, when he saw he was healed, came back, praising God in a loud voice. He threw himself at Jesus' feet and thanked him—and he was a Samaritan.
> Jesus asked, "Were not all ten cleansed? Where are the other nine? Was no one found to return and give praise to God except this foreigner?" Then he said to him, "Rise and go; your faith has made you well."

Perhaps this is a lesson in human ingratitude. On the other hand, maybe it's a picture of ten people having such a good time that they "forget" the cause of their happiness. Human forgetfulness and/or procrastination is probably a big reason why so many humans fail to show real gratitude for good things done in their lives.

**That One Solitary Life**—One of the most famous writings about the sum of Jesus' life is from an anonymous author. It's called "One Solitary Life." This is how it goes:

> He was born in an obscure village, the child of a peasant woman. He worked in a carpentry shop until he was thirty, and then for three years he was an itinerant preacher.
>
> When the tide of popular opinion turned against him, his friends ran away. He was turned over to his enemies. He was tried and convicted. He was nailed upon a cross between two thieves. When he was dead, he was laid in a borrowed grave.
>
> He never wrote a book. He never held an office. He never owned a home. He never went to college. He never traveled more than two hundred miles from the place where he was born. He never did one of the things that usually accompanies greatness.
>
> Yet all the armies that ever marched, and all the governments that ever sat, and all the kings that ever reigned, have not affected life upon this earth as powerfully as has that One Solitary Life.

**Theology: His Greatest Theological Thought**—Karl Barth (1886–1968), a Swiss theologian, is considered by many to be the greatest theological writer of the twentieth century. He strove hard to recover from liberalism the reality of a relationship with God and Christ. He spoke often of the Bible as a "witness to the word," the "word" being Christ himself. He delved deeply into the nature of Christ's person and character, and the meaning of revelation and inspiration. He wrote many books on the subjects about which he had a passion. On a trip to the United States, a reporter asked him what was the greatest theological thought he had ever had. Barth considered a moment and then said, quoting the famous children's hymn, "Jesus loves me, this I know, for the Bible tells me so."

**Thirty Pieces of Silver**—How much was the money worth that Judas Iscariot was paid to betray Jesus? Was it predicted? Zechariah 11:12–13 records the prophecy about how much would be paid to Judas Iscariot to betray Jesus: "I told them, 'If you think it best, give me my pay; but if not, keep it.' So they paid me thirty pieces of silver. And the LORD said to me, 'Throw it to the potter'—the handsome price at which they priced me! So I took the thirty pieces of silver and threw them into the house of the LORD to the potter."

The fulfillment is found in Matthew 26:14–16: "Then one of the Twelve—the one called Judas Iscariot—went to the chief priests and asked, 'What are you willing to give me if I hand him over to you?' So they counted out for him thirty silver coins. From then on Judas watched for an opportunity to hand him over."

The thirty pieces of silver would probably be worth about thirty dollars by today's standards.

**Tomb and Cross Location**—Where was Jesus crucified, and where was his tomb located? The site of Jesus' crucifixion was "Golgotha," or "Calvary," or the "Place of the Skull," a small hill outside Jerusalem. His tomb was located near Golgotha, according to John 19:41–42; it was hewn out of rock and owned by Joseph of Arimathea, a wealthy member of the ruling body of the Jews, the Sanhedrin. It was a "new" tomb, according to Luke 23:53, and no one had ever been buried in it. This was a rather amazing and exact fulfillment of Isaiah 53:9, which said, "He was assigned a grave with the wicked, and with the rich in his death, though he had done no violence, nor was any deceit in his mouth." Jesus was to be buried with the robbers crucified with him, presumably in a pauper's grave or perhaps in Gehenna, but Joseph interceded and volunteered his own tomb, thus making a double fulfillment.

Today, the Church of the Holy Sepulchre in Jerusalem marks the places where Jesus was crucified and buried. The site is known to go back to A.D. 41–44, when Herod Agrippa erected a third wall around Jerusalem, taking the church from outside the city to inside. In A.D. 326, the emperor Constantine had the church built over the spot where Jesus was crucified and buried. It had three different levels, accommodating Golgotha and the tomb. The Persians burned down the site in 614, but it was later restored. In 1009, the caliph Hakim destroyed most of the building, but it was again restored in 1048, with the Crusaders restoring the rest of it from 1099 to 1149. Since that time, the church has been preserved to this day.

Is this the true site of Jesus' death and resurrection? It cannot be proved, but the tradition goes back at least to the reign of Constantine.

**Torture: Rough Him Up, Why Don't You?**—Before the Romans crucified Jesus, they played with him, and their playing was not nice. We find the details in Matthew 27:26–31:

> Then he released Barabbas to them. But he had Jesus
>   flogged, and handed him over to be crucified.
> Then the governor's soldiers took Jesus into the Praeto-
>   rium and gathered the whole company of soldiers
>   around him. They stripped him and put a scarlet robe
>   on him, and then wove a crown of thorns and set it on
>   his head. They put a staff in his right hand and knelt in
>   front of him and mocked him. "Hail, king of the Jews!"
>   they said. They spit on him, and took the staff and
>   struck him on the head again and again. After they had
>   mocked him, they took off the robe and put his own
>   clothes on him. Then they led him away to crucify him.

Jesus was most likely flogged with a "cat-o-nine-tails," a device with three to nine strands studded with pieces of bone, metal, and other sharp substances. The Jews normally gave thirty-nine lashes, one short of the standard forty in case a lash was accidently missed in the counting. The soldiers tied the victim by the hands and lifted him up on a pole several inches off the ground. While hanging there, a professional soldier whipped him, lashing and then jerking the lash over his body to rip the flesh. When the flogging was done, the victim's back, arms, and legs were little more than bloodied flesh with much of the skin abraised off. Often victims were in such shock from loss of blood that when released, they fell to the ground and were left to die. In Jesus' case, he was led off to his execution, forced to carry the crossbeam of the cross.

**Transfiguration**—When Jesus was transfigured, Peter wanted him to stay that way. We find the story in Matthew 17:1–8, where Jesus was "transfigured" before three disciples—James, Peter, and John:

> After six days Jesus took with him Peter, James and John
>   the brother of James, and led them up a high mountain
>   by themselves. There he was transfigured before them.
>   His face shone like the sun, and his clothes became as
>   white as the light. Just then there appeared before them
>   Moses and Elijah, talking with Jesus.
> Peter said to Jesus, "Lord, it is good for us to be here. If
>   you wish, I will put up three shelters—one for you, one
>   for Moses and one for Elijah."

> While he was still speaking, a bright cloud enveloped
> them, and a voice from the cloud said, "This is my Son,
> whom I love; with him I am well pleased. Listen to
> him!"
> When the disciples heard this, they fell facedown to the
> ground, terrified. But Jesus came and touched them.
> "Get up," he said. "Don't be afraid." When they looked
> up, they saw no one except Jesus.

Apparently, Peter thought the kingdom of God had come on earth, and Moses and Elijah would be staying. That is probably the reason he offered to build three shelters. A big question is, How did the disciples recognize Moses and Elijah? Perhaps Jesus spoke to them by name or revealed their identity by some other means. It's interesting that these two characters from the past appear, for each had an incomplete ministry while on earth. Moses was prevented from going into the land of Israel after the forty years of wandering in the wilderness because of a serious mistake he made in anger (see Num. 20:7–13). Thus, he never completed his mission of taking the people of Israel all the way to the Promised Land.

Elijah, similarly, lost heart for his prophet's position as he saw the Northern Kingdom slip into greater and greater idolatry under the leadership of King Ahab and his pagan wife, Jezebel. God allowed him to pass the prophet's mantle to Elisha and then took Elijah up into heaven in a flaming chariot (see 2 Kings 2:9–12). He did not complete several duties God had given him earlier. In addition, it was Elijah that Jews expected to appear shortly before the coming of the Messiah (see Mal. 4:5–6). As a result, it is particularly appropriate that these two men appeared with Jesus, because that moment might have been regarded as a completion of each of their ministries.

**Traps**—When the Sadducees, who didn't believe in the resurrection, tried to catch Jesus in a trap, he slipped through their hands on one deft word. We find the story in Matthew 22:23–33, where the Sadducees devised a tricky question. A woman was married to a man who died before she had children. Under Jewish law, when a man had no heirs, his oldest brother was required to mate with the widow and impregnate her to give the deceased brother an heir. This was because Jewish law featured stringent requirements about who could inherit what parcels of land. A man without an heir simply vanished, so God provided a way for that man to gain an heir (see Deut. 25:5–10, a passage on the law of "levirate marriage"). In the Sadducees' setup, this woman ended up marrying seven brothers in the name of levirate marriage without producing an heir. She then died (no wonder!).

Now this is where the trap is laid. The Sadducees did not believe there was an afterlife or a resurrection. So they asked, "Now then, at the resurrection, whose wife will she be of the seven, since all of them were married to her?" (Matt. 22:28). The purpose of all this was to show the stupidity of the idea of a resurrection, because such cases as the one just offered showed the hopeless tangle that would result. The Sadducees clearly were quite proud of this illustration, which supported their idea that resurrection was impossible because of all the problems associated with it. In other places in scripture, we find similar situations where people find fault with the idea for other reasons (see 1 Cor. 15:35–50, where the apostle Paul deals with a Greek-inspired problem with the idea of the resurrection).

Jesus answered the Sadducees as follows: "You are in error because you do not know the Scriptures or the power of God. At the resurrection people will neither marry nor be given in marriage; they will be like the angels in heaven. But about the resurrection of the dead—have you not read what God said to you, 'I am the God of Abraham, the God of Isaac, and the God of Jacob'? He is not the God of the dead but of the living."

After all this trouble, Jesus came up with a fairly simple explanation that put the Sadducees on the run: "When the crowds heard this, they were astonished at his teaching. Hearing that Jesus had silenced the Sadducees, the Pharisees got together" (Matt. 22:33–34). Luke 20:39–40 is even more direct: "Some of the teachers of the law responded, 'Well said, teacher!' And no one dared to ask him any more questions."

Apparently, Jesus knew how to deal with hecklers quite well!

**Travel: How Far Did Jesus Go in the World?**—Jesus never traveled outside of Israel during his three-year ministry, confining himself to the forty-by-eighty-mile region of Galilee, Samaria, Judea, and the east side of Galilee. However, his parents did take him out of Israel when they fled to Egypt during his infancy, a journey of several hundred miles, depending on where they lodged, which is not known.

**Trial**—Jesus was actually tried before several different people in five phases:

1. Annas, the former high priest, examined him first (John 18:12–14, 19–23)

2. Caiaphas, the high priest, with the Sanhedrin (Matt. 26:57–68)
3. Pontius Pilate (John 18:28–38)
4. Herod Antipas (Luke 23:6–12)
5. Pilate again, who pronounced the death sentence (John 18:36—19:16)

Jesus' trial before the Jews (first two trials above) were illegal on two counts. One, criminal trials were not allowed at night; two, criminal trials had to be performed at the Temple and in public during the day. Moreover, the Jews had no power to pass a capital punishment; only the Romans could carry out an execution. Thus, the Sanhedrin, the great court of Israel and its ruling body consisting of seventy-one members, waited until morning to actually pass sentence (see John 27:1). Then they sent Jesus to Pilate so that they could carry out a public execution.

The question of what issue the Sanhedrin would use to incite capital punishment was a tricky one. When Jesus was brought before the Sanhedrin after midnight on Friday morning, they wanted to destroy him because of blasphemy, because he "made himself out to be God." However, they knew the Gentile Pontius Pilate would not understand the heinous sin of blasphemy, so they went to him and charged Jesus with claiming to be "king" in place of Caesar, an act of rebellion punishable by crucifixion. Even then Pilate wanted to let Jesus go because he learned Jesus meant he was a king, but "not of this world." Pilate obviously thought Jesus a fool, but because of the crowd screaming for Jesus' death, he decided to "wash his hands" of the whole matter and get rid of the problem by sending him to his death (see John 19:11–25).

**Trinity: Never Mentioned**—Though Jesus is called the second member of the Trinity—the Godhead, which consists of the Father, Son, and Holy Spirit—the word *Trinity* never occurs in the Bible. Several passages, though, clearly support the idea of a Trinity. The only Old Testament passage that lists all three members of the Trinity in one verse is Isaiah 48:16: "Come near me and listen to this: 'From the first announcement I have not spoken in secret; at the time it happens I am there.' And now the Sovereign LORD has sent me, with his Spirit." The three noted here are: "Sovereign LORD"—God the Father; "me"—the Son; and "his Spirit"—the Holy Spirit.

Several New Testament passages also list all three:

*Matthew 3:16–17:* "As soon as Jesus was baptized, he went up out of the water. At that moment heaven was opened, and he saw the Spirit of

God descending like a dove and lighting on him. And a voice from heaven said, 'This is my Son, whom I love; with him I am well pleased.'"

*Matthew 28:19:* "'Therefore go and make disciples of all nations, baptizing them in the name of the Father and of the Son and of the Holy Spirit.'"

*Romans 8:9:* "You, however, are controlled not by the sinful nature but by the Spirit, if the Spirit of God lives in you. And if anyone does not have the Spirit of Christ, he does not belong to Christ."

*1 Corinthians 12:3–6:* "Therefore I tell you that no one who is speaking by the Spirit of God says, 'Jesus be cursed,' and no one can say, 'Jesus is Lord,' except by the Holy Spirit. There are different kinds of gifts, but the same Spirit. There are different kinds of service, but the same Lord. There are different kinds of working, but the same God works all of them in all men."

*2 Corinthians 13:14:* "May the grace of the Lord Jesus Christ, and the love of God, and the fellowship of the Holy Spirit be with you all."

*Ephesians 4:4–6:* "There is one body and one Spirit—just as you were called to one hope when you were called—one Lord, one faith, one baptism; one God and Father of all, who is over all and through all and in all."

*1 Peter 1:1–2:* "Peter, an apostle of Jesus Christ, To God's elect, strangers in the world, scattered throughout Pontus, Galatia, Cappadocia, Asia and Bithynia, who have been chosen according to the foreknowledge of God the Father, by the sanctifying work of the Spirit, for obedience to Jesus Christ and sprinkling by his blood: Grace and peace be yours in abundance."

*Jude 1:20–21:* "But you, dear friends, build yourselves up in your most holy faith and pray in the Holy Spirit. Keep yourselves in God's love as you wait for the mercy of our Lord Jesus Christ to bring you to eternal life."

All these passages contain oblique mentions of the Father, Son, and Spirit as equal in authority, power, and the right to worship. It is from these and many other passages that define the Father, Jesus, and the Spirit all as being equally God that we get the teaching of the Trinity. The formal teaching is that God exists as three persons, all distinct and equal and all deriving the same "essence"—divinity. Although God exists as these three persons, God remains one God in essence, not three gods, as some have accused Christians of believing in. Some have tried to illustrate the idea through water, which can exist in frozen, liquid, and gaseous forms; and the egg—shell, albumin, and yolk. Others have compared the idea of the Trinity to human marriage in which two persons come together and form a third "persona" between them in unity and love.

**Turning People Away!**—Although he was open to anyone following him, Jesus always laid out the cost. Some turned away as a result, as indicated by this passage in Matthew 8:18–22:

> When Jesus saw the crowd around him, he gave orders to cross to the other side of the lake. Then a teacher of the law came to him and said, "Teacher, I will follow you wherever you go."
> Jesus replied, "Foxes have holes and birds of the air have nests, but the Son of Man has no place to lay his head."
> Another man, one of his disciples said to him, "Lord, first let me go and bury my father."
> But Jesus told him, "Follow me, and let the dead bury their own dead."

Jesus was not afraid to let people go their own way when they considered following him too great a price.

**Twain's Favorite Pun on Jesus**—Mark Twain said Jesus was against polygamy on the basis of his statement in the Sermon on the Mount, "No man can serve two masters."

**Two Thieves**—A legend has it that the thieves on the two crosses next to Jesus were named Titus and Dumacus. They were very old, but the story is that when Joseph and Mary fled into Egypt, these two highwaymen assaulted them. Dumacus wanted to kill Joseph, Mary, and the child. But Titus was taken with the child's beauty and spared them. He said, "O blessed child, if the day should ever come when I shall need mercy, then on that day remember this deed." He was the one to whom Jesus said, "Today you will be with me in Paradise" (Luke 23:43).

**Unusual Faith: Faith on Top of a Pillar**—Simeon the Stylite (390–459) was the son of a shepherd. He moved to Antioch in Syria, where he was converted and became an Anchorite (hermit), living in various monasteries for the next twenty years. About 423, he ascended a pillar at Telanissus and for the next thirty-six years lived in great austerity, preaching from the top of the pillar on a platform some sixty feet above the desert floor. He preached to thousands who came to see and learn from him. His spirituality and personal knowledge of Jesus were extensive.

**Vacations**—There are some who refuse to take vacations or periods of rest, saying, "The devil never takes a vacation." But when you study the Gospels, you'll find at least eight times when Jesus either alone or with his disciples went aside to rest, pray, and think.

*Matthew 14:13:* "When Jesus heard what had happened, he withdrew by boat privately to a solitary place. Hearing of this, the crowds followed him on foot from the towns."

*Matthew 14:23:* "After he had dismissed them, he went up into the hills by himself to pray. When evening came, he was there alone."

*Mark 1:35:* "Very early in the morning, while it was still dark, Jesus got up, left the house and went off to a solitary place, where he prayed."

*Mark 1:45:* "Instead he went out and began to talk freely, spreading the news. As a result, Jesus could no longer enter a town openly but stayed outside in lonely places. Yet the people still came to him from everywhere."

*Mark 6:31:* "Then, because so many people were coming and going that they did not even have a chance to eat, he said to them, 'Come with me by yourselves to a quiet place and get some rest.'"

*Luke 5:16:* "But Jesus often withdrew to lonely places and prayed."

*Luke 9:10:* "When the apostles returned, they reported to Jesus what they had done. Then he took them with him and they withdrew by themselves to a town called Bethsaida."

*John 6:15:* "Jesus, knowing that they intended to come and make him king by force, withdrew again into the hill by himself."

**Veil of Temple: The Veil Torn in Two**—That veil was thick enough that two teams of horses could not pull it apart, but when Jesus died it was ripped in half. Matthew 27:51 says, "At that moment the curtain of the temple was torn in two from top to bottom. The earth shook and the rocks split."

In the Temple, the veil was the line of demarcation between the people and God. Only the high priest could go beyond the veil and that only once a year. Hebrews 9:2–7 explains what this was all about:

> A tabernacle was set up. In its first room were the lamp-stand, the table and the consecrated bread; this was called the Holy Place. Behind the second curtain was a room called the Most Holy Place, which had the golden altar of incense and the gold-covered ark of the covenant. This ark contained the gold jar of manna, Aaron's staff that had budded, and the stone tablets of the covenant. Above the ark were the cherubim of the Glory, overshadowing the place of atonement. But we cannot discuss these things in detail now.

> When everything had been arranged like this, the priests entered regularly into the outer room to carry on their ministry. But only the high priest entered the inner room, and that only once a year, and never without blood, which he offered for himself and for the sins the people had committed in ignorance.

The writer to the Hebrews goes on to explain that this veil separated God from men. But Christ entered through it, made the perfect sacrifice for sin, and paved the way for any person to come into the presence of God without having to make other sacrifices. This idea is the essence of Christ's salvation—that any person can come to God, know God, be intimate with God, love God, and be forgiven by God. Thus the veil was torn in two at Christ's death to indicate that God had made this intimacy possible.

**Veil of Veronica: Was This Jesus' Real Face?**—The Veil of Veronica was first noticed as an artifact in Rome about the twelfth century. It came to be associated with St. Veronica. The legend says that while Jesus carried his cross to Golgotha, a woman in the crowd named Veronica offered him her kerchief to wipe his brow. He did so and returned the kerchief to her. When she looked at the cloth later, she discovered that Jesus' face was clearly imprinted on it. The legend grew over the years saying that she was the woman whom Christ healed of a twelve-year-long hemorrhage (Matt. 9:20) and that she was also the wife of Zacchaeus, the short-legged tax collector who became one of Jesus' converts.

Papal bulls issued in 1143 stated that the scrap of cloth should be known as the "true image of the Lord" and associated it with the legendary St. Veronica. Every church in Europe eventually contained a reproduction of the veil, though today it is no longer publicly shown and must be viewed through a golden plate, like an icon. Strangely enough, the face on the veil corresponds very closely to the face on the Shroud of Turin. Some scholars today believe that the veil was even copied from it. The eyes on the face are closed, and the visage is long and narrow with no ears exposed. The beard is divided into three parts (though on the Shroud of Turin it is divided into two). The marks of Jesus' injuries during his scourging and crucifixion are most apparent. Today, the veil resides in Rome.

Some of the faithful will be tempted to believe that this story could be true, whereas others will quickly and easily dispose of it as bogus. It would appear that we have either a fantastic miracle here or a crafty fabrication by some forger steeped in his art. It's your choice what to believe.

**Virgin Birth: Was Jesus Really Born of a Virgin?**—There are several references in scripture to Jesus being born of a virgin. The prophecy cited is from Isaiah 7:14, where Isaiah tells King Ahaz, one of the errant kings of Israel: "Therefore the Lord himself will give you a sign: 'The virgin will be with child and will give birth to a son, and will call him Immanuel.'" The word here used for "virgin" is the Hebrew word *almah*, which can mean virgin, young woman, or maiden; however, it normally refers to a woman who is not yet married. However, the prophecy seems to apply to two events: a young woman giving birth to a son during King Ahaz's time (fulfilled by Isaiah's son—see Isa. 8:3); and a virgin giving birth to the Messiah, who would be called "Immanuel," which means "God is with us." These kinds of double fulfillments were common in the Old Testament.

When Matthew cites the reference in Matthew 1:23, he quotes the passage from the Septuagint, a Greek translation of the Old Testament made by loyal Jews living in Egypt in approximately 300 B.C. In Matthew's quotation, there is no ambiguity in the meaning of the term for "virgin"—the Greek word *parthenos*, which always means a "virgin," a young woman who has never had sexual relations.

The only other references to Jesus' virgin birth occur in Luke 1:26–38, where the Virgin Mary is told by the angel Gabriel she will conceive a son who is to be the Savior and King of the Jews. When she questions the angel, she learns she will conceive through the power of the Holy Spirit and will remain a virgin. The purpose of this was so that her son would be both completely human and divine, and also without sin.

These are the only passages clearly delineating the doctrine of the virgin birth of Christ. One other passage, though, indicates that the Jews might have known some of the circumstances of Jesus' birth. We find in John 8:41, where Jesus accuses the Pharisees of being born of the devil, this exchange takes place: [Jesus said], "You are doing the things your own father does." "We are not illegitimate children," they protested. "The only Father we have is God himself."

In another passage, Mark 6:3, Jesus is referred to as "Mary's son," as if there was a cloud of suspicion hanging over the nature of Jesus' birth.

The reference to "illegitimate children" could be an oblique accusation that the Pharisees thought Jesus was illegitimate. This is congruent with Jewish tradition that Jesus was born illegitimately.

The virgin birth is a key doctrine of the Christian faith. Without it, there is no substantial proof that Jesus was anything other than a normal human being, corrupted by original sin and subject to all the infirmities of humankind. How was divinity conferred on him if not through a virgin birth? Also, if he did have original sin and was a sinner like the rest of humanity, how then could he pay for the "sins of the world"? Would he not have had to pay for his own sins first?

Both sides of the issue have difficult problems to solve. To those believing in a virgin birth, the problem is the whole mechanism of how God impregnated Mary and how Jesus could be God and man in one person. To those not believing in it, the problem is how Jesus could be sinless, God, and the Savior of the world all in one without it.

**Virgin Mary: She Knew the Cost**—Even when God called her to bear Jesus, Mary knew it was impossible, for she was a virgin. As the angel Gabriel laid out the plan of action, Mary was amazed and asked, "How will this be, since I am a virgin?" (Luke 1:34).

Gabriel answered her: "The Holy Spirit will come upon you, and the power of the Most High will overshadow you. So the holy one to be born will be called the Son of God. Even Elizabeth your relative is going to have a child in her old age, and she who was said to be barren is in her sixth month. For nothing is impossible with God" (vv. 35–37).

Apparently, Mary was satisfied with this explanation, for she said to Gabriel, "I am the Lord's servant. May it be to me as you have said" (v. 38).

Doubts often come after the fact, and it appears that Mary suffered through some. She decided to solve the problem by visiting her relative, Elizabeth, in the south near Jerusalem. At the time, Elizabeth was pregnant with John the Baptist, another miraculous birth though not virginal. When Mary came to her door, this is what happened, according to Luke 1:39–45:

> At that time Mary got ready and hurried to a town in the
> hill country of Judah, where she entered Zechariah's
> home and greeted Elizabeth. When Elizabeth heard
> Mary's greeting, the baby leaped in her womb, and
> Elizabeth was filled with the Holy Spirit. In a loud
> voice she exclaimed: "Blessed are you among women,
> and blessed is the child you will bear! But why am I so
> favored, that the mother of my Lord should come to
> me? As soon as the sound of your greeting reached my
> ears, the baby in my womb leaped for joy. Blessed is
> she who has believed that what the Lord has said to her
> will be accomplished!"

When Mary heard those words, her doubts were set free, and she exploded into a great psalm of praise called the "Magnificat" (from the first word of the Latin, which means "magnifies"). Apparently, Mary's doubts were dealt with, and she never turned back from the course she was set on.

**Voice from Heaven**—God spoke from heaven three times during Jesus' ministry. They are as follows:

At Jesus' baptism, according to Matthew 3:13–17:

> Then Jesus came from Galilee to the Jordan to be bap-
> tized by John. But John tried to deter him, saying, "I
> need to be baptized by you, and do you come to me?"
> Jesus replied, "Let it be so now; it is proper for us to do
> this to fulfill all righteousness." Then John consented.
> As soon as Jesus was baptized, he went up out of the
> water. At that moment heaven was opened, and he saw
> the Spirit of God descending like a dove and lighting
> on him. And a voice from heaven said, "This is my Son,
> whom I love; with him I am well pleased."

The second time occurred at the transfiguration on the mountain where Jesus took Peter, James, and John and met with Moses and Elijah. According to the story in Matthew 17:1–6:

> After six days Jesus took with him Peter, James and John
> the brother of James, and led them up a high mountain

by themselves. There he was transfigured before them. His face shone like the sun, and his clothes became as white as the light. Just then there appeared before them Moses and Elijah, talking with Jesus.

Peter said to Jesus, "Lord, it is good for us to be here. If you wish, I will put up three shelters—one for you, one for Moses and one for Elijah."

While he was still speaking, a bright cloud enveloped them, and a voice from the cloud said, "This is my Son, whom I love; with him I am well pleased. Listen to him!"

When the disciples heard this, they fell facedown to the ground, terrified.

The last instance was somewhat different and strange. Each of the two above examples seems appropriate and well-advised, being done at pivotal moments of Jesus' ministry and life. The third, though, occurs in John 12:27–33. Jesus is speaking:

"Now my heart is troubled, and what shall I say? 'Father, save me from this hour'? No, it was for this very reason I came to this hour. Father, glorify your name!"

Then a voice came from heaven, "I have glorified it, and will glorify it again." The crowd that was there and heard it said it had thundered; others said an angel had spoken to him.

Jesus said, "This voice was for your benefit, not mine. Now is the time for judgment on this world; now the prince of this world will be driven out. But I, when I am lifted up from the earth, will draw all men to myself."

He said this to show the kind of death he was going to die.

God often does things in threes although they may be different in texture and situation, for example: the Trinity; the disciples divided into three groups of four each; human history in three stages—all of history, the millennium, eternity; Jesus and the two thieves on Calvary; and the three miracle-working periods of Israel's history—Moses' day, Elijah and Elisha's time, and the time of Jesus and the early church. There seems no distinct rhyme or reason for the three occasions in which God spoke from heaven except that two were public (the baptism and the description of Jesus' death) and one private (the transfiguration). Each confirmed the reality of the Father's approval of Jesus as Savior, Lord, and King.

**Walking on Water**—When Jesus walked on water, strange events occurred, according to Matthew 14:22–33. This is what happened:

> Immediately Jesus made the disciples get into the boat and go on ahead of him to the other side, while he dismissed the crowd. After he had dismissed them, he went up into the hills by himself to pray. When evening came, he was there alone, but the boat was already a considerable distance from land, buffeted by the waves because the wind was against it.
>
> During the fourth watch of the night Jesus went out to them, walking on the lake. When the disciples saw him walking on the lake, they were terrified. "It's a ghost," they said, and cried out in fear.
>
> But Jesus immediately said to them: "Take courage! It is I. Don't be afraid."
>
> "Lord, if it's you," Peter replied, "tell me to come to you on the water."
>
> "Come," he said.
>
> Then Peter got down out of the boat and walked on the water to Jesus. But when he saw the wind, he was afraid and, beginning to sink, cried out, "Lord, save me!"
>
> Immediately Jesus reached out his hand and caught him. "You of little faith," he said, "why did you doubt?"
>
> And when they climbed into the boat, the wind died down. Then those who were in the boat worshiped him, saying, "Truly you are the Son of God."

Although some scholars have suggested that Jesus was not really walking "on" the water but "by" the water or perhaps in a shallow part of it, the story does not support that idea. How could Peter sink and almost drown in water only shin deep? Galilee is a deep lake that drops off quickly from the shore; it is some 690 feet below sea level. Nearby, Mt. Hermon rises 9200 feet above sea level. This leaves the lake vulnerable to sudden and high winds raging through the gorges around the lake. Matthew says the boat was a "considerable distance from land." There are no real sandbars or islands in the lake that could have made walking "by" the water possible. Furthermore, the disciples interpreted Jesus' walking on the water as a sign of his being the "Son of God." These were fishermen, men who knew the lake well and would not be hoodwinked by a trick.

**War: No Battles on December 25**—No great battles have ever been waged on December 25 in recorded history, though many have been fought on December 24 and 26.

**War: We Need This Kind of Truce**—The "Truce of God" was established by the Roman Catholic Church in the tenth century, mainly in France. The idea was to lessen the impact of warfare among feudal lords and nobles on the common people. Fighting was prohibited from Saturday night to Monday morning, on church grounds and holy places at all times, with other special prohibitions around holy days such as Easter and Christmas. The practice died out in the eleventh century presumably because feudal nobles and lords preferred to fight anywhere and anytime the urge struck.

**Washing Feet: Jesus Once Stripped Down to Wash His Disciples' Feet**—In John 13:2–17 we read:

> The evening meal was being served, and the devil had already prompted Judas Iscariot, son of Simon, to betray Jesus. Jesus knew that the Father had put all things under his power, and that he had come from God and was returning to God; so he got up from the meal, took off his outer clothing, and wrapped a towel around his waist. After that, he poured water into a basin and began to wash his disciples' feet, drying them with the towel that was wrapped around him.
>
> He came to Simon Peter, who said to him, "Lord, are you going to wash my feet?"
>
> Jesus replied, "You do not realize now what I am doing, but later you will understand."
>
> "No," said Peter, "you shall never wash my feet."
>
> Jesus answered, "Unless I wash you, you have no part with me."
>
> "Then, Lord," Simon Peter replied, "not just my feet but my hands and my head as well!"
>
> Jesus answered, "A person who has had a bath needs only to wash his feet; his whole body is clean. And you are clean, though not every one of you." For he knew who was going to betray him, and that was why he said not every one was clean.

> When he had finished washing their feet, he put on his
> clothes and returned to his place. "Do you understand
> what I have done for you?" he asked them. "You call
> me 'Teacher' and 'Lord,' and rightly so, for that is what
> I am. Now that I, your Lord and Teacher, have washed
> your feet, you also should wash one another's feet. I
> have set you an example that you should do as I have
> done for you. I tell you the truth, no servant is greater
> than his master, nor is a messenger greater than the
> one who sent him. Now that you know these things,
> you will be blessed if you do them.

The Lord of the universe washing his disciples' grungy feet! It's astonishing to imagine, let alone see in real life! But that is what Jesus did. He set the example and then advised us to follow it.

**Way of the Cross**—The "Via Dolorosa," or way of sorrows, can be plotted in modern Jerusalem, from the one-time Roman barracks where the soldiers humiliated Jesus after his sentencing, down through the streets to Golgotha where he was crucified. This path is often called "The Stations of the Cross"(see entry). Each point is plotted as a guide to believers to help them experience and in some way relive what Christ went through in dying for the sins of the world.

**Weather**—Though some have tried to discredit Jesus' miracles of healing as psychosomatic healings, several of the more amazing miracles concerned other phenomena. Twice he fed thousands of people, starting only with a few fish and pieces of bread. Once he walked on water. On another occasion, he turned water into wine. He even caused at least two miraculous catches of fish in which his disciples, having fished all night without success, were told to try in a different spot. In each case, hundreds of fish were caught within seconds.

The most amazing of all the miracles, perhaps to fishermen as hardened and tough as Jesus' primary disciples Peter, Andrew, James, and John, was the stilling of a storm. We find the story in Matthew 8:23–27 as follows:

> Then he got into the boat and his disciples followed him.
> Without warning, a furious storm came up on the lake,
> so that the waves swept over the boat. But Jesus was
> sleeping. The disciples went and woke him, saying,
> "Lord, save us! We're going to drown!"

> He replied, "You of little faith, why are you so afraid?"
> Then he got up and rebuked the winds and the waves,
> and it was completely calm.
> The men were amazed and asked, "What kind of man is
> this? Even the winds and the waves obey him!"

Galilee was renowned for its "furious storms" because it was over six hundred feet below sea level and the high hills around it (reaching up over nine thousand feet) formed funnels for the wind. Often a storm came up suddenly. Fishermen always needed to be watchful in case they were caught far out on the lake in such a torrent.

In this case, Jesus was so tired from the day's activities (according to scripture, it was one of his most strenuous days) that he fell asleep in the stern of the fishing craft. His disciples rowed across the lake. A storm reared up, however, and began swamping the boat. At first the disciples tried to handle it as they normally would, but their efforts proved futile. In desperation, they woke Jesus. (He must really have been tired to have missed all this activity!) Jesus calmly asked them why they were so afraid; then he spoke to the storm, saying, "Peace, be still." Other passages reveal that an immediate calm resulted.

The disciples' response was understandable amazement. At this point, they didn't really know the true nature of Jesus as the God-man. But even if they had, would they have believed he could stop a storm at a word?

**Weeping: Did Jesus Ever Cry?**—Only two scenes in the New Testament show Jesus weeping. The first is found in John 11:35 where Jesus "wept" as he gazed on the tomb of Lazarus, a close friend of his. Why did he weep? Certainly not because he was grief-stricken at the loss of his friend, for in a few minutes he would raise Lazarus from the dead. Undoubtedly, the reason he wept was that he saw pain in the eyes and hearts of Lazarus's two sisters, Martha and Mary. People can identify with such weeping, for who has not "hurt" when one sees a child crying because of pain, or a bereaved and lonely person weeping because of his or her loss? A mere commercial today can sometimes bring tears to the viewers (remember the old ATT commercials—"Reach out and touch someone"?) because of the compassion we feel in our hearts for those in mortal pain. This is what Jesus must have felt.

What made it all the harder was the fact that both women believed that Jesus could have prevented Lazarus's death. When Lazarus was ill they sent him a message, saying, "Lord, the one you love is sick" (John 11:3). When Jesus received the message, he told his disciples, "This sickness will not end in death" (v. 4), and he waited two more days before traveling to Bethany where Lazarus lived. Thus, when he arrived, Jesus learned that Lazarus had actually been dead for four days. Perhaps from the moment Jesus received the message he already knew Lazarus was dead. But Jesus must have had a plan in mind, one that would prove his power and his love to those who looked on.

Why did he wait four days? Jews believed that the spirit of a dead person hovered around the body for four days after death. Wanting to dispel any possibility of false beliefs about his powers, Jesus probably waited the full four days so that everyone would see that Lazarus was irrevocably dead, something he didn't do in the other two episodes where he raised people from death (Jairus's daughter and the widow of Nain's son).

When he finally arrived at the tomb and saw the people weeping—for Lazarus had been a good man, a good brother, and a good friend—Jesus was overcome. Their pain became his pain.

The second instance where Jesus wept is found in Luke 19:41. There, Jesus stood on a hill overlooking Jerusalem and spoke of how the city would be destroyed because of its unbelief. Then he wept, crying out that he had wished many times to gather the people of Jerusalem under his arms like a mother hen gathers her chicks in the rain. This time Jesus wept for his own pain in being rejected by the people of Jerusalem.

One more reference says that Jesus wept rather often: "During the days of Jesus' life on earth, he offered up prayers and petitions with loud cries and tears to the one who could save him from death" (Heb. 5:7). The prophet Isaiah also said that the Messiah would be "a man of sorrows, and familiar with suffering" (Isa. 53:3).

The message in Jesus' tears is a potent one: "I know what it is to hurt as you hurt, and I join you in your pain."

**Where Is Jesus Now?**—Two passages reveal where Jesus is now. The first comes from Acts 7:55–58, where Stephen, about to be stoned, cries out:

> "Look," he said, "I see heaven open and the Son of Man standing at the right hand of God."
> At this they covered their ears and, yelling at the top of their voices, they all rushed at him, dragged him out of the city and began to stone him.

The other passage comes from Hebrews 10:12–13, where the

author says, "But when this priest had offered for all time one sacrifice for sins, he sat down at the right hand of God. Since that time he waits for his enemies to be made his footstool."

Jesus himself, when questioned at his trial by the high priest, was asked who he really was. According to Matthew 26:62–64, this is what was said:

> Then the high priest stood up and said to Jesus, "Are you not going to answer? What is this testimony that these men are bringing against you?" But Jesus remained silent.
>
> The high priest said to him, "I charge you under oath by the living God: Tell us if you are the Christ, the Son of God."
>
> "Yes, it is as you say," Jesus replied. "But I say to all of you: In the future you will see the Son of Man sitting at the right hand of the Mighty One and coming on the clouds of heaven."

To stand at the right hand of God was a place not only of honor, but also of power and authority. Jesus at God's right hand represents his right to rule and act in human history as he pleases.

**Whipping**—When Roman soldiers flogged a prisoner like Jesus in preparation for crucifixion, they used a whip with three leather strands. Each strand was tied at points into knots holding pieces of metal and bone. The idea was to lash with the whip and then rip it sideways, tearing the flesh of the victim as much as possible.

The victim himself was tied to a pole or beam so that his weight would be held even if he lost consciousness, which he frequently did. This position allowed the whip to lash around the body, striking legs, arms, chest, stomach, and face. Such a flogging tore the flesh in long strips of skin that caused profuse arterial bleeding. If a man wasn't killed by the flogging, he had the cross to look forward to (see entry under **Torture**).

**Widow's Mites: Jesus Noticed Even the Smallest Gifts**—When a widow dropped two "mites" into the gift treasury, Jesus proclaimed that she had actually given more than all the rich men who paraded their wealth and dumped in fortunes. According to Mark 12:41–44, this is what happened:

> Jesus sat down opposite the place where the offerings were put and watched the crowd putting their money into

the temple treasury. Many rich people threw in large amounts. But a poor widow came and put in two very small copper coins, worth only a fraction of a penny.

Calling his disciples to him, Jesus said, "I tell you the truth, this poor widow has put more into the treasury than all the others. They all gave out of their wealth; but she, out of her poverty, put in everything—all she had to live on."

True giving in the eyes of God is a matter of the sacrifice of the individual in relation to what he or she possesses, not the amount given.

**Wine Drinking**—In the early days of the church, there were Aquarians who did not want to drink wine in the Lord's Supper, so they substituted water. They were very ascetic, refused wine and meat, and often never married. Maybe that's why they died out!

**Wise Men: Did They Know More Than the Hebrew Prophets?**—Their three gifts—gold, frankincense, and myrrh—indicate an insight into who Jesus was that many missed. Gold was a gift for a king. Frankincense was given to a priest. Myrrh was for someone who was to die. In each case, the "wise men" recognized these elements of Jesus' position and nature: King of Kings who rules over all; the priest who intercedes for us before God; and the Savior who would die for the sins of the world.

**Wise Men: Young, Middle-aged, and Old**—An old legend says the first Wise Man was young, in search of a king, and brought gold. The second was middle-aged, with difficult questions on his mind; he brought frankincense to worship God, whom he hoped would answer his questions. The third was an old man with many sinful years behind him; he longed for a Savior, and thus brought myrrh for healing the Savior's sufferings.

**Wit: Jesus the Wit**—To many, Jesus was not only a miracle worker but an orator and a witty one at that. He had a "way with words," and many of his lesser known statements have come into our own language as witticisms. A sampling follows (NASB):

"Look at the birds of the air, that they do not sow, neither do they reap, nor gather into barns, and yet your heavenly Father feeds them. Are you not worth much more than they?" (Matt. 6:26)

"Which of you by being anxious can add a single cubit to his life's span?" (Matt. 6:27)

"Why do you look at the speck in your brother's eye, but do not notice the log that is in your own eye?" (Matt. 7:3)

"What man is there among you, when his son shall ask for a loaf [of bread], will give him a stone?" (Matt. 7:9)

"However you want people to treat you, so treat them." (Matt. 7:12; by its better known version: "Do unto others as you would have them do unto you.")

"It is easier for a camel to go through the eye of a needle than for a rich man to enter the kingdom of God." (Matt. 19:24)

**Work: Gave Manual Work Dignity**—At the time of Jesus' life on earth, manual work was considered by the Romans and others to be beneath them, something only slaves had to do. There were over 7 million slaves in the Roman Empire, most of them conquered peoples who were forced to serve hard masters. They performed all menial as well as important duties in the empire, from washing people's feet when they came to visit, to acting as physicians, teachers, and tutors. Jesus' work as a carpenter became for all the ages a symbol of the importance and goodness of such work.

In fact, Jesus had quite a bit to say about work. Note the following parables:

*Parable of the Tares* (Matt. 13:24–30): Jesus shows that Satan tries to foil the work of God's kingdom, but that the workmen should be patient, knowing that God will sort the true from the bad at the end.

*The Unmerciful Servant* (Matt. 18:23–35) warns masters and overseers to be kind and gentle or Christ will come and punish them for their evil ways.

*The Hiring of the Laborers* (Matt. 20:1–16) demonstrates that God is always looking for people to work in the kingdom and that God will give them all eternal life and will reward them regardless of how much of their lives they actually did work.

*The Two Sons* (Matt. 21:28–32) pictures two sons, one of whom said he'd perform his father's work but didn't, and the other who refused, then went and did it anyway. Jesus shows here that deeds are more important than impetuous words.

*The Wicked Husbandmen* (Matt. 21:33–45) exposes all who would scandalize God's kingdom by hurting God's servants. It warns any who attack God's workers that God will deal with them personally.

*The Parable of the Talents* (Matt. 25:14–30): Jesus told the people to be faithful to the gifts God has given them, to invest and use them wisely for the kingdom of God, for God will one day reward them for their work.

*The Rich Fool* (Luke 12:16–21) is about a successful businessman who has great income and wealth but fails to give God a place in his life. He ends up losing his soul for his oversight.

*Tower Builder* (Luke 14:28–30) shows the importance of planning and making sure you can see a project through before you ever start it.

*The Lost Sheep* (Luke 15:3–7) pictures a shepherd who cares so much for the one sheep that has gotten away that he goes out and retrieves it.

*The Unjust Steward* (Luke 16:1–8) illumines the importance of using your power, position, and possessions for advancing the kingdom.

*The Rich Man and Lazarus* (Luke 16:19–31) demonstrates the shallowness and folly of worldly might and wealth when not shared and used for the kingdom of God.

Very clearly, Jesus was concerned about how people used their time and money in their work. In the New Testament, you also find many admonitions about the glory and privilege of work:

*Ephesians 6:5–8:* "Slaves, obey your earthly masters with respect and fear, and with sincerity of heart, just as you would obey Christ. Obey them not only to win their favor when their eye is on you, but like slaves of Christ, doing the will of God from your heart. Serve wholeheartedly, as if you were serving the Lord, not men, because you know that the Lord will reward everyone for whatever good he does, whether he is slave or free."

*Colossians 3:22–24:* "Slaves, obey your earthly masters in everything; and do it, not only when their eye is on you and to win their favor, but with sincerity of heart and reverence for the Lord. Whatever you do, work at it with all your heart, as working for the Lord, not for men, since you know that you will receive an inheritance from the Lord as a reward. It is the Lord Christ you are serving."

*1 Timothy 6:1–2:* "All who are under the yoke of slavery should consider their masters worthy of full respect, so that God's name and our teaching may not be slandered. Those who have believing masters are not to show less respect for them because they are brothers. Instead, they are to serve them even better, because those who benefit from their service are believers, and dear to them. These are the things you are to teach and urge on them."

There are also admonitions to employers as well (see entry under "Bosses").

**Worldliness: Totally Otherworldly**—When a visitor to St. Catherine's Greek Orthodox Monastery (founded in the sixth century at the foot of Mt. Sinai in Arabia) met monks there in 1946, he discovered that most of them had never heard of World War II, and many knew nothing about World War I. Who says all Christians are too worldly?

**Worldliness of Jesus**—If Jesus wasn't worldly, he at least knew the ways of the world. Jesus, though poor, possessing nothing, and not interested in worldly position and power, still understood its trappings and ways. One of his parables illustrates this. It is found in Luke 16:1–9:

> Jesus told his disciples: "There was a rich man whose manager was accused of wasting his possessions. So he called him in and asked him, 'What is this I hear about you? Give an account of your management, because you cannot be manager any longer.'
> "The manager said to himself, 'What shall I do now? My master is taking away my job. I'm not strong enough to dig, and I'm ashamed to beg—I know what I'll do so that, when I lose my job here, people will welcome me into their houses.'
> "So he called in each one of his master's debtors. He asked the first, 'How much do you owe my master?'
> "'Eight hundred gallons of olive oil,' he replied.
> "The manager told him, 'Take your bill, sit down quickly, and make it four hundred.'
> "Then he asked the second, 'And how much do you owe?'
> "'A thousand bushels of wheat,' he replied.
> "He told him, 'Take your bill and make it eight hundred.'
> "The master commended the dishonest manager because he had acted shrewdly. For the people of this world are more shrewd in dealing with their own kind than are the people of the light. I tell you, use worldly wealth to gain friends for yourselves, so that when it is gone, you will be welcomed into eternal dwellings."

Although some may scoff at this parable, saying it indicates that Jesus advocated stealing and chicanery, it actually does just the reverse. What Jesus was saying here was that an unbeliever found a way to use his position and authority to help himself. In the same way, Jesus meant that believers should use their position, power, and wealth to influence people for the kingdom of God—certainly not by doing anything dishonest, but by using righteous influence and "wheeling and dealing" in order to help advance God's kingdom.

**Writers: He Believed**—Words from Dostoyevsky in his master novel *The Brothers Karamasov* are these lines: "I believe there is nothing lovelier, deeper, more sympathetic and more perfect than the Savior; I say to myself with jealous love that not only is there no one else like him, but that there could be no one. I would say even more. If any one could prove to me that Christ is outside the truth, and if the truth really did exclude Christ, I should prefer to stay with Christ and not with the truth. There is in the world only one figure of absolute beauty: Christ. That infinitely lovely figure is as a matter of course an infinite marvel." Dostoyevsky and his fellow writer, Leo Tolstoy, imbued their characters with the faith they themselves espoused and lived in daily life.

**Writers:** see **Gibran**.

**Writers: "Life Is Difficult"**—That is the first line of M. Scott Peck's classic "The Road Less Traveled," which has been on best-seller lists for over ten years. In the book, Peck develops a theology of life, suffering, and the problem of problems through a lens of faith, which he says he reached during the writing of the book.

**Writers: A Thought from the King of Thinkers**—Blaise Pascal (1623–1862), a French mathematician and thinker, is most famous for his posthumously published *Pensées* (1670), in which he outlines his thoughts about faith and life. He blazed a trail as a mathematical prodigy, contributing to the modern understanding of calculus, the theory of probability, and the properties of the cycloid. His work in physics and the study of fluids led to the invention of the hydraulic press. However, his climactic conversion to faith in Christ in 1654 led to his entrance into the convent of Port Royal. There he devoted himself to religious writing. One of his writings about Jesus is helpful:

> Jesus Christ, without worldly riches, without the exterior productions of science, was infinitely great in his sublime order of holiness. He neither published inventions nor possessed kingdoms, but he was humble, patient, pure before God, terrible to evil spirits, and without spot of sin. Oh, with what illustrous pomp, with what transcendent magnificence did he come attended, to such as beheld with the eyes of the heart, and wit those faculties which are the judges and discerners of true wisdom.

**Writing: Jesus Wrote Only Once**—Although the four Gospels are about Jesus' life, he did not write a word of them. The only time Jesus is recorded as writing was in John 8, where Jesus wrote on the ground as he confronted the Pharisees about a woman who had committed adultery. Some speculate that he was writing out words for different kinds of sin and then pointing to the specific people. He had just said, "Let him who is without sin cast the first stone."

**Writings: Did Jesus Write Anything in the Bible?**—see **Letter from Heaven**.

**WWJD: What If We Did Everything as Jesus Would Do?**—When Charles M. Sheldon challenged his congregation to bring their behavior into conformity with Jesus' character, they began to ask a question: "What would Jesus do?" Sheldon wrote the novel *In His Steps* to show the amazing results when Christians take seriously the call to follow Christ. It became one of the best-selling books of all time.